Timely Reading

Blanche of Castile overseeing the education of Saint Louis. Bibliothèque nationale, Manuscrits, N.a. lat. 3145. By permission of the Bibliothèque nationale.

Timely Reading

BETWEEN EXEGESIS
AND INTERPRETATION

Susan Noakes

Cornell University Press

Ithaca and London

CORNELL UNIVERSITY PRESS GRATEFULLY ACKNOWLEDGES
A GRANT FROM THE ANDREW W. MELLON FOUNDATION
THAT AIDED IN BRINGING THIS BOOK TO PUBLICATION.

First published 1988 by Cornell University Press.

International Standard Book Number 0-8014-2144-6
Library of Congress Catalog Card Number 87-47862

Printed in the United States of America

Librarians: Library of Congress cataloging information
appears on the last page of the book.

The paper in this book is acid-free and meets the guidelines for
permanence and durability of the Committee on Production Guidelines
for Book Longevity of the Council on Library Resources.

For Clayton
Colleague, listener, computer whiz,
friend, husband

Contents

Preface

> I must therefore warn that well-known character, the general
> reader, that I am here embarked upon a most distasteful
> business: taking down the picture from the wall and looking
> on the back; and, like the inquiring child, pulling the musical
> cart to pieces.
>
> ROBERT LOUIS STEVENSON, "On Some Technical
Elements of Style in Literature"

In this book I argue that reading is a historically evolving process in that readers as a group change over time, and each reader
changes over small periods of time, from day to day, hour to hour. I
therefore focus attention throughout on a paradox: reading intrinsically brings with it a reminder of loss of earlier readers and earlier
reading selves, as well as the sense of plenitude and enrichment more
traditionally, and necessarily, associated with reading by Western culture. Examining this paradox enables me to articulate a model of the
reading process which accounts for its complex temporal structure, as
well as for its inherent impulse to suppress awareness of the character
of its own temporality.

Though I draw on the work of several schools of contemporary
literary and textual theory (including semiotics, feminism, phenomenology, hermeneutics, and deconstruction), I hope the model
developed here will interest not only literary theorists but also others
with a serious interest in the role that reading plays in Western society.
Having noted the frustration of colleagues in such disciplines as history, anthropology, psychiatry, and philosophy as they attempt to understand the increasingly specialized concepts and terms characteristic
of literary theory today, I have tried to write in *lingua franca*. This is a
risky business (as Dante knew): complex concepts are most precisely

discussed with specialized terms, and the considerable advances recent Western theory has made in formulating the relations of literary to other forms of human activity have produced a range of new concepts that are indeed subtle. Yet I have felt the risk of some imprecision worth taking, for the implications of the model of the reading process articulated here are broad, extending beyond the academy into the civic domain (especially in education and the law), and their development requires the collaboration of students of many disciplines outside literary theory proper.

The book might seem to be ordered chronologically; after an introduction setting forth its concepts and sources, it proceeds from a general treatment of changes in reading in the thirteenth century to discussions of two writers of the fourteenth, Dante and Boccaccio, followed by one from the very early fifteenth, Christine de Pizan; it then jumps half a millennium to examine two nineteenth-century authors, Nerval and Baudelaire. But chronology in this case is merely a matter of convention. As the leap from the fifteenth to the nineteenth century in itself would suggest, no attempt is made to trace the general history of readers or reading. Such an attempt would in any case be premature, given not only the paucity of research so far undertaken on such primary materials as exist but also, and more fundamentally, the lack of an accepted theoretical model that might give shape and direction to this research.

It is toward the development of such a model, a model of "timely reading," that the sequence of chapters in fact moves, deriving its elements from the literary works discussed and stressing several themes that their authors have used in exploring the temporal character of reading: the feminine unreliability of readers who distort stable, male-established authority and authorship; the enduring nature of those aspects of words which are perceptible to the senses (sound, written characters), in contrast to the transitory nature of their meaning; the search for an ever-receding meaning in a text, especially a text associated with an earlier generation; and, of special importance, reading by an author of his or her own previously written text, "now" found to mean something different from what it "used" to mean. Although the presence of such themes in the work of authors of several periods attests to the continuing awareness over many centuries of the temporal character of reading, two points in the examination of this awareness stand out, marking Western culture's general ambivalence about the value of reading: the attempt to disguise or deny the inevitable time-dependent evolution of reading, an attempt dramatized most conspicuously in the polemical rhetoric that founds Renaissance humanism; and the growth of an acute anxiety about the instability of the reader and the reading process, a hallmark of literary modernism. These two points inform my decision to examine works composed, on the one hand, in the late medieval and early Renaissance period and, on the other, in the late, transitional stage of romanticism.

My choice of texts takes me far from the standard canon. This is particularly conspicuous in my selection of Christine de Pizan and, to some extent, of Nerval, long taken to be a writer of secondary importance. Even when I treat major writers, I deal with their lesser-known works. For example, Boccaccio appears in these pages as an editor, theorist, and commentator rather than as author of the *Decameron*. Similarly, Baudelaire is studied primarily in relation to a short story now read only by specialists and to some material among his essays, art criticism, and translations; his lyrics are considered comparatively briefly. Even when treating one of the most canonical of all European works, Dante's *Comedy*, I have stressed what most specialists have traditionally seen as an aspect less important than his (purportedly) central concern with theology: intertextuality and especially wordplay.

This focus on what is marginal to the canon is necessary to my subject, for texts and aspects of texts that are minor by canonical standards are precisely those in which the complex relationship of reading to time emerges most clearly. More "successful" works or aspects of works, I would argue, succeed precisely *because* they camouflage the problems in this relationship. They leave unchallenged the very notion on which the concept of canon is based. Canonical works, "major" works of literature, are those claimed to be "timeless"; that is, when read by properly educated readers they will be found to have value and beauty in the twentieth century as they did in, for example, the eighteenth. The "timelessness" of canonical works depends on the assumption that the reader has an essence unchanged by the contingencies of history, an essence often described as something fundamentally human that endures even as readers cross temporal and cultural boundaries. The reading process, too, must be assumed to be essentially unchanging if the notion of a timeless canon is to prevail. Like the many feminist and Third World critics who have challenged the foundations of the notion of canonicity, I take the view here that works enter the canon because they conform to an ideology that canonical literature serves. The ideology that concerns me here is an ideology that relates less directly to government and conquest than those cited by other critics of the notion of canon and more directly to reading itself. The Western ideology of reading presents this carefully taught activity as if it were instead a natural one, as value-free as, for example, tradition claims perception to be. Instead, I argue here that reading must be understood as the constantly transformed product of historical change, not a timeless process focused on timeless texts but rather a "timely" activity—the most complex encounter with time in which many Westerners consciously engage.

As a ten-year veteran of the "canon wars" whose efforts to enrich the canon in areas ranging from freshman humanities courses to Ph.D. examination lists have achieved only the most limited and short-lived victories, I have come to believe that those who would urge reconsideration of the canon must adopt a new strategy. Attention must be directed first to a critique of the ideology of reading that authorizes the present canon; only after such a critique has matured and gained acceptance will it be possible to expand the canon itself. I speak of the desire to enrich and expand the canon because I could not (as my choice of texts makes clear) support efforts to throw Dante, say, off anyone's reading list to be replaced by Catherine of Siena, or to "make room at the other end" of the list for some examples of the "emergent literatures." Many dreary debates about the impossibility of including, on a twenty-eight-week reading list, works by other than white, male writers, because such inclusion would inevitably mean the dropping of an essential link in the chain of tradition, have left me convinced that the only tenable position is one that asks both purveyors and consumers of reading lists to go beyond their present level of effort. Thus, I do not propose to impoverish the canon but rather to instill additional energy and excitement into the reading process so that students and scholars are ready to read more, and with greater intensity.

It must also be borne in mind that the canon has always changed with time. A mere seventy years ago, for example, the *American College Course: Three Centuries of French Literature,* privately printed for members of the American College Society in 1916, asserted that "the three greatest French poets of the nineteenth century are Lamartine, Hugo and Musset" (p. 176). A late chapter on "minor writers" explains: "The nineteenth century in French literature has been decidedly an age of fiction. . . . The achievement of the century in poetry, however, is not inconsiderable. Besides Hugo, who . . . is undoubtedly France's greatest poet, there were De Vigny, De Musset, and Gautier. . . . [but] their fiction . . . on the whole was more remarkable than their poetry" (p. 395). Where are Baudelaire, Mallarmé, Rimbaud, and Verlaine? The final chapter, on "recent and contemporary French writers," mentions in passing "the strange and weirdly fascinating verses of Verlaine . . . and Mallarme [*sic*]" and remarks: "The works best worth reading and remembering in this group are [by] Leconte de Lisle and Herédia. The weirdest are Baudelaire's 'Flowers of Evil'" (p. 428). Rimbaud was apparently too "weird" to deserve mention.

What this suggests, I believe, is that canon-worthiness is in the eye of the beholder. In an effort to contribute to the evolution of the readers who create the canon, then, I have made a central historical concern of this book a tracing of the transformation of fictive representations of the reader. I measure the beginning of this transformation from the birth of the nonclerical, vernacular reader, roughly contemporary with the reign of Saint Louis. I locate important early turning-points in it in Dante's and Christine de Pizan's benevolent condescension toward their readers, qualified by their awareness of the writer's role as servant to the royal or noble patrons who are intended to be among those readers. At the opposite pole I locate Baudelaire's angry, rather than benevolent, condescension to his reader, qualified by his awareness of his need to divest the voyeuristic reader of money by putting on a titillating display.

While I draw connections between this transformation and economic and historic developments in the relation between reader and author, my fundamental explanatory framework remains an analysis of Western models for the reading of texts and the fundamental ambivalence about time which these models share. Central to this analysis is a heuristic distinction between the two poles I characterize as "exegesis" and "interpretation." I associate the first of these above all with Boccaccio's humanistic quest for the perfectly reconstructed text; he sees the text as a dismembered body which it is the skilled reader's task to heal. I associate the latter primarily with Baudelaire's occasionally exuberant celebration of a kind of reading that knows no rules or boundaries; he envisions texts as bodies that the skilled reader will metamorphose into new shapes without end.

This heuristic distinction permits me to construct a model of reading as an activity that can derive its energy only from a constant shuttling back and forth between these two poles. Indeed, I claim that pure exegesis and pure interpretation are not merely stultifying; if the model of reading I present here is valid, they are, by my definition, impossible. Accordingly, I treat three other writers who represent recognition of the legitimacy and necessity of both exegesis and interpretation as goals to be pursued, though not achieved. Nerval appears as a reader torn asunder by their opposing forces and as a writer capable of bringing these forces into a delicate rhetorical balance; Dante and Christine as paradigmatic figures who develop models of reading that integrate exegesis and interpretation without seeing the two as mutually competitive. Christine I take to present these poles as symbiotically connected, while for Dante they are fully dialectical.

Overall, my argument shows, I hope, that dichotomous models of the temporality of reading are destructive when they fail to include some vehicle that makes resolution of the dichotomy possible. I conclude by treating in some detail currents in literary theory that hold promise for the construction of such a vehicle. If, however, some of my readers travel in boats unprepared for the choppy waters of recent literary theory, I can assure them that my argument is conceptually completed with the chapter on Baudelaire. All the rest is annotation.

Development of the ideas in this book was nurtured over many years by many people. My greatest debt is to my husband, Clayton Koelb, who tirelessly gave both moral and technical support, even when the pressures of his own projects and complex schedule were intense. I shall never understand where he finds his reserves of generosity, persistence, and patience, but I'll be grateful for them, always.

I must also thank my mother, Vivian Noakes, who taught me when I was very little that poems and libraries are especially important. Though she continues to think that the influence of my late father, Leroy F. Noakes, directed me toward scholarship (a perception no doubt true), the literary focus of that interest originated with her. In addition, her willingness to provide summer-long daily care for her grandson made crucial revisions possible.

Friends of almost twenty years' standing, Adriana and Roberto Mancini, kept alive a nourishing source of connection with the Tuscan language and cultural tradition, even when the circumstances of professional life in the United States made that connection difficult to maintain. *Invece di tante lettere . . .*

Herman Sinaiko's patience and responsive intelligence taught me, while still an undergraduate, that I could indeed build my own path through texts of philosophy and literary theory, if I were patient enough with myself.

The late Paul de Man found time to read and comment on a series of revisions and kept me from losing faith in the project at a moment of considerable professional discouragement.

A grant-in-aid from the American Council of Learned Societies allowed me to conduct the research on manuscripts of Boccaccio and Christine de Pizan that made Chapters 3 and 4 possible. An award from the National Endowment for the Humanities in support of a translation of Emilio Betti's *Teoria generale della interpretazione* gave me the opportunity to develop an understanding of the connections between hermeneutics and semiotics. The University of Kansas General Research Fund supported significant work toward the concluding chapter.

SunHee Kim Gertz, Harvey Graff, and Alan Nagel provided many useful comments on earlier versions.

William J. Kennedy and Laurence M. Porter, readers for Cornell University Press, helped me strengthen the book's overall structure and rhetoric and remove from it errors too embarrassing to mention. For selecting them as readers and for his patience, good humor, and tact, I must thank also the Press's editor Bernhard Kendler.

A short, unannotated version of Chapter 1 appeared as "The Fifteen Oes, the *Disticha Catonis,* Marculfius, and Dick, Jane, and Sally" in The University of Chicago Library Society *Bulletin* 2 (1977), 2–15; I am grateful to the Library's Development Office for permission to use this material. I also thank the Trustees of Boston University for permission to include in Chapter 5 portions of "Self-reading and Temporal Irony in *Aurélia,*" *Studies in Romanticism* 16 (1977), 101–19. Portions of Chapter 2 appeared in "The Double Misreading of Paolo and Francesca," *Philological Quarterly* 62 (1983), 221–39. Portions of the Conclusion appeared in "Literary Semiotics and Hermeneutics: Towards a Taxonomy of the Interpretant," *American Journal of Semiotics* 3 (1985), 109–19. Portions of the material on Newman, the Paolo and Francesca and Geryon episodes in Dante, Nerval's *Aurélia*, and Baudelaire's *La Fanfarlo* are much reworked versions of parts of my doctoral dissertation. All translations are mine except where otherwise identified.

SUSAN NOAKES

Lawrence, Kansas

Timely Reading

Introduction: "What has virtue to do with a Reading-room?"

I do not know of a single instance where an author has been so eccentric as to report without any intention to deceive that he now means by his text what he did not mean.

E. D. HIRSCH, JR.

The foregoing words appeared in print in 1967,[1] just before the deluge: that is, just before Jacques Derrida's philosophical work began to be known in the United States, just before the "Yale School" came to be, and just before American literary theory became violently polarized. It is important to remember that Hirsch, among the first native American theorists in his generation to prowl the unfamiliar landscape of European philosophy, was not addressing a problem *about to be* articulated and explored by a new critical movement; he was instead describing the preceding forty-year (to use his term) "assault" from within on literary theory. More broadly, "the sensible belief that a text means what its author meant" (p. 1) had, according to Hirsch, been under "attack" since the poets T. S. Eliot and Ezra Pound had argued that the best poetry is "cut off from the life of its author," a doctrine that fostered the illogical inference that *all* literature is necessarily cut off from its author's life. In Hirsch's account this dictum merely garnered support from similar notions advanced by Martin Heidegger, Northrop Frye, and misinterpreters of W. K. Wimsatt and Monroe

---

1. E. D. Hirsch, Jr., *Validity in Interpretation* (New Haven, Conn.: Yale University Press, 1967), p. 9.

Beardsley's famous essay, "The Intentional Fallacy." It would thus be now roughly sixty years, spanning three generations of literary theorists, since it was first asked whether a text's meaning is equivalent to what an author originally intended it to mean, and still no generally accepted answer has been found.

What I propose to do here may be seen as a new attempt to answer this question, and examining an instance of the limit case proposed by Hirsch in the sentence cited as epigraph will provide a good starting point. I have no desire to contradict Hirsch when he says he doesn't know of such an instance. No doubt within the limits set by his usage of key terms, the instance I discuss could be explained away with his distinction between "meaning" ("what the signs represent") and "significance" ("a relationship between that meaning and a person, or a conception, or a situation, or indeed anything imaginable"; p. 8)— although one would have to ignore the nearly twenty years of subsequent study of sign structure, to which the present book also seeks to contribute. Hirsch's identification of this limit case as touchstone still stands.

Despite his rhetoric, the limit case is not a *reductio ad absurdum*; neither of the names that first came to my mind on reading Hirsch's sentence can fairly be called "eccentric." Both Dante Alighieri and John Henry Cardinal Newman have earned central positions in the canon, and the seriousness of their commitment to writing, and to writing as a vehicle for the conveyance of meaning, is not open to question. Nor would the term "fickle," also used by Hirsch to describe the hypothetical author in such a limit case, suit either Dante or Newman, for, although both are famous as converts (political and religious, respectively), neither converted lightly.[2]

Newman's Timely Self-Reading

The Newman text to be examined as limit case is *An Essay in Aid of a Grammar of Assent* (1870). Etienne Gilson, introducing a popu-

---

2. Hirsch also overlooks the important literary-historical tradition of revision, where the changed meanings may be erased (as in Tasso) or not (as in Montaigne). Indeed, the whole foundation of literary modernism is the attempt to create a text that later means something it didn't mean at first. It can be argued that French modernism, in particular, grows out of such revisions as Lautréamont's (*Poésies* vs. *Les Chants de Maldoror*) and Arthur Rimbaud's (*Une Saison en enfer* vs. the verse).

lar edition of the *Grammar*,[3] calls it "the first sketch of what philosophers today call a phenomenology of religious belief," the word "phenomenology" suggesting an analogy between Newman's concerns and
matters that lie outside the religious domain. One of the principal
questions Newman had to confront, because he was writing the *Grammar* and because it had to be part of the *Grammar*'s subject matter, was
the relation between belief and writing. His text is recognized as an
important treatment of this problem. Jacques Lacan, for example, criticizing Claude Lévi-Strauss's failure to deal with the problematic role
of the subject, points to the *Grammar* as a text that confronts an important aspect of that problem.[4] Both the *Grammar*'s contemporary authority and its present interest in an extratheological context are based
on Newman's recognition of the complexity of his position as both the
one investigating and the one investigated. A respected stylist, educa-
tor, and literary theorist, Newman shows his concern with the notion
that structures of language reflect structures of thought, not only in the
title but throughout the *Grammar*, and in many of his other writings as
well. For all these reasons, then, a brief look at several excerpts from
his *Grammar* and other works that treat related themes can offer terms,
quandaries, examples, and notions to make visible certain of the issues
involved in "timely reading."

The first pertinent passage has to do with writing in the form that
most obviously interested Newman in the *Grammar*: scripture. Since
Newman's personal history included both Protestant and Catholic periods (a fact well known to his audience), and since that audience had
both Protestant and Catholic components, he had to address the question of how the foundations of each group's beliefs relate to scripture.

> There is another great conflict of first principles, and that among
> Christians, which has occupied a large space in our domestic history,
> during the last thirty or forty years, and that is the controversy about
> the Rule of Faith. I notice it as affording an instance of an assumption
> so deeply sunk into the popular mind, that it is a work of great difficul-
> ty to obtain from its maintainers an acknowledgment that it is an

3. Image Books edition (Garden City, N.Y.: Doubleday, 1955), p. 20. Citations in
my text refer to John Henry Newman, *An Essay in Aid of a Grammar of Assent* (Notre
Dame, Ind.: University of Notre Dame Press, 1979).
4. Jacques Lacan, *Écrits* (Paris: Seuil, 1966), p. 862. Lacan is discussing the position
of an informant who, during the time of describing to the anthropologist the rituals in
which she or he ordinarily participates, necessarily abandons assent to these rituals.

assumption. That Scripture is the Rule of Faith is in fact an assumption so congenial to the state of mind and course of thought usual among Protestants, that it seems to them rather a truism than a truth. If they are in controversy with Catholics on any point of faith, they at once ask, "Where do you find it in Scripture?" and if Catholics reply, as they must do, that it is not necessarily in Scripture in order to be true, nothing can persuade them that such an answer is not an evasion, and a triumph to themselves. Yet it is by no means self-evident that all religious truth is to be found in a number of works, however sacred, which were written at different times, and did not always form one book; and in fact it is a doctrine very hard to prove. So much so that years ago, when I was considering it from a Protestant point of view, and wished to defend it to the best of my power, I was unable to give any better account of it than the following, which I here quote from its appositeness to my present subject.

"It matters not," I said, speaking of the first Protestants, "whether or not they only happened to come right on what, in a logical point of view, are faulty premises. They had no time for theories of any kind; and to require theories at their hand argues an ignorance of human nature and of the ways in which truth is struck out in the course of life. Common sense, chance, moral perception, genius, the great discoverers of principles do not reason. They have no arguments, no grounds, they see the truth, but they do not know how they see it; and if at any time they attempt to prove it, it is as much a matter of experiment with them as if they had to find a road to a distant mountain, which they see with the eye; and they get entangled, embarrassed, and perchance overthrown in the superfluous endeavour. It is the second-rate men, though most useful in their place, who prove, reconcile, finish, and explain. Probably, the popular feeling of the sixteenth century saw the Bible to be the Word of God, so as nothing else is His Word, by the power of a strong sense, by a sort of moral instinct, or by a happy augury."

That is, I considered the assumption an act of the Illative Sense;—I should now add, the Illative Sense, acting on mistaken elements of thought. [Pp. 296–97]

Newman is citing, in 1870, one of his own works published in 1837, both because he now still means by it what he did then and because he does not. The 1837 material presents the lack of a logically demonstrable foundation for Protestant belief in Scripture as an argument for the intuitive, self-evident truth of that belief; in the 1870 context the same passage tangentially assumes that belief to be "mistaken" because the "elements of thought" that form its foundation are mistaken. Nonetheless, in 1870 Newman takes the words he wrote in 1837 to suggest a truth of which he was, in 1837, unaware. While Newman the reader of 1870 reads his words of 1837 as meaning something he "now" knows to be mistaken (that Scripture is the Rule of Faith), this is not why he quotes them in 1870; he quotes them because he "now" reads them as also meaning something very important which he did not *then* know they meant: specifically, that there is such a thing as an "illative sense" (from the Latin past participle of the root of "infer") and that it shapes the assumptions with which one begins a line of reasoning, as well as one's intermediate and final conclusions.

Although a tracing of his own path to the rejection of this proposition is certainly an important part of the larger agenda of the book, Newman's immediate goal in this chapter is not to prove or disprove that proposition. The object of the chapter, titled "The Illative Sense," is rather to explain his idea that there exists a sense in the reasoning faculty of each individual which makes final judgments as to "the validity of an inference in concrete matter" (p. 271), a sense—more highly developed in some than in others—that Newman calls "illa-tive." In the section of this chapter under discussion, Newman is showing that the illative sense is at work when judgments are made as to first principles; that is, it comes into play not just in the conduct and conclusion of arguments, in the middles and ends, but also at the very beginnings. He advances the controversy over the Rule of Faith as an instance of a conflict at the level of the elements of an argument on which the illative sense must act, an instance which, together with others he presents, shows that those who make arguments assume the right to make assumptions: that is, to rule out some propositions as irrelevant or absurd. The passage Newman quotes argues in 1837 that though the premises of the early Protestants were faulty, their conclu-sions were right. In 1870 it serves to show that while both the premises and the conclusions of the Protestants were faulty, they employed not the Bible as their Rule of Faith, but rather the illative sense.

It is no coincidence that Newman's illustration in this rhetorically complex passage concerns (in 1837) written authority and that he cites it *as* written authority in 1870. The issue Newman raises is fundamen-tal to literature as well as religion, for the assumption he attributes to Protestants, that words in a book are intimately and necessarily linked to truth, suggests the more general assumption that words effectively work as names of things, ideas, and so on, an assumption "so deeply sunk" into the mind of any reader that it is difficult—or, rather, im-possible—to acknowledge that it is an assumption until and unless one stops reading and writing, however temporarily. One must ask, with Newman, how people come to take what they read to be true, perhaps more true than what they experience, and, more fundamentally, how they come to believe that language works, that it names things and ideas in such a way that anyone other than the namer (and other than the namer at the moment of naming) will connect the very same things and ideas with the naming words. To ask why people come to believe that language works does not imply an attempt to convince them that they should not, any more than Newman's asking how one comes to believe in God (the overall question of the *Grammar*) implies that believing in God is an error.

The strategy Newman adopts in 1837 to account for the assumption that scripture is the Rule of Faith is likewise instructive. He does not attempt to identify the roots of the assumption but instead suggests that they are somehow linked to "the popular feeling of the sixteenth century." With this casual historical reference to the beginnings of the Reformation, Newman replaces argument with a well-known fact, whose pertinence to the matter at hand he does not demonstrate. Yet his introduction of history changes the character of the argument that precedes it, dignifying it and lending it a certain plausibility, simply because a relation between the argument and such a well-known fact is implied. This strategic maneuver is a very simple example of a common literary device: using history to create a transition between one idea and another (often suggesting a cause-and-effect relationship) or to begin a narrative by linking one event to another. The maneuver effected by his citation of his own work in 1870 mirrors his use of it in the 1837 passage. This kind of maneuver takes on an especially compelling character when it is thus linked to autobiography. As he argues in 1870 for the existence and importance of the illative sense, the historical event (the existence of a "sense" about scripture in the sixteenth century, brought in as a substitute for argument) and an autobiographical event (Newman's assertion in 1837 that there exists such a "sense") seem, dimly, to become meaningful, reversed reflections of each other.

The way in which this particular example of self-citation is to function can be made clearer after a look at another example of the same strategy, taken from an earlier chapter in the same book. Self-reading is an important rhetorical device in the *Grammar*, and the way it is used suggests the role that writing plays in Newman's argument at a level less obvious than that of scriptural authority. In founding his *Grammar of Assent* upon the contrast between notional assent (assent to notions) and real assent (assent to things—the same as belief; pp. 48, 87), Newman cites a letter he published in 1841, written while he was working on Tract XC,[5] a landmark in the history of the Oxford Movement: it showed that the Thirty-nine Articles of the Church of England were susceptible of a Catholic interpretation and eventually led to Newman's break with Anglicanism. The letter cited thus comes from a period in which his skills as an interpreter and a writer were implicated in the crucial event of his public life. Still a Protestant clergyman, he published the letter under the pen name Catholicus, an epithet that anticipates by four years his conversion, which is dated at 1845. The subject matter of the letter is even more important than its date and pseudonymous attribution. It concerns the possible ill effects of the establishment of a public library and is one of a series of seven letters opposing Sir Robert Peel's views on "the Tamworth Reading Room." The issue is whether reading has a good or bad influence on an intellectually defenseless group, the working class. Newman, as "Catholicus," asks, "What has virtue to do with a Reading-room?" and argues that secular knowledge does not promote ethical behavior. From a theological standpoint, then, he is in 1841 questioning the hierarchical superiority of knowledge over belief, in a context that concerns secular books rather than theology.

In 1870 Newman introduces into the *Grammar* a lengthy passage from the 1841 letter in the following terms: "I insisted on this marked distinction between Beliefs on the one hand, and Notional Assents and Inferences on the other, many years ago in words it will be to my purpose to use now. I quote them because, over and above their appositeness in this place, they present the doctrine on which I have been insisting, from a second point of view, and with a freshness and force which I cannot now command, and, moreover, (though they are my own, nonetheless, for the length of time which has elapsed since their publication) almost with the cogency of an independent testimony" (p. 88).

Here, Newman is very far from saying that the words he wrote "then" mean something else "now," but what he does say about the relation between his words of an earlier time and his present intentions

5. Francis X. Connolly, Introduction, *A Newman Reader* (Garden City, N.Y.: Doubleday, 1964), p. 29. The Reading Room letters are reprinted in Newman, *Essays and Sketches*, (New York: Longmans Green, 1948), 2:173–214.

is nonetheless instructive. He says that self-citation—citation of his own words from an earlier time—lends authority to his argument for two reasons. The first is implicit: what appeared "many years ago in words" transcends, in meaning and truthfulness, the present and perhaps polemical moment. The second is explicit: the words of his youth have a vigor no longer at his disposal. To describe his younger and older selves, Newman uses a commonplace employed, especially by the romantics, to compare the words of writers to those of literary precursors.[6] The passage of time is taken to increase (whereas in some other settings it might be thought to decrease) the value or force of words; time is taken to change the significance of words.

In addition, Newman suggests that because the same person speaks the same message at two different times, offering "almost . . . an independent testimony," that message is truer than if spoken by that person at only one time; the passage of time makes it possible to describe one self as two. This elaboration of two distinct moments into an intrapersonal differentiation between two distinct selves is unusual only because of the frankness with which Newman states it in a non-fictional context. Even though the differentiation of one self into two, purportedly distinguished by chronological position, is merely a corollary of the principle that the passage of time is regarded as changing the import of words, literary texts more often represent this corollary than illustrate the principle itself.

The greater visibility of the corollary as compared to the principle follows a pattern demonstrated by Walter J. Ong, later refined and linked especially to the nature of language by Louis Marin. In *Ramus, Method, and the Decay of Dialogue*,[7] Ong showed how processes of thought not intrinsically and necessarily spatial in nature came to be described in spatial terms and then accepted as in fact spatial in nature. He enunciated this difficult concept by presenting the move toward the spatialization of thought as linked to a particular period in history, rather than as a more general mental strategy. Marin, in his brilliant analysis of the Port-Royal texts, the *Grammaire* and *La Logique*, discussed the efforts of the Port-Royalists to come to grips with "the temporalization of the act of verbalization," the necessary dependence

6. The *loci classici* of this romantic commonplace are the studies that Harold Bloom began with *The Anxiety of Influence* (London: Oxford University Press, 1973). The gesture is also similar to that of a medieval writer citing his or her *auctoritas*.

7. Walter J. Ong, *Ramus, Method, and the Decay of Dialogue* (Cambridge, Mass.: Harvard University Press, 1958).

of meaning on memory, pointing out that the problem was not simply a psychological one but also had, for them, metaphysical and epistemological implications. It is Marin's idea that the Port-Royalists solved the problem by "transferring the temporal aporias of the totality and complexity of the representation to space. . . .Space is then the backdrop against which the figure rises, the scenery in which the figures take form and the stage on which they are represented while taking on meaning and value."[8] Although the texts by Nerval and Baudelaire discussed later in this book "dramatize" (to continue Marin's metaphor) the spatialization of temporal problems inhering in language by using human "figures," characters, rather than the categories of grammar or logic, the pattern remains the same as that suggested by Ong and Marin: there is a movement away from awareness of the temporal doubt and confusion at the root of language toward a concrete spatialization of what is accepted as an adequate approximation of that doubt.

This pattern appears in Newman's *Grammar* in his definition of mind, based on the idea of multiple selves within one person: "The mind is like a double mirror, in which reflections of self within self multiply themselves till they are undistinguishable, and the first reflection contains all the rest" (p. 162). In a lecture of 1858, Newman wrote of another doubled relationship involving thought, and in this case also he did not ascribe any temporal character to the doubling; the spatialization of what Marin's Port-Royal logicians recognized as a temporal problem is thus fully realized. In the 1858 lecture thought is seen as one half of a unity, the other half of which is language. The metaphor that incorporates language is material, geometric:

> Thought and speech are inseparable from each other. Matter and expression are parts of one: style is a thinking out into language. This is what I have been laying down, and this is literature; not *things*; not on

8. Louis Marin, *La Critique du discours: Sur la "Logique de Port-Royal" et les "Pensées de Pascal"* (Paris: Minuit, 1975), pp. 165–66. Psychoanalysis also treats the convertibility of temporal and spatial modes, though from a different perspective; the application of this perspective to literary language is illustrated by Paul de Man, "Ludwig Binswanger et le problème du moi poétique," in Georges Poulet et al., *Les Chemins actuels de la critique* (Paris: Union générale d'Editions, 1968), pp. 43–58, esp. 52–53; translated by the author as "Ludwig Binswanger and the Sublimation of the Self," in *Blindness and Insight* (New York: Oxford University Press, 1971), pp. 36–50, esp. 44–46. See also Roman Ingarden, *The Cognition of the Literary Work of Art*, trans. Ruth Ann Crowley and Kenneth R. Olson (Evanston, Ill.: Northwestern University Press, 1973), p. 110 n. 11.

the other hand mere *words*; but thoughts expressed in language. Call to mind, Gentlemen, the meaning of the Greek word which expresses this special prerogative of man over the feeble intelligence of the inferior animals. It is called Logos: what does Logos mean? it stands for both *reason* and for *speech*, and it is difficult to say which it means more properly. It means both at once: why? because they are in a true sense one. When we can separate light and illumination, life and motion, the convex and the concave of a curve, then will it be possible for thought to tread speech under foot, and to hope to do without it—then will it be conceivable that the vigorous and fertile intellect should renounce its own double, its instrument of expression, and the channel of its speculations and emotions.[9]

Both these passages convert a temporal split into something spatial, though neither alludes to time. In the definition of the mind as a double mirror, Newman is talking about sequential selves or, to put it another way, the self at different moments. These selves may be made to "relive" in memory, and the mind may be thought of as the locus in which the process of remembering occurs. The selves are not, however, simultaneously existing, different selves but rather selves of different times. In the passage about thought and language as doubles, any recognition of the possibility of a temporal problem in the relation of thought to speech is suppressed, and the two become the "doubles" of myth and fairytale. Only when the temporal aspect of the relation between language and thought (which in this passage is then equated with reason) is suppressed can the two be taken as doubles.

It is important to contrast Newman's attitude toward the relation of language and thought as presented in this passage with the attitude toward the same relation as he presents it in the two passages cited earlier. There, in his criticism of the Protestant Rule of Faith and in the Reading Room controversy, Newman calls attention to this relationship and also shows a consciousness of temporality, whether in argument or imagery or in the context in which he introduces his quotations. But when he describes the relation of language to mind as simple and harmonious, he suppresses that temporal consciousness entirely. In this regard, his way of dealing with the relation between time and (his own) language is anything but "eccentric"; it is paradigmatic.

9. John Henry Newman, *The Idea of a University* (New York: Rinehart, 1960), p. 308.

Exegesis and Interpretation

The foregoing exploration of passages from Newman's writings has introduced several topics that recur in the chapters to come, including doubles, pseudonyms, and libraries. More important, it has suggested four general notions basic to the problem I am treating. First, the belief that language does "work" is an unproven assumption that avoids basic questions about *how* it works. Second, the creation of a historical narrative structure may be a strategy that circumvents argument. Third, the passage of time may be taken to change the meaning of words. Fourth, the passage of time can be converted into a spatial construct, especially comprising images of multiple rather than sequential selves, through a process that makes it easy completely to forget about the experience involved in temporal relationships.

Of these four notions, the third, directly tied to the epigraph of this chapter, provides the clearest introduction to the project of this book: analysis of the timeliness of reading—that is, of the temporal situation[10] that constitutes, motivates, and defines reading. Newman's use of self-citation suggests that this situation is founded on the tension between two poles, poles that I will call "exegesis" and "interpretation," taking this terminological distinction from theological hermeneutics to respond to a need within literary hermeneutics.[11] "Ex-

10. This rather special use of "situation" is to be contrasted with Maurice Merleau-Ponty's use of the term, which is discussed in the Conclusion; for now, it is enough to recall the word's etymological relation to "site," suggesting the similarity of reading to a structure whose shape and orientation are determined by a particular place, which here represents time.

11. "In theological discussion. . . exegesis normally meant determining what meaning the text has for its own author and intended readers, interpretation sought the meaning the text could have for the current age, and hermeneutics concerned the rules to apply in order to get from the former to the latter": Paul J. Achtmeier, *An Introduction to the New Hermeneutic* (Philadelphia: Westminster Press, 1969), pp. 13–14. Cf. David Hoy, "Literary History: Paradox or Paradigm," *Yale French Studies* 52 (1975), 268–86: "The task of a theory of literary interpretation becomes one of coming to terms with the tension between the immanence of literature and the historicity of interpretation" (pp. 269–70). As Hoy's usage illustrates, however (like Emilio Betti's, discussed in the Conclusion), the word "interpretation" is often used even within hermeneutics to designate what is here termed "exegesis." A parallel dichotomy, though with a personalistic rather than temporal basis, is discussed by Patrocinio P. Schweickart, "Toward a Feminist Theory of Reading," in *Gender and Reading: Essays on Readers, Texts, and Contexts*, ed. Elizabeth A. Flynn and Patrocinio P. Schweickart (Baltimore, Md: Johns Hopkins University Press, 1986), pp. 31–62, esp. 55. A similar pattern is suggested, in the same volume, by Elizabeth A. Flynn, "Gender and Reading," pp. 267–88, esp. 267.

egesis" is a form of reading that emphasizes the words' temporal distance from the reader; "interpretation" emphasizes their closeness. For example, if Newman in 1870 had read his words of 1837 in order to recall as fully as possible what his views and circumstances had been in 1837, he would have been reading exegetically. When he looked for a truth for 1870 in the 1837 text, he was interpreting it.

These two forms of reading result from two kinds of relationship between reader and text, and their distinction has more than just practical significance for literary criticism. The reader who relates to a text in both ways will privilege neither text nor self with genetic priority or hierarchic superiority but will judge each in appropriate contexts. Such an ability to move, consciously, between these two poles would markedly alter the role that written language plays in culture. It would also help identify other problems inherent in reading, for variations of kind in the relationship between a single reader and a text reveal most about the nature of reading itself.

At this initial stage, however, the character of these two poles needs to be further delineated through some discussion of the similarities between exegesis and interpretation. Purely exegetical activity mirrors purely interpretive activity. An exegete is concerned with the text's historical character and position but not with her or his own. Thus, an exegete, although perhaps labeled a "historicist," will in fact try to evade history in the most fundamental way. At moments when the exegete realizes that the total historical reconstruction of a text is impossible, she or he becomes an interpreter. While perhaps continuing to give the text's historicity a passing nod, out of scholarly habit, the interpreter's principal goal will be to identify a relationship between the text and what is contemporary to the interpreter. While not denying that the text has its own historical character, the interpreter is likely to be skeptical about her or his ability to know it, implying that it is not the interpreter who evades history but history that evades the interpreter. At both exegetical and interpretive poles, then, the reader's stance with regard to history is unsteady, serving to impel a restless movement, a kind of oscillation between the two.[12]

---

12. A parallel to the "oscillating" movement between exegetical and interpretive modes of reading is Elaine Showalter's model of the female reader as operating inside two traditions at once and keeping two "oscillating" images of a text simultaneously in view; in "Review Essay: Literary Criticism," *Signs* 1 (1975), 435–60, she terms it "hermeneutic sleight of hand." Whereas Showalter is concerned with two perspectives discriminated according to patterns of gender dominance, my concern is with two perspectives that the reader attempts to discriminate temporally.

These two poles share yet another parallel difficulty. The exegete's historical position constitutes a claim of self-effacement. But the subject of the verb "to read" cannot disappear, although tradition identifies the illusion of doing so as a source of pleasure. The illusion of self-effacement, or rather of absorption of the exegete's self by one identified with the text or author, is a denial of differentiation, temporal and otherwise, from the text in favor of the production of an illusion of multiple selves. On the other hand, when an interpreter ceases to maintain this differentiation between text and self, the text necessarily becomes a projection of the interpreter's categories. Although some interpreters may erroneously claim that such a projective relationship to the text is "dialectical" (as some exegetes may call their antihistorical activities "historicism"), their difficulties in differentiating themselves from the text raise grave doubts about their abilities to fulfill their primary goal, the establishment of a dialectical relationship between themselves and contemporary culture. Ultimately, the interpreter who does not also read as an exegete has no text. Similarly, the exegete, who must first of all establish or choose the edition of a text to work from, cannot have a text without first making a judgment about that text's meaning which is necessarily interpretive.

Exegesis and interpretation, then, are two distinct kinds of reading that cannot be kept separate, for one mirrors and depends upon the other. Insofar as they are distinct, the tension between them must form the foundation of any analysis of the nature of reading, yet their inseparability is among the principal factors that make such analysis difficult. There does exist a more attractive approach to this foundation: one might ask whether the structure and goals of the relationship between reader and text have changed in the course of history—not the history of an individual's reading but rather the history of an entire culture's reading activity. This is the question with which my argument begins.

Chapter 1

A Sketch of a Fragment
from a Story of Reading

Once upon a time there was a prince named Louis whose
mother wanted him to learn how to read.

What I wish I could do in this chapter[1] is to give a full explanation of what is happening in the miniature that appears as frontispiece
to this book. Instead, much of the chapter must be taken up in explaining why neither I nor anyone else can give that full explanation and
why it is nonetheless useful to attempt it. Explaining what is happening in the picture would inevitably mean making a narrative, just as
storytellers do when they begin with "once upon a time." This narrative would involve not only the ordering of some facts about the
childhood of Saint Louis, if the necessary facts could be found, but also
the placing of these facts in a historical context by connecting the kind

1. An excerpt from an earlier version appeared in the University of Chicago Library
Society *Bulletin* 2 (Winter 1977), 2–15. I am grateful to Ruth Dean, Peter F. Dembowski, Harvey Graff, Bert Hall, Sandra Hindman, George Huppert, M. B. Parkes,
Robert Rosenthal, and Richard H. Rouse for their comments on it; I have unfortunately
been unable to pursue many of them because of this chapter's limited scope. For a
survey of studies in medieval literacy, see Harvey Graff, *Literacy in History: An Inter-
disciplinary Research Bibliography* (New York: Garland, 1981), esp. pp. 146–79, 88–102.
Jesse H. Gellrich, *The Idea of the Book in the Middle Ages* (Ithaca: Cornell University
Press, 1985) treats several issues discussed in this and the following chapter. Brian
Stock, *The Implications of Literacy* (Princeton, N.J.: Princeton University Press, 1983),
treats the period immediately preceding that of Saint Louis, the eleventh and twelfth
centuries, as characterized by a growing dominance of written over oral tradition. A
useful survey that spans both the classical and modern eras is Jane P. Tompkins, "The
Reader in History: The Changing Shape of Literary Response," in *Reader Response
Criticism*, ed. Jane P. Tompkins (Baltimore, Md.: Johns Hopkins University Press,
1980), pp. 201–32.

of duration known as "historical period" with the moment in time that the miniature may be said to represent. If the narrative were to be an extended one, moreover, including many chapters in the story of reading, it would involve comparing the period of the miniature with other periods and comparing the location or setting represented in the miniature with others. It might involve inferring that if a certain thing were known to be done in a certain way in a time *before* the period of the miniature and in a time *after* it as well, the thing might have been done in the same way in Saint Louis's day. In short, writing such a narrative would necessitate drawing many inferences, most involving manipulations of time.

Although I think the writing of such a narrative would be very risky, one of the reasons I wish I could do it is the great difference I see between two of the most famous "fictive readers"[2] in the history of European literature: those addressed by Baudelaire and by Dante. The work of each of these authors is generally regarded from a literary-historical viewpoint as a major landmark. Dante marks a kind of apex for medieval literature and, specifically, the beginnings of poetry written in a vernacular language oriented less toward entertaining its readers than toward edifying them. Baudelaire marks the beginning of modernism and, with it, of a new and more troubled attitude toward the relation between poetry and ethical instruction. *Les Fleurs du mal* and the *Commedia* are strikingly similar: each is perhaps the masterpiece of moral analysis and criticism of its age; each represents depravity in the most shocking terms; each also evokes bliss; each is known above all for the power of its language. Both authors stress from the outset an intimate kinship between themselves and the reader, Baudelaire by calling the reader "mon semblable, mon frère" (one like me, my brother) and Dante by the famous trick of the *Commedia*'s first lines: "Nel mezzo del cammin di nostra vita / Mi ritrovai per una selva oscura / Chè la diritta via era smarrita" (In the middle of the journey of our life / I found myself in a dark wood / For the straight way was lost).

Yet authorial apostrophes in these two works directly address readers who, though sharing a taste for the same kind of shocking, analytical, beautiful poetry, are completely different sorts. Dante evokes a reader who is reverent and attentive, not just to the poet's message and

2. The term is introduced by Lowry Nelson, Jr., "The Fictive Reader and Literary Self-Reflexiveness," in *The Disciplines of Criticism*, ed. Lowry Nelson, Jr., Thomas Greene, and Peter Demetz (New Haven, Conn.: Yale University Press, 1968); Dante is discussed on pp. 184–87.

the words that embody it but also to the very letters and sounds of those words. He describes his reader as sitting at a desk studying the work, looking hard for Dante's meaning under the covering of his unfamiliar terms; Dante also stresses that the reader must bring adequate equipment to make a successful reading of the *Commedia* possible. Baudelaire's famous prefatory poem "Au lecteur," by contrast, describes a reader who is anything but studious and disposed to equip himself for a difficult journey. The chief characteristic of Baudelaire's reader is "ennui": he picks up *Les Fleurs du mal* out of boredom. Far from earnestly seeking the "straight way," he is a "hypocrite." No willing student of the author, he rather engages with him in the most bitter kind of sibling struggle. If Dante treats his reader like a cherished younger brother whom he must admonish and prod to see that he "turns out well," Baudelaire evokes rather the relationship of Cain and Abel.

Much of this difference between fictive readers may stem from authorial idiosyncrasy; nevertheless, I feel compelled to ask whether some of it is not attributable as well to differences between actual readers, as a class, in early fourteenth-century Tuscany and mid-nineteenth-century Paris. Specifically, I would ask whether the difference between these fictive readers is paralleled by any differences in the ideological, material, or institutional aspects of reading—other than the differences in literary style, genre, subject matter, and so on, which are the traditional objects of literary study. I mean such things as the moral value assigned to reading within a culture, the appearance of the book and its effect on reading, and reading pedagogy. The question I am raising is similar to one posed by Walter Ong, who has emphasized the need, within the context of rhetorical studies, "to broach directly the question of readers' roles called for by a written text, whether synchronically as such roles stand at present or diachronically as they developed through history."[3]

It is commonly assumed, I think, that literature has changed with time, and that readers as participants in political life and economic life, for example, have changed as well. But it is less commonly assumed that readers have changed as readers, that the way they have carried on

3. Walter J. Ong, "The Writer's Audience Is Always a Fiction," *PMLA* 90 (January 1975), 9–10. A French example is chosen here to stand for the case of Dante's Italian reader—whose circumstances were necessarily different; cf. J. K. Hyde, *Society and Politics in Medieval Italy* (London: Macmillan, 1973), pp. 6–7—to emphasize that the point is applicable generally, not to Italy alone.

the process of reading has changed. Instead, it is generally supposed that the reading process has remained stable while the character of literature and of life has changed. One reason for this assumption is that few details about the reading process in most periods have been gathered and analyzed, so that a credible narration of reading's history as one of change rather than changelessness may at present seem unattainable. I am suggesting that instead of looking at the few commonly known facts about the reading process in earlier periods and assuming that they indicate an activity rather like the one practiced today, it would be more instructive to assume earlier reading to be unlike reading today. In the terms outlined in the Introduction, I am proposing to begin study of the temporal situation of reading by trying an exegetical rather than an interpretive approach to the narration of the story of reading.

While some historians of education, media, and culture have interested themselves in the periodization and localization of the ideological, material, and institutional developments that I wish to relate to the history of reading, historians of literature generally have not. This is particularly true if their own reading has primarily been limited to European works published since about 1500. This chapter is intended primarily to raise questions in their minds, although its argument must be qualified by an important caveat. When a narrative addressed to adults begins with "once upon a time," it purposely calls itself into question in many ways, one of which must above all be stressed here: if something is reported to have occurred "*once* upon a time," it need not have happened that way again. If one could know that Saint Louis once read the Psalter in a certain manner, that would not necessarily imply that anyone else ever read it just so, before his time or after. My goal is to help open possibilities for conceptualizing such discrete moments in the history of reading rather than to establish general patterns.

To keep from being misled by what the Middle Ages would deplore as excessively "literal" reading of the story to be narrated in this chapter, one must bear in mind that it initiates an argument about those aspects of temporality that are repressed or forgotten in reading. Its narrative must therefore not be read as a way to minimize the difficulties inherent in the drawing of inferences about any facet of the temporality of reading, including its history, but rather as a way to recall such difficulties and make them accessible to further reflection. Experience of the temporality of reading is available to all readers, although some may more often welcome that experience and others more often turn away from it. Nonetheless, any reader who is to go on reading must turn away from temporality while reading. Narrating an episode from the history of reading is useful: it reminds readers of the temporality they must often forget. Narratives of this kind thus serve as mnemonic devices evoking a theoretical problem, even though they are incapable of reconstructing a moment that is lost. They can make more comprehensible the difference between Dante's reverent, studious reader and Baudelaire's bored, hypocritical one. With this in mind, I turn back to my sketch of a fragment from a story of reading.

A Legend of Saint Louis

Once upon a time there was a prince named Louis whose mother wanted him to learn to read. Born in 1214 and crowned king of France at his father's death twelve years later, Louis appears at the center of the frontispiece miniature wearing not a crown but a halo, recalling the saintly life that led to his canonization just a few years before 1300— the fictive date of Dante's *Commedia*. He is holding a book, and his mother, Blanche of Castile, is overseeing what he is doing with it. In his right hand Louis holds what seems to be a *festuca*, a pointer used for picking out words or letters; a tonsured cleric holds a bundle of sticks. The sticks, together with the seated rather than kneeling position of all three figures, suggest that what is in progress may be a reading lesson rather than an episode of prayer, although the exercise is nonetheless clearly devotional in intent.[4] Prayerbooks were so commonly used for the teaching of reading that they were also known as "primers" or "first books,"[5] confirming that a depiction of the reading of devotions and of a reading lesson might amount to the same thing. The eyes of mother and cleric (whom I take, then, to be a tutor) meet over the child's head, as if assenting gravely to the seriousness of the task. Their

4. Walter J. Ong, *Rhetoric, Romance, and Technology* (Ithaca: Cornell University Press, 1971), p. 125, mentions "bundles of switches as regular classroom equipment" in pictures of Renaissance classrooms, tracing the common Renaissance practice of physical punishment to the extensive, ritualized, medieval equation of flogging with learning. Guillaume de Saint-Pathus, confessor to Louis's wife, stresses in his biography of the saint that Louis reported being beaten by his master several times: *Vie de Saint-Louis*, ed. H.-F. Delaborde, Collection de textes pour servir à l'étude et à l'enseignement d'histoire (Paris: Picard, 1899), p. 18.

5. On the controversial etymology of "primer," see Edwyn Birchenough, "The Prymer in English," *Transactions of the Bibliographical Society: The Library*, ser. 4 (1938), 177–78.

symmetrical postures frame Louis's activity. His line of vision converges with those formed by the forefingers of Blanche and the cleric, pointing, like so many *festucae*, to the page, mirroring the activity of the reader of the Book of Hours in which the miniature appears.

The triangle of figures recalls one of the most wide-ranging of the questions one must ask about reading in the period 1100–1500: what was the composition of the reading public? What was the social identity of those who concerned themselves with reading? If there is evidence that members of a particular group in a particular period received some basic instruction in literacy, does this mean they are to be seen as part of the literary public? Does it imply that literary works of that period are to be read now with their background and values in mind? The groups represented in the miniature are women, kings, and clerics. Nonetheless, what role women and kings played in developing literacy is especially unclear.

A few remarks on literacy in relation to the class to which Prince Louis belonged may give some idea of the difficulties involved in defining the social composition of the reading public in the late Middle Ages. Although it has often been suggested that Carolingians considered reading an unmanly activity, best left to women and priests who stayed at home while the warriors went off on the business that mattered, by 1200 it seems to have been a commonplace that a young man in training for knighthood should learn letters in order to be able to say the Latin prayers fixed by the Church.[6] But this recitation need

6. Cf. *Jourdain de Blaye*, ed. Peter F. Dembowski (Chicago: University of Chicago Press, 1969), p. 35 (line 698). The biography of Saint Louis by his confessor, Geoffrey of Beaulieu, indicates that the king was able to translate some Latin into French for the benefit of his entourage and that he could write with his own hand: Gaufrido de Belloloco, *Vita Ludovici Noni* (Paris: Imprimerie Royale, 1840), chaps. 14, 23, reprinted in *Receuil des historiens des Gaules et de la France* 20, (1968). M. T. Clanchy, *From Memory to Written Record: England 1066–1307* (London: Edward Arnold, 1979), p. 186, noting that even Henry I and Henry II received instruction in Latin, points out that from "King John's reign [which ended a decade before Louis's began] onwards elementary instruction in Latin [for English kings] was taken for granted" and infers that the "example set by the kings inevitably gave the [English] baronage and gentry a motivation to learn some Latin." M. B. Parkes, "The Literacy of the Laity," in *The Medieval World*, ed. David Daiches and Anthony Thorlby (London: Aldous Books, 1973), 2:555–77, presents evidence of a certain level of practically oriented literacy among the English peasantry of the period; some of Clanchy's material supports Parkes's conclusion. Blanche was by no means the only medieval mother to take an active role in her child's education: cf. Clanchy, *From Memory to Written Record*, p. 196, and Dhuoda, discussed below. Contemporary complaints of an illiterate parish clergy, surprising in a period of

not have implied that such a young man could construe even simple Latin or understand the meanings of the Latin words he learned to recite. Even aristocrats with a reputation for learning may not have known how to read for themselves, like that learned man of the twelfth century, the possessor of a fine library, who continued to follow the Roman practice of having his dependents read to him and did not himself know how to read.[7] In a treatise on the subject of the perfect prince which Louis was to commission around 1260, Vincent of Beauvais quotes what was already an old proverb: "Rex illiteratus est quasi asinus coronatus" (an unlettered king is like a crowned ass); yet in the early fifteenth century Christine de Pizan still found it necessary to urge that the kings of France should learn to read for themselves the laws they had to sign, so that they need not depend on clerks and ministers for a knowledge of the contents.[8] Louis is known to have read aloud to a group while translating from Latin into French for the benefit of ignorant courtiers,[9] but his level of learning seems to have struck contemporary observers as remarkable, almost on a par with his "miracles." Contemporary awe at his reading and praying may even explain the choice of subject for the miniature. It is therefore impossible to generalize about other monarchs or nobles. For women the evidence is even more sparse and difficult to interpret, and much the same is true for such other groups as merchants, artisans, and peasants.

The presence of the pointer in the prince's hand is interesting; perhaps he would have used such an implement when his master "taught him letters," to use the phrase of Guillaume de Saint-Pathus. We do not know just how a thirteenth-century prince would practice his

---

increasing literacy, are discounted by Janet Coleman, *English Literature in History, 1340–1400: Medieval Readers and Writers* (London: Hutchinson, 1981), pp. 35–37, which cites increased competition for clerical positions from about 1100 to the Reformation as the motivation for increased complaints about the qualifications of those who held coveted posts.

7. Parkes, "The Literacy of the Laity," p. 556. Carlo M. Cipolla, *Literacy and Development in the West* (London: Penguin Books, 1969), p. 40, compares such a man to a wealthy person who does not learn how to drive because driving is the province of the chauffeur.

8. Christine de Pizan, *Le Livre des faits et des bonnes meurs du bonne roy Charles V*, ed. Suzanne Solente (Paris: Champion, 1936–40). Clanchy, *From Memory to Written Record*, pp. 161–62, points out that it was during Louis's lifetime that the vernacular became a language of record acceptable at court: "The earliest petitions to St. Louis in 1247 are written in Latin, whereas those of two decades later are in French."

9. Gaufrido de Belloloco, *Vita Ludovici Noni*, p. 15.

ABC's. One very old method required the pupil to pick out with his pointer all the examples of the letter A on a page, then all the B's, and so on. Other aids the tutor might or might not have employed included an alphabet or syllabary written across the top of the first page of the book to be used as a primer[10] or letters carved out of ivory, like dice. In the miniature he may well be at a more advanced stage, actually reciting or reading; the pointer might then serve to help him keep his place. If so, this suggests that the reading is proceeding slowly, whether because the prince is a beginning reader or because a slow pace was thought appropriate to devotional reading.

To wonder how the prince might have "learned his letters" is to turn one's attention from general questions of social and pedagogical history to the very physical aspect of medieval manuscripts. Certainly such a focus is not inappropriate to the student of medieval literature. Dante, particularly at certain points in the *Commedia*, obliges his reader to contemplate with reverence the very letters of his text. While the theoretical concerns of this book may seem remote from consideration of material details, it is just such physical features that can best serve the mnemonic function this narrative proposes to fulfill, given their marked differences from the physical features of books today. As L. M. J. Delaissé points out, the designation "book" is now commonly denied to manuscript books,[11] as if, because their letters were copied by hand rather than printed by a press, they are somehow less complete or permanent. What were these handwritten letters like, and might their character have in some way affected the reading process? The noted paleographer E. A. Lowe remarked of the script of Saint Louis's day: "The Gothic script is difficult to read. It has the serious faults of ambiguity, artificiality, and overloading. It was the child of an age that was not bent on achieving the practical, the age of St. Louis and St. Francis. It is as if the written page was made to be looked at and not read. Instead of legibility its objective seems to be a certain effect of art and beauty."[12]

10. Sandra Hindman informs me that such ABC's appear in manuscript schoolbooks prepared for the Emperor Maximilian I in the later fifteenth century. This method, as well as the use of the Christ's-cross or crisscross, is found in hornbooks, a later development.

11. L. M. J. Delaissé, "Towards a History of the Medieval Book," *Miscellanea André Combes* (Rome: Libreria editrice della Pontifica Università Lateranense, 1969), pp. 423–35.

12. E. A. Lowe, "Handwriting," in *The Legacy of the Middle Ages*, ed. C. G. Crump and E. F. Jacobs (Oxford: Clarendon Press, 1962), p. 223.

One might infer, then, that Louis would have had to spend more time learning his letters than a child might today. Moreover, there was not just one category of Gothic script but many, each serving a different textual function and occupying a different place in a kind of hierarchy of scripts.[13] Different fonts are used in today's printed books to distinguish, for example, chapter headings or foreign words; the greater range of differences among the various Gothic scripts was due to some extent to scholastic emphasis on an analytical approach to texts, which suggested the importance of thus discriminating their parts visually. To reach full literacy, then, a Gothic reader would have to master a kind of semiotics of scripts, not only identifying the various forms a letter might take but knowing what these forms meant within the text structure. Such a hierarchy of scripts obtained, however, only within books copied by professional scribes trained to use them. The scripts they wrote may be generally classified as text or book hand. Very different was the class of Gothic cursive hands. Cursive, that is, "running," hands are comparable to what schoolchildren today call "writing" as learned in the middle grades as distinct from the "printing" to which primary schoolers are limited. Cursive hands were long limited to use in documents drafted in the rush of business. They nonetheless came, rather later than Saint Louis's time, to be used also to copy books. M. B. Parkes points out that this development was particularly advantageous to the "pragmatic reader," one who, unlike the scholarly reader or the cultivated reader in pursuit of recreation, had learned to read in the transaction of business: "Instead of having to master the difficult alphabets of the several varieties of the text hand, [the pragmatic reader] could read a book in the alphabet with which he had become familiar in the course of reading and drafting documents."[14]

But in the early thirteenth century a knowledge of several text hands and cursives was necessary if one were to read more than a very limited number of books and documents. An acquaintance with regional variations in Gothic script would have been useful, too, and consultation of documents of past generations would require knowledge of pre-Gothic scripts. The early thirteenth-century reader of vernacular litera-

13. For an introduction in English to this topic, see Sandra Hindman and James Douglas Farquhar, *Pen to Press* (College Park: Art Department, University of Maryland; Baltimore: Department of the History of Art, Johns Hopkins University, 1977), pp. 55–56.
14. Parkes, "The Literacy of the Laity," p. 563.

ture, moreover, had to acquire an additional skill. In Latin books it was by this time well established that words should be separated from each other by spaces and not run together, as had been the practice from Roman times. But the older practice persisted to some extent in the vernacular manuscripts that the laity might be most likely to read.[15]

Such compounding of the difficulties of fully learning one's letters no doubt affected the attitudes toward reading of even those who emerged victorious over the deciphering process that dominated the Gothic schoolroom. Learning to discriminate and identify letter forms is necessarily a process of trial and error for any child in any age, but today it is shaped by school materials (and even television programs) that stress clarity in letter forms and familiarity and appeal in their semantic associations. Reading is fun, children are told in countless ways. The learning process is structured so that rewards come rapidly: identification of, implying mastery over, favorite objects ("'I' is for ice cream cone"). Everything is done to make trials few and errors easy to avoid (although no way has yet been found to make reading continue to be this easy beyond the letter-learning stage). Louis had a harder time and probably never thought reading "fun." While he clearly valued it, it is doubtful that he would have expected it to bring immediate rewards.

But perhaps it was language and not letter forms that most forcefully shaped Louis's early expectations about what kind of activity reading was to be. His first reading materials were written in Latin, not his mother's tongue. Although the translation of such elementary reading materials as *Cato's Distichs* suggests that there was some introductory reading education based on vernacular languages as early as the second half of Louis's century,[16] initiation into reading by means of Latin texts may have continued to be the norm in some places as late as 1450— perhaps even later.

In such circumstances, "reading" did not necessarily mean "understanding": some pupils learned their letters, were able to copy Psalms, and could identify and recite these Psalms—all without knowing what

---

15. Paul Saenger, "Silent Reading: Its Impact on Late Medieval Script and Society," *Viator* 13 (1982) 406.

16. Henri Pirenne, "L'Instruction des marchands au moyen âge," *Annales d'histoire économique et sociale* 1 (1929), 13–28, at p. 28, mentions that Flemish versions of *Cato's Distichs* were available in this period. I am aware of examples, though not many, from the fourteenth century, in English, French, Provençal, and Tuscan. In the absence of central governmental control of education, pedagogical practice in this and other respects varied from place to place.

the words meant. Pierre Riché describes the reciting of Latin without understanding as common in the seventh and eighth centuries ("The text remained a dead letter for those who received only elementary instruction"),[17] and lack of understanding of the Latin Pater Noster, a text frequently used as first "reader," was still common enough in the first half of the fifteenth century to be a particular focus of Lollard scorn.[18]

Throughout the Middle Ages there was thus a continuous tradition of education in letter recognition and Latin memorization which did not, in many cases, lead to what would today be described as the ability to read. The tradition derived from the belief that there is in certain forms of language a power that transcends human reason, a belief akin to that which Newman saw (paradoxically) as fundamental to those heirs of Lollardy, the sixteenth-century Protestants. It is an attitude toward language which goes far deeper than sectarian polemics; it sees language as valuable not merely through its priority to meaning but even despite its complete lack of attainment of meaning. When a child's first book is written in a language other than its mother's—as is likely in colonial or postcolonial cultures or in households transplanted to a country different from that of the parents' birth—that fact affects the child's attitudes toward reading and written language. When the first language read is primarily associated with worship, the child's associations with worship affect the attitude toward reading, and written language will continue to possess the special power or status associated with worship. The very difference between Latin and the vernacular enhanced this power by association. Although medieval reading masters might argue that Latin was easier to learn because it was more regular in spelling and syntax and smoother in sound than the vernaculars of the day, Latin still differed in many and disconcerting ways from the languages lay children (those not raised in monasteries) spoke before beginning their schooling. In one area (for example, the Germanic) the syntax of Latin might seem in many respects intuitively familiar, while the vocabulary might seem almost wholly foreign. Elsewhere (for example, where the vernacular was a Romance language), beginning readers might readily understand a large number of cognate words but be puzzled about the ways the parts of a sentence fit together.

17. Pierre Riché, *Education and Culture in the Barbarian West*, trans. John J. Contreni (Columbia: University of South Carolina Press, 1976), p. 468.
18. Margaret Aston, "Lollardy and Literacy," *History* 62 (1977), 366.

The picture is not, however, one of unrelieved difficulty, for a few small concessions were made to the tastes of pupils of Louis's age. There is reason to think that, like medieval readers at all levels, children were fond of acronyms and similar devices. For example, after working through the standard prayers, creed, and other elements of the catechism, some pupils went on to a series of prayers to Jesus, each one beginning with "O"; these prayers, known from the mid-twelfth century, were later printed by Caxton as *The Fifteen Oes of Jesus.* Presumably, in the midst of their burdensome and solemn task, the children could take some pleasure in the return of the fat, round letter. A similar sensitivity to the power of visual games to stimulate interest is found in one of the earliest of medieval instructional books. Considerably above the level of a primer, it was written in southern France by the Princess Dhuoda for her fifteen-year-old son William—some four hundred years before Blanche of Castile took charge of Louis's education. Dhuoda concludes her prefatory epigram with this hint:

> A littera D. delta incipe legendo,
> M. Moyda hactenus conclusa sunt.
>
> (Begin reading at the letter D,
> And you will find the end when you get to M.)[19]

If William followed the clues, he found that the initial letters of every other line formed the message "Dhuoda dilecto filio Uuilhelmo salutem. Lege" (Dhuoda sends greetings to her beloved son William. Read).[20] Perhaps his mother designed this acrostic to capture his attention, start him studying the text, and lead him to her injunction to read. A less imaginative but still useful device opens the *Liber Catonianus*, the first book used in many medieval grammar schools. Its first section, the *Disticha Catonis*, is a collection of distichs, each a unit of minimal and manageable length. Their form makes them readily quotable, though the sentiments are somewhat leaden:

19. *Dhuoda, Manuel pour mon fils,* Sources Chrétiennes 225, ed. Pierre Riché (Paris: Editions du Cerf, 1975), p. 78. Riché, p. 79 n.2, indicates that *moyda* is Dhuoda's way of writing *meta*, indicating the Greek letter mu; he suggests that she may be playing on *meta*, "the limit or end of a book."

20. Ibid., pp. 72–78. Peter F. Dembowski has pointed out to me a parallel device in the openings of many stories in the *Legenda aurea*, which rapidly became favorite reading material among the laity.

> Instrue praeceptis animum, ne discere cessa
> nam sine doctrina vita est quasi mortis imago.

(Instruct the mind according to principles, and never cease training it, for without learning life is like an image of death.)[21]

On the whole, however, Louis's task even at the primer level must have been hard. As a rank beginner he was presented with texts that teachers today would regard as far above his conceptual level, such as the Psalms and the *Disticha Catonis*. Many of their phrases would have remained incomprehensible; short of ignoring them, he could have done little except puzzle over them and store them in his memory for correlation to other phrases that paralleled them in language, if not necessarily in meaning.

The next striking aspect of the mechanics of medieval reading, from today's viewpoint, must be the habit of sub-vocalization. Silent reading was the exception rather than the rule. In the thirteenth century it was still assumed that the breviary would be read orally, even when one cleric read alone. Only in the mid-fourteenth century did the nobility of France begin to accept silent reading.[22] The consequences of this fact are so far-reaching that I am tempted to add to the now familiar opposition between oral and written culture a third category and call the late Middle Ages—the period in which an abundant written literature emerged out of oral forms—a "reading-aloud culture." Reading aloud no doubt fostered sensitivity to the phonic elements of a text, so that authors could count on their readers to be alert to them. More generally, it is clear that when reading normally employed the faculties of speech and hearing as well as sight, it was not only a slower but also a more active process than it is now, when silent reading is the norm.

Moreover, whereas reading is today considered above all not only a silent but also a solitary activity, in the late Middle Ages it was most often depicted as shared, especially when the readers were lay persons rather than clerics. M. T. Clanchy asserts that by about 1300 "private reading must still have been a luxury, largely confined to retiring ladies and scholars. Books were scarce and it was ordinary good manners to share their contents among a group by reading aloud."[23] The circum-

---

21. *Disticha Catonis*, ed. Marcus Boas (Amsterdam: North-Holland, 1952), p. 152.
22. Saenger, "Silent Reading," p. 407.
23. Clanchy, *From Memory to Written Record*, p. 198.

stances of shared reading experience no doubt varied a great deal. Even in a monastery, monks in the refectory listened together in silence to the texts read during meals. In cultivated secular circles, lay people listened to romances and discussed them together, if we can take as representative of real life scenes from *Troilus and Criseyde* and other works. Indeed, the custom described earlier of having books read aloud rather than reading them oneself lent itself to the practice of group listening. Reading in such gatherings differed markedly from solitary reading. That members of the group could elaborate or comment upon the text made reading a community experience. In such circumstances the interpretation of the text developed by any single reader or listener was the product not of her or his understanding of the text alone but of a combination of questions and insights supplied by others. Again, the more widespread practice of group rather than solitary reading suggests a more active approach to books; only a very highly trained and experienced reader can raise in solitude the range of questions likely to be generated by a group.

The late medieval reader's efforts to read actively were further stimulated by the glosses and illuminations that appeared increasingly even in lay books. In use from antiquity, these two forms of textual complement were employed in new ways in the late Middle Ages. Starting in the century before Louis's birth, the way scholarly texts were laid out began to change markedly, perhaps reflecting the new scholarly methods and changed attitudes toward study associated with scholasticism; from the mid-fourteenth century there were analogous changes in the presentation of books for lay readers, encouraging development of increasingly sophisticated styles of reading.

Illuminations had long served a dual function: they were ornamental, being incorporated into books that producers or patrons wished to render more precious; and they clarified the organization of expensive books by marking, for example, the beginnings of chapters. As lay readers came gradually to constitute a more substantial part of the reading public, however, illuminations came to fulfill the third function of completing and explaining, often in considerable detail, the meaning of the text. Some explanatory cycles of miniatures seem to have been planned by the authors or translators themselves, from a wish to help their nonscholarly readers understand the text in question. For example, in manuscripts containing the French translations of Aristotle's *Nichomachean Ethics* and *Politics*, executed in the 1370s under the direction of the translator Nicole Oresme at the commission of

Charles V of France, illustrations functioned—according to Claire Richter Sherman—as "visual definitions of unfamiliar terms and concepts . . . [as] a consequence of the new [secular] audience for whom the translations were intended."[24] In these and other similarly conceived manuscripts of the period, an illumination might point to a less obvious interpretation of a passage or add to the passage's context a parallel concept from another source.

Similarly, glosses in vernacular books for the laity, developing out of the tradition of grammatical and historical commentary on scripture done by and for scholars, sometimes elaborated upon a text by directing the reader's attention to related passages or by adding to a particular passage an outside parallel focused on one of its less obvious concepts. The authors of texts on occasion even created such glosses themselves to complement their texts conceptually.

To integrate illuminations and glosses, the techniques of laying out pages were much refined during the late Middle Ages, bringing illuminations and glosses physically or visually closer to the texts they elaborated and thus rendering the organization of the page more complex. When visually closer to its focus, complementary material was more useful to the reader; indeed, some books obliged the reader to read the gloss or illumination together with the text. Such developments in the *mise-en-page* of books for the laity encouraged the reader to interrupt the reading process as a scholar does, to puzzle over the relationship of complement to text and then the meaning of the text itself.

Paralleling conceptual systems that complemented the text on the page were the systems for reorganizing and expanding textual meaning in which cultivated lay readers were formally and informally trained. One of these was mnemonics, studied as an integral part of rhetoric: students learned techniques for storing and recovering related material with the help of no device more distant than memory.[25] Another was allegory, which provided ways to look for the multiple levels of mean-

24. I am particularly grateful to Sandra Hindman for introducing me to this topic. See her "Authors, Artists, and Audiences" in Hindman and Farquhar, *Pen to Press*, pp. 157–211; and *Text and Image in Fifteenth-Century Dutch Bible Illustration*, Corpus Sacrae Scripturae Medii Aevi, Series Miscellanea 1 (Leiden: Brill, 1977). This approach is also stressed by James Douglas Farquhar, in Hindman and Farquhar, *Pen to Press*, pp. 81–83; and Claire Richter Sherman, "Some Visual Definitions in the Illustrations of Aristotle's *Nichomachean Ethics* and *Politics* in the French Translation of Nicole Oresme," *Art Bulletin* 59 (1977), 320–30; the passage quoted appears at p. 330.

25. Frances Yates, *The Art of Memory* (Chicago: University of Chicago Press, 1966).

ing presumably hidden beneath the literal level of a text. A third, typology, stimulated the reader to think in historical parallels, seeking in other periods—the individual or collective past, the present, the apocalyptic future—episodes similar to the one the text presented. Those readers not trained in the more sophisticated forms of these systems in schools could nonetheless have learned the basic patterns quite effectively through a common cultural experience: attendance at sermons, the construction of which was governed by these systems. To a reader experienced in applying them, any text, no matter how elaborate in itself, would have been functionally partial; only when the reader had complemented it would the text have become complete.[26]

A reader knowledgeable in such systems and accustomed to testing interpretive hypotheses actively would have been equipped to address questions to any book encountered. Indeed, such a reader might ask of any single text a great range of questions that would seem to modern readers inappropriate: questions about ethics while reading a book about animals, for instance. Medieval books bore no Dewey decimal numbers to tell readers whether a book was fiction or nonfiction, about geography or mythology. While there certainly were categories according to which books were ordered, they were broader than those in common use today. Since books were scarce, readers had to address all their many questions to just a few and get out of them all they could. New kinds of books, however, might be made up to suit the individual reader's purposes, by binding parts of old ones together or by compiling and copying. In rare-book libraries today such manuscripts are often misleadingly labeled "miscellanies," even though many were made to meet the most specialized needs of an individual reader, representing in concrete form that reader's active interrogation of available reading matter.

Whether a thirteenth-century book was copied by a professional or, in rare circumstances, a lay reader, its cultural position differed from that of a book today. While not all books were objects of reverence, attitudes toward them would necessarily have been affected by the devotional character of the first books to which readers were exposed, and, as the child grew, the pious context for reading established by the primer was reinforced. This was especially true for the great majority

26. The classic treatment of medieval attitudes toward the book is Ernst Robert Curtius, "The Book as Symbol," in *European Literature and the Latin Middle Ages*, trans. Willard R. Trask (1953; rpt., New York: Harper & Row, 1963), pp. 302–47.

of readers, educated by churchmen who emphasized meditation as a component of reading.[27] In monasteries, meditation played an even larger part in what may properly be termed there a "theology of reading": the novice was to learn to reflect on every word or phrase, for each was a potential vehicle by which God might send personal inspiration.

Religious ideas about education also shaped the way the aristocracy learned to read during Louis's period, for training in reading formed a coherent system, unfolding step by step from primary level to the most advanced schools, so that methods of study practiced at the highest level influenced elementary teaching in a direct way impossible in today's less homogeneous society. Hugh of St. Victor, a leading figure in an important school of biblical scholars, wrote extensively on methods of textual interpretation and on more general issues relating to university-level students; Vincent of Beauvais borrowed entire chapters from Hugh's *Didascalicon* in compiling for Louis's children his *De eruditione filiorum nobilium (On the learning of the sons of the nobility);* [28] and William of Tournai applied certain of Hugh's ideas to younger people in his *De instructione puerorum (On the education of boys),* written in the mid-thirteenth century. Their use of Hugh's ideas suggests that the educational system, so long as it remained in the hands of churchmen whose principal interest was religious, could mold reading as an activity consistent in its technique and ends, from primer to university. Indeed, the method employed in analyzing any text, even at the most advanced levels, was based on the study of grammar as learned in the grammar school, a program on which pupils embarked after learning letters and Latin recitation in the manner described earlier. Interpretation of meaning began with grammatical commentary and moved step by step, toward an understanding of the whole.

The way people first learned to read religious works must have influenced the way they later read secular, vernacular texts as well. The habit of meditative, oral reading substantially affected, among other things, the reader's habitual pace. Speed reading would have been out of the question; the more skillful reader was the slower one. While a

27. The monastic and scholastic reading traditions are contrasted by Jean Leclercq, *The Love of Learning and the Desire for God,* trans. Catherine Misrahi, 2d ed. (New York: Fordham University Press, 1974), pp. 18–22; on "active" reading see also pp. 88–90.

28. Vincent of Beauvais, *De eruditione filiorum nobilium,* ed. Arpad Steiner, Medieval Academy of America Publ. No. 32 (Cambridge, Mass.: Medieval Academy of America, 1938), p. xiv.

beginner might see a word and, having few resources for elaborating upon it, proceed quickly to the next, the skillful reader would find something to ponder.

Some texts, sacred and otherwise, were even thought to have both exoteric and esoteric meanings; only those readers granted sufficient grace in their meditation would arrive at the latter. A work of secular literature, moreover, was not a vehicle by which an author communicated a personality, and readers did not read from an interest in the peculiar insights of an individual, as they later learned to do. Overshadowing the importance of any individual author was the divine Author of what was called, according to a widespread medieval commonplace, the Book of the World. This notion of all earthly events as part of a narrative "written" by God is the basis of the system of typological commentary, mentioned earlier, which implied that the more grace a Christian was granted to learn to read books written under God's direction, the better able that reader would be to decipher the world as a book written directly by God.

Reading Styles and Reading Ideologies

The style of reading I have been describing, though vastly different from that of today, was very well suited to the reader Dante evokes. Those who, in the twentieth century, have learned to read by quickly spotting familiar, often-repeated words ("Look!" "See!") have acquired a quick sense of mastery of and identification with the contents of their first books. Such associations are perhaps appropriate to the founding of a reading style suitable for the enjoyment of novels or modern lyrics. They are quite inappropriate for the arduous journey through the *Commedia*.

To account for the differences between Dante's fictive reader and Baudelaire's, then, one must look not merely to authorial idiosyncrasy but also to identifiable historical change. Authors may seem to create fictive readers, but in another sense readers are the ones who call authors into being. For example, Baudelaire's fictive reader, an emblem of solitude, is utterly impossible to imagine in the group setting typical of reading in Saint Louis's day. Lay readers simply did not, indeed generally could not, read silently and alone. The kind of book *Les Fleurs du mal* is could not in any sense have existed in the thirteenth century, not only because there was no writer like Baudelaire but also (and more important) because there could have been no readers like the reader Baudelaire addresses and needs.[29]

To be sure, questions can be raised about one detail or another in the sketch I have drawn. No one factor—either the ABC approach, the variations in script, or the use of a nonnative language—in itself constitutes an essential difference between late medieval reading and reading in, say, the mid-nineteenth century. The ABC method, for example, is far from unique to the Middle Ages and is still employed today. The association of reading with a language other than the mother tongue is to be found where the vernacular is exclusively a spoken tongue, or where an elite that controls education uses a language different from that of the masses,[30] or where a language peculiar to religious practice is the first one encountered in written form.

But while no single factor emerges as a defining characteristic, the combination of several demonstrates clearly that reading is a historically evolving process. It also suggests that differentiating moments in its history and coming to understand them as historical reading "styles" (much as one differentiates "styles" in, say, prose composition) is a necessity for students of literature. The reading style described in this chapter is appropriate to many works of medieval literature. It is founded on the circumstances of contemporary education and shaped by the need to decipher unfamiliar letter patterns, words, and meanings. To define such reading styles one must consider many factors, including not only education but also the physical characteristics of contemporary books, the mechanics of reading, and, more generally, the ways in which cultural ideologies express themselves as ideologies of reading.

29. Hans-Robert Jauss has set forth the mutual production of meaning by reader and text in relation to Baudelaire's work; see esp. the summary of his treatment of Baudelaire in *Aesthetic Experience and Literary Hermeneutics*, trans. Michael Shaw (Minneapolis: University of Minnesota Press, 1982), pp. 83–84: In "Le Cygne" and "before the eye of the reader, there takes place a retransformation of the world of objects which has become alien. . . .But now it is only remembrance from which the counterimage of the new and the beautiful. . . arises. . . . The harmonizing and idealizing power of remembrance is the newly discovered aesthetic capacity which can replace the extinct correspondence of soul and timeless nature by the coincidence of present existence and prehistory, modernity and antiquity, historical now and mythical past." Cf. also pages 263–93, Jauss's study of French lyric poetry of 1857 (the year of publication of *Les Fleurs du mal*) in relation to the ideology of the hearth, urging the bourgeois reader to withdraw from the chaotic urban world into an interior world of intimacy and recollection.

30. Clanchy, *From Memory to Written Record*, p. 161, discussing the century following Louis's, points to the situation of the trilingual jury foreman in England.

Styles and ideologies of reading must be conceived as necessarily always changing. For example, the modern notion of reading as a skill that equips and even stimulates the reader to explore topics distant from daily concerns is the product of an ideology that values change and individual growth. Newman, in "The Reading-Room Controversy," questions the relevance of such an idealogy in Victorian England, and it certainly would be applied inappropriately to readers in late medieval France.[31] The reading skills acquired by many of Saint Louis's contemporaries were only partial. The reader's training beyond the Pater Noster might be limited to a specific class of material and specific elements of vocabulary: devotional and chivalric for the aristocracy, agricultural and fiscal for reeves, commercial for merchants. If reading was in any sense a "window to the world" in the thirteenth century, as it has often been claimed to be since the Industrial Revolution, then the world in question was an extraterrestrial one only. The notion that reading "opens new worlds" is a later one, shaped in part by the claims of Renaissance printers and writers who urged that the contemporary reader (and writer), already standing on the shoulders of those giants, the Ancients, could thereby see beyond them.[32] More immediately, it is part of a post-Enlightenment ideology of reading.

It is difficult to find models to represent the change from one reading style and one reading ideology to another. The most widely accepted model is, quite literally, "mechanical": where changes in reading habits have been noted, they have most often been seen as products of technological change. The advent of printing has been credited with changes in both reading style and reading ideology: for example, a general shift from oral to silent reading, and a new tendency to seek out books that question rather than confirm religious orthodoxy.[33] Similarly, the successive advents of what might broadly be called filmed, televised and computerized texts have been taken to cause changes in reading style and ideology, though such changes have

31. Ibid., pp. 197–98: "A knight of the eleventh century who learned the rudiments of Latin in childhood would not have found this skill had much application in daily life, nor did it open to him the cultural heritage of his people, because Latin was a foreign language and books were not generally available. By thirteen hundred the situation had changed, but not radically. . . . Literacy for purposes of recreation or self-improvement. . . was still not very useful, although that too was beginning to change."

32. This is an early version of the notion of the productivity of the sign; see the discussion of the semiotization of the reading process in the Conclusion.

33. Saenger, "Silent Reading," pp. 412–14.

rarely been seen as reason to celebrate. Although such technologically oriented interpretations have much to recommend them, they must be framed within a larger context.

The history of reading must be seen not merely as a corollary to a history of technology; indeed, the history of the technologies of reading is itself but a corollary to the history of reading as a cultural, literary, and ideological problem. Rather than accepting a change in reading technology as a cause of change in reading style and ideology, one must instead investigate first the needs that made society generate a demand for any change in reading technology, then the discrepancy between the extent to which the change simply fulfilled those needs and that to which it altered or suppressed them in unforeseeable ways, and finally the ways in which society mythologized the change once it was made. The many differences in the mechanics of reading between today and Louis's day are merely indicators of fundamental changes in reading style and ideology.

Still, the notion that printing more than anything else changed the nature of reading is a powerful one, because it helps one to evade awareness of the temporal nature of reading. The printing press was taken up as myth and emblem by readers aware of and uncomfortable with the timeliness of reading. The Romans who looked back across a wide sea at Greek literature had much earlier experienced such awareness and discomfort. Indeed, awareness of the timeliness of reading had asserted itself on many occasions in those several periods described as "renaissance" (for example, Insular, Carolingian, Cluniac) or "humanistic." In the fifteenth century, however, it reached a climax. Renaissance humanists energetically sought out lost texts and labored to establish through comparison and inference the correct (that is, original) readings of them. When they did so, they acted on the belief that handwritten books expose readers to the perils of temporality, and that a method for transmitting texts without alteration would prevent intellectual decline or even make progress possible. Perhaps the most succinct statement of this powerful yet misleading notion comes a generation or two after the introduction of printing in Europe. It is found in a manuscript schoolbook written in the late fifteenth century: "Iff bookys [i.e., the editions] of olde auctors were not corrupt and sum of them fals, I wolde not doubte that men now in this tyme sholde overpasse them or els be equall with them, for mennys wyttes be as goode now as they were then."[34] The inadequacy of the process by

34. *A Fifteenth-Century School Book from a Manuscript in the British Museum (MS.*

which the supposed tools of learning are produced thus comes to be seen as the cause of what is perceived as a decline in learning: the process is inadequate because it does not eliminate the loss associated with the passage of time.

Printing was widely taken to circumvent such temporal loss: Gutenberg's press would seize an author's words just as written and transmit them, unchanged, to a reader anywhere, anytime. Many early printers stressed such superhuman accuracy in the colophons with which they identified their books.[35] No matter that there were fifteenth-century scribes who produced copies far more accurate than those produced by presses of the era: a mechanism that would dissociate reading from temporal loss was what many wanted, and that is what some of them thought they got.

This view of the printed book engenders through metonymy an image favored by I. A. Richards, one of the founders of twentieth-century Anglo-American criticism: "A book is a machine to think with."[36] A machine does not have the same temporal character as a mind: each time one sets a machine in motion, it is the same. To be sure, it is not eternal, but like eternal things it does escape mortality. Richards's attitude is very different from that adopted by Baudelaire in the essay "The Painter of Modern Life." Reflecting on the temporal relation between an artwork and life, Baudelaire uses "modern" in a sense closer to the original medieval meaning of the word—"contemporary"—than to the sense in which it is commonly used today. He suggests that authentically "modern" life—that is, the life of the present moment—is in its very essence transitory, fleeting, contingent. Thus, the best "painter" of this life is not one who paints slowly and carefully, elaborating an illusion on canvas, but rather one who sketches.

The approach to literary criticism suggested here, by way of the historical study of reading, is very far from Richards's approach. It seeks not to avoid history by use of some sort of "machine" but rather to turn toward history even in the midst of reading, an activity that

---

Arundel 249), ed. William Nelson (Oxford: Clarendon Press, 1956), p. 23. "Fals" means "incorrectly transcribed," or *depravati* in the Latin of this bilingual text.

35. The role of this mythology in Caxton's preface to his second edition of the *Canterbury Tales* was discussed by M. B. Parkes in a paper read at the Pen to Press Symposium at College Park, Maryland, in October 1977.

36. I. A. Richards, *Principles of Literary Criticism* (1925; rpt. New York: Harcourt, Brace, n.d.), p. 1.

intrinsically suppresses temporality. Yet, even taking as my emblem
not a printing press or machine of any kind, but Baudelaire's famous
term "sketch," I have still not produced a narrative that attains sketch
status in Baudelaire's laudatory sense. My narrative of a fragment from
the history of reading remains closer to the temporal inauthenticity of
painting. It is not a disinterested mirroring but rather a deliberately
constructed "plot," built, like many simple narrative plots before it,
upon an opposition between two characters, one sympathetic and the
other unsympathetic. Dante's reader—whom he evokes as earnest,
active, struggling to accomplish a difficult and praiseworthy goal—is
the protagonist whose motives and limitations have been detailed
while the hypocrite reader detested even by his creator Baudelaire has
stood in the background, creating with his somber force a kind of
chiaroscuro effect that helps Dante's reader shine.

To develop such a contrastive "plot," I have stressed only change in
reading style; that is, I have been almost exclusively exegetical. Using
the same two poles, one could of course stress continuity instead,
taking an interpretive approach rather than an exegetical one. One
could point out, for example, that just as Saint Louis's contemporaries
needed special training to read pre-Gothic script if they were not to
rely exclusively on the authority of experts to read the past, modern
readers can read what history has left behind only if they expend great
effort in learning how to do so. In fact, in 1850 Baudelaire's contemporary Gérard de Nerval published the first version of *Angélique*, a story
that dramatizes just such a modern reader struggling to read the past.[37]

My purpose in pushing as far as possible toward exegesis rather than
interpretation of reading has not, however, been to show that exegesis
of the reading process is better, more fruitful, more interesting than
interpretation of it. I do not want merely to initiate some new variant
of philology which, taking a strongly rhetorical stance, would see
readers as elements intrinsic to the words they read and try to docu-
ment their evolution, as an etymologist traces the evolution of a word.
To be sure, I have chosen to excavate the elements of this chapter's
"plot" in a historical period that is particularly well suited to such
exegetical archaeology: the era of the rise of the vernacular literatures.
It is generally accepted that at this time a new secular reading public

37. See Gérard de Nerval, *Oeuvres*, ed. Albert Béguin and Jean Richer (Paris: Edi-
tions Gallimard, Bibliothèque de La Pléiade, 1966), 1:1248, on the first appearance of
Les Faux Saulniers, parts of which Nerval later published in *Les Filles du feu, Les
Illuminés, La Bohème galante,* and *Loréley*.

was coming to birth. The period thus provides a protagonist with whom modern readers can feel sympathy, as with a distant forebear, since modern readers characteristically think that they, too, are secular readers.

But seeing that readers of a distant age read very differently from readers of today is not in itself a compelling goal. Nor would one want to undertake this kind of historical study simply to seek some kind of connection between readers "then" and readers "now," to help latter-day readers imagine themselves in the situation of the readers who were the author's contemporaries. Rather, the interesting, important, compelling fact is this: although now, with Saint Louis in mind, one finds it quite obvious that reading is a historically evolving process, *no one is in the habit of thinking of reading in this way.* The essential question then becomes, why not? Why does one not think of the history of reading?

This "not-thinking" the history of reading is no accident. If readers lack a continuous awareness of the history of reading, their oversight is not casual. It is an aspect of that turning away from the temporality of reading which itself makes reading possible. Thinking through an episode in the history of reading, such as the narrative of Saint Louis as beginning reader, is but one step in the effort to turn back toward that temporality—and not the most fundamental one.

It is necessary to go back to the (logically prior) question raised earlier. Why and especially how is awareness of the historical development of reading suppressed? Narrating the history of reading, however challenging such a task may be, is much simpler and more straightforward than attempting to answer this question, which takes as its object not merely the history but the very temporality of reading. Certain directions toward an answer have been suggested by writers whose awareness of the temporality of reading is particularly acute. It is to an examination of these directions, as seen in the texts of such writers, that I now turn.

Chapter 2

Dante's Stories of Reading

> to broach directly the question of readers' roles called for by a
> written text. . . .
>
> WALTER J. ONG, "The Writer's
> Audience Is Always a Fiction"

The story of Paolo and Francesca[1] is not only the most widely known episode of the *Commedia* but also among the most famous of all literary depictions of reading: the final phrase that Dante puts into Francesca's mouth—"Galeotto fu 'l libro e chi lo scrisse" (a Galeotto [panderer] was the book and the one who wrote it; *Inferno* v. 137)[2]—has almost the status of a proverb in literary circles. Even cursory examination of the episode, however, shows that its concern is less with the general relation of book and author to reader than with one very specific aspect of that relation: its complex temporality.

Both Francesca and the narrator-pilgrim are from the outset painfully aware of the discrepancy between the time *of* which she tells, when she and Paolo, still alive, embraced rapturously on earth, and the time *in* which she tells, when she and Paolo, dead with no hope of resurrection, are buffeted by the winds of Hell. This discrepancy is the very same one noted by Hirsch in the passage quoted as epigraph to the

---

1. See Susan Noakes, "The Double Misreading of Paolo and Francesca," *Philological Quarterly* 62 (1983), 221–39 for a more extensive treatment. My understanding of the relation between temporality and language for Dante is shaped by the teaching of John Freccero; see his *Dante: The Poetics of Conversion*, ed. Rachel Jacoff (Cambridge, Mass.: Harvard University Press, 1986).

2. Citations from the *Commedia* are from Giorgio Petrocchi, ed., *La Commedia secondo l'antica vulgata* (Turin: Giulio Einaudi, 1975). English translations are those of John D. Sinclair, *The Divine Comedy of Dante Alighieri*, 3 vols. (New York: Oxford University Press, 1939; rpt. 1975), except for *Inferno* xvi.127 ff., where I have preferred to give my own more literal translation.

Introduction ("an author . . . so eccentric as to report without any intention to deceive that he now means by his text what he did not mean") but cast in slightly different terms. This "author," already eccentric in being a she and therefore a person whose reliability and veracity are, especially in medieval tradition, somewhat suspect, reports that the plot she "wrote" and acted out in the past now means something different. Francesca, the first of the souls the pilgrim will speak with in Hell, like all the others he will meet after her, offers a reading of the story of her life on earth, a story that the pilgrim, too, must learn to read.

Awareness of the discrepancy between the time of which Francesca tells and the time in which she tells and implicitly reads is intensified by the double allusion with which she begins her answer to the pilgrim's question (v. 118–20) as to how she and Paolo came to the love that has brought them damnation. Francesca responds:

> Nessun maggior dolore
> che ricordarsi del tempo felice
> ne la miseria; e ciò sa 'l tuo dottore.
>   Ma s'a conoscer la prima radice
> del nostro amor tu hai cotanto affetto,
> dirò come colui che piange e dice.

(There is no greater pain than to recall the happy time in misery, and this thy teacher knows; but if thou hast so great desire to know our love's first root, I shall tell as one may that weeps in telling.)

[v. 121–26]

Francesca's remark that the pilgrim's "doctor," Vergil, knows the pain of remembering happiness in misery does not simply or even principally refer to Vergil's own eternally liminal position of exclusion from salvation; rather, it suggests the famous passage from his *Aeneid* with which Aeneas begins the tale of Troy. Francesca is in fact quoting Vergil's Aeneas:

> infandum, regina, iubes renovare dolorem,
> Troianas ut opes et lamentabile regnum
> eruerint Danai. . . .
> . . . quis talia fando
> . . . duri miles Ulixe temperet a lacrimis? . . .
>   . . . .

sed si tantus amor casus cognoscere nostros
et breviter Troiae supremum audire laborem,
quamquam animus meminisse horret luctuque refugit,
incipiam.

(Unutterable woes, O queen, you urge me to renew: to tell how the
Greeks overturned the power of Troy, and its deplorable realms. . . .
Who of hardened Ulysses' band, can, in the very telling of such woes,
refrain from tears? . . . . But since you are so desirous of knowing our
misfortunes, and briefly hearing the last effort of Troy, though my
soul shudders at the remembrance, and hath shrunk back with grief,
yet will I begin.)

[*Aeneid* II.3–5, 10–13][3]

Francesca's allusion is a double one because Dante has already, four
cantos earlier, opened his own narrative by allusion to this same prefatory speech; Francesca's lines, spoken as the pilgrim enters Hell, thus
echo the *Commedia*'s prologue as well as Aeneas's:

Ahi quanto a dir qual era è cosa dura
esta selva selvaggia e aspra e forte
che nel pensier rinova la paura!
    Tant'è amara che poco è più morte;
ma per trattar del ben ch'i'vi trovai,
dirò de l'altre cose ch'i' v'ho scorte.
                . . . .
    così l'animo mio, ch'ancor fuggiva,
si volse a retro a rimirar lo passo
che non lasciò già mai persona viva.

(Ah, how hard a thing it is to tell of that wood, savage and harsh and
dense, the thought of which renews my fear! So bitter it is that death is
hardly more. But to give account of the good which I found there I
will tell of the other things I noted there. . . . so my mind, which was
still in flight, turned back to look again at the pass which never yet let
any go alive.)

[I. 4–9, 25–27]

Each of the three instances in this play of citation and allusion emphasizes the discrepancy between the time *of* which and the time *in*

---

3. All references to the *Aeneid* are to F. A. Hirtzel, ed., *P. Vergili Maronis Opera*
(Oxford: Clarendon Press, 1900; rpt. 1963); English translations are from *The Works of
Virgil Literally Translated into English Prose*, trans. [Joseph] Davidson and T. A. Buckley
(London: George Bell, 1891).

which a narrator narrates.[4] Francesca's participation in this intertextual play is ultimately much more important than her quotation and imitation of the lyric poets of the *dolce stil nuovo*. Her declaration "quel giorno non vi leggemmo più avanti" (that day we read in it no farther) further develops the theme of the temporality of reading. Perhaps occasionally snickered at as a euphemism for the start of physical contact between the lovers, the phrase's significance lies in its indication of the end of the couple's participation in the temporal sequence of the book they read and their return to lived as opposed to literary time.

But beyond these evident indicators of the episode's temporal thematic lies a more complex development of Dante's thinking about the temporal relation among author, words, and readers. While the episode is an obvious condemnation of literal reading, it also offers an entirely new definition of reading according to "the letter and not the spirit." Dante here shows that literal reading, reading on the surface where the mere letters are, is not a spatial but a temporal error. What's more, in his view no reader can avoid such temporal error; it is a necessary condition of all reading, a kind of inescapable, original sin characteristic of all readers. His later development in the *Paradiso* of terms, images, and concepts introduced in the Paolo and Francesca episode further shows, paradoxically, that whereas all interpretation is provisional—that is, subject to change at a later time—interpreters are nonetheless obliged to act as if it is not provisional if they are indeed to interpret. Francesca's story thus becomes Dante's way to demonstrate how it is that readers can read with an awareness of constant change only if they stop trying to get meaning from the words of a text: only, that is, if they stop reading.

The Double Misreading of Paolo and Francesca

To understand the more complex aspects of Dante's inquiry into the problem of reading and time, one must look once again at this familiar canto and ask what about it is original, is uniquely Dante's contribution. Dante was hardly the first to tell a tale in which reading precedes and causes adultery. This plot appears in so many permutations in the late Middle Ages that it attains the status of a com-

---

4. Giuseppe Mazzotta, *Dante, Poet of the Desert* (Princeton, N.J.: Princeton University Press, 1979), pp. 165–79, shows how the relation between *Inferno* v and the *Aeneid* is mediated by Augustine.

monplace.[5] It expresses the concern of those who adopt it with an important development in the history of reading: the increasing number of lay readers who lack the moral discipline and hermeneutic training of clerical readers. Certainly there were other times when the character of the reading public changed dramatically (for example, a pronounced change occurred early in the nineteenth century, as I argue in Chapter 6), but some late medieval writers addressed this change with special explicitness and urgency because it appeared to them to have consequences not only in this world but also in the next.

Dante shared this concern, for he wrote his masterpiece at a crucial period in the history of reading, at the climax of a century that had seen the beginnings of what M. B. Parkes calls the "emergence of the general reader."[6] In Dante's native Tuscany especially, the period was a particularly important one in the history of reading because it saw the beginnings of government-supported schools for the laity and marked, according to Dante's own account in *De Vulgari Eloquentia*, a turning-point in the history of the literary vernacular.[7] But Dante does not simply adopt, without considering its meaning, the topos that connected lay reading—especially by women—with the temptation to

5. Examples of the topos in important works of the later Middle Ages include the following: (1) The correspondence attributed to Héloise and Abélard, which may be interpreted as being about seduction by letters and esp. by complex Ciceronian rhetorical devices. It had attained by Petrarch's time a literary importance far exceeding that of mere biography; the letters formed the closest thing to an epistolary novel the Middle Ages had. (2) The allusion to and citation of Héloise in the *Roman de la Rose*. On the parallel between Héloise and Francesca, see Peter Dronke, "Francesca and Héloise," *Comparative Literature* 27 (1975), 113–35, also valuable for its history of readings of the passage and for the indication of many classical allusions in *Inferno* v; see esp. page 120 with conclusions about the "double structure" of the episode. (3) Chrétien's *Cligès*. Often interpreted as an anti-Tristan, it involves the efforts of Fénice, the beloved of Cligès and wife of Cligès's uncle, not to follow in the footsteps of Iseut, a literary model she explicitly rejects. (4) Chaucer's *Troilus and Criseyde*. Criseyede's reading of the *Roman de Thèbes* is interrupted at a crucial moment: had she continued, she would have come to an allegorical passage whose elements later appear to Troilus in a dream. Although Cassandra interprets the dream correctly, Troilus, also unaware of the *Roman de Thèbes*, rejects her interpretation. I am grateful to Alice Miskimin for bringing this analogue to my attention. *The Nun's Priest's Tale* provides another variant. See also the intriguing discussion of the contrast between Dante's view of textual temporality and Chaucer's in Karla Taylor, "A Text and Its Afterlife: Dante and Chaucer," *Comparative Literature* 35 (1983), 1–20.
6. Parkes, "The Literacy of the Laity," p. 572.
7. I have summarized the development of lay literacy in Tuscany in "The Development of the Book Market in Late Quattrocento Italy," *Journal of Medieval and Renaissance Studies* 11 (1981), 23–55.

seduction, and he does not present the topos in general terms. The author of the *Commedia* depicts Paolo and Francesca as reading not just any romantic fiction but, philologists agree, the Vulgate cycle *Lancelot del Lac*.[8] The passage they read concerns a love based on reading or, more precisely, on the interpretation of words, a premise that Dante uses to create a kind of *mise-en-abîme* in which the story his characters read comments on their own situation.

Dante cites the following details in Paolo and Francesca's reading of the *Lancelot* text: (1) What they read about Lancelot is "how love seized him" (v. 128). (2) Francesca says they were "conquered" by a particular brief passage, "solo un punto" (v. 132), the one point at which a "desired smile" is kissed by "cotanto amante," a lover of masculine gender: the point at which Lancelot kisses Guinevere. (3) Furthermore, Francesca says they got no farther in their reading of the Lancelot story than that kiss, for at the moment they read of it, they mimicked it, stopping their reading; consequently, they never found out how the story ends.

Scholars have pointed out a major discrepancy between Francesca's paraphrase of the episode of the kiss in the Lancelot romance and that episode itself. As in other instances, Dante creates a misquotation by an erring character to make a literary and moral point. In the romance the trembling Lancelot is seized and kissed by Guinevere; in Francesca's paraphrase the roles are reversed, and Francesca's trembling mouth is kissed by Paolo.

Just why Dante has Francesca paraphrase this crucial moment in the Lancelot narrative, the very one mirrored in her narrative, becomes clear to the reader who recalls the Vulgate *Lancelot* and specifically two other elements of its plot that Francesca cites: the context of the "single point" that conquered Paolo and Francesca, and "how love seized Lancelot." The interrelation of this paraphrased moment and these two additional elements, on the one hand, and the terms of Francesca's narrative, on the other, articulate several aspects of the complex tem-

8. H. Oskar Sommer, ed., *The Vulgate Version of the Arthurian Romances*, pts 1,3, *Le livre de Lancelot del Lac* (Washington, D.C.: Carnegie Institute of Washington, 1910). Pertinent arguments are summarized in Ernst Walser's review of the monograph "Galeotto fu il libro e chi lo scrisse," by Heinrich Morph, *Giornale storico della letteratura italiana* 70 (1917), 196–98. Also in agreement are Renato Poggioli, "Tragedy or Romance? A Reading of the Paolo and Francesca Episode in Dante's *Inferno*," *PMLA* 72 (1957), 350n; and Anna Hatcher and Mark Musa, "The Kiss: *Inferno V* and the Old French Prose *Lancelot*," *Comparative Literature* 20 (Spring 1968), 97–109. The latter article may be consulted for a bibliographical survey of the problem.

porality of reading, particularly the instability of the meaning of the text and the unreliabilty of the reader—most prominently, in this classic episode, the feminine reader.

As the narrator of the prose *Lancelot* moves toward the kiss episode, he makes it clear in many ways that neither Lancelot nor Guinevere is to be seen in the sentimental light that modern interpretations, especially, cast upon them. Lancelot is presented as foolish and bumbling; Guinevere is manipulative and disdainful. As she watches Lancelot and a companion approach across a meadow, she insults him by remarking that he does not look as impressive as she had expected; and once he reaches her, things go from bad to worse. As she interrogates him at length about his identity and achievements, his terror far exceeds the conventional bounds of knightly reticence, until he is embarrassed to the point of swooning by the presence of a former mistress, the Lady of Malohaut.

Indeed, the harsh Guinevere who kisses Lancelot in the *Vulgate* cycle episode is not Arthur's queen at all; she is an impostor, something of a witch. But because they stop reading at the moment of the kiss, Paolo and Francesca do not learn of her appalling identity. Nor do they find out that Lancelot is severely punished for his lustful faithlessness to a holy quest and his role in the quest assumed by Gallehaut; the cause of his punishment is explicitly pointed out by a priest who energetically berates the fallen knight. In short, the prose *Lancelot* cited by Dante had transformed the traditional Lancelot story (already condemned by the papacy a hundred years before the *Commedia* was written)[9] into a religious attack on chivalric values, showing that adulterous love brings only unhappiness.[10] Paolo and Francesca are thus depicted as reading a text designed expressly to keep potential adulterers out of Hell. That they are in Hell shows that they did not have the ears to hear the guidance they most needed, that they were blind to the text's meaning.

Moreover, with the line "di Lancialotto *come amor lo strinse*" (of

9. Alderino Bondi, "'Galeotto fu il libro e chi lo scrisse,'" *Il nuovo giornale dantesco* 1 (1917), 85–87.

10. Since 1960 a good deal of textual criticism of the *Lancelot en prose* has appeared, and its attribution has been much debated. This research has led to an entirely new view, presented by Henri de Briel and Manuel Hermann, in *King Arthur's Knights and the Myths of the Round Table: A New Approach to the French Lancelot in Prose* (Paris: Klincksieck, 1972), pp. 8–9. They suggest that it was composed for religious ends by Templars, Templar sympathizers, or Cistercians: "The authors of the Vulgate Version, far from glorifying this affair, condemned it consistently. . . . They utilized such love to show that it only led to failure."

Lancelot, how love constrained him; v.128; emphasis added), Dante creates a very precise *mise-en-abîme* to demonstrate that torment results from misreading a text meant to edify. When he has Francesca report that she and Paolo were reading about the way in which love took hold of Lancelot, he focuses attention on the important moment in the well-established ritual of any courtly encounter—known, in the technical language of courtly love familiar to Dante's readers, as the *amoris ascensio* (kindling of love). *Their* curiosity about the *amoris ascensio* of Lancelot is exactly paralleled by the *pilgrim's* reciprocal curiosity about their own *ascensio*:

> a che e *come* concedette amore
> che conosceste i dubbiosi disiri?

(*how* and by what occasion did love grant you to know your uncertain desires?)

[v.119–20; emphasis added]

Both the pilgrim's "come" (v.119) and Francesca's (v.128) mean "in what way"; the repetition of the word marks the parallel.

The pilgrim's question draws attention, by means of this *mise-en-abîme*, to a crucial event in the Lancelot text. Lancelot's account of the *amoris ascensio* is the turningpoint of the kiss episode in the prose romance and, indeed, according to Lancelot himself, the ground of the entire narrative. In the *Paradiso*, the importance of this moment will be recalled and further highlighted when the poet alludes to Guinevere's inquiry about Lancelot's *amoris ascensio* as the "primo fallo scritto di Ginevra" (the first fault written of Guinevere)[XVI.15]. The question, not the kiss, is her first recorded fault.[11]

The story of his *amoris ascensio* which Lancelot tells Guinevere in answer to her question—how?—bears all this narrative weight, in both the prose romance and the *Commedia*, because it is pregnant with meaning: Lancelot explains that Guinevere elicited his love by naming him her "*ami*," but Guinevere, who is represented as not even recognizing Lancelot at his approach, replies that she cannot remember ever calling him by this term of endearment. Lancelot responds by narrating his leave-taking from Arthur and Guinevere, at which time Guinevere named him her knight and "fair sweet *ami*." Lancelot de-

---

11. Contrary to what many commentators say, it is the question, not the kiss, that makes the Lady of Malohaut cough: Sommer, *Lancelot*, p. 261, line 14.

scribes the word *ami* as not only awakening his love but also protecting him in tribulation and enabling him to perform all the feats that are the stuff of the romance. But Guinevere's response is like that of the ladies who will tell Prufrock, "That is not what I meant, at all." She is amazed that he has taken a word from a general and conventional context and interpreted it as having an individual and intimate meaning. She makes it clear that, for her, words may be nothing but words, with no relation to anything "besides the saying of them" (p. 261, lines 37–41). In the terms adopted earlier, Lancelot has failed to "read" exegetically.

To read about "how love constrained Lancelot," then, is to read about how the naive may mistake words intended to have only a conventional sense for words intended to have a personal sense. Although Lancelot's misinterpretation of what Guinevere says leads, in the short run, to desirable results, in the long run he suffers for it. Lancelot's misreading, then, is to mistake a phrase spoken "to many a knight" for one spoken only once, uniquely for him.

The text, and the particular passage of the text, that Dante presents Paolo and Francesca as reading thus voices two warnings: first, against adultery; second, against the misreading as words directed uniquely to one individual of words repeated as part of a convention. Dante depicts the pair as blind to both these warnings and condemned eternally for their blindness. The misreading of detail which Dante attributes to Francesca and Paolo—reversing the roles of Lancelot and Guinevere— points to their dual misreading on a larger scale. Francesca's exclamation, "Galeotto fu 'l libro e chi lo scrisse," expresses an appalling blindness that she has carried with her into Hell, for it is she and Paolo (rather than a textual or authorial panderer) who have undone themselves by misreading a work written to edify them.

The pilgrim's fainting "like a corpse" is an understandable response to such evidence of readerly blindness.[12] Such blindness suggests that even works like those of Dante himself, if read by those determined to

12. There would be very little reason for the pilgrim-poet to faint upon hearing Francesca's accusation if she were merely condemning romances. The Church had been pointing out their dangers for a century, and to condemn them would have been only to repeat a tired commonplace about literature and morality. Moreover, since Dante had never written a romance (if, as is sometimes suggested, he once translated the *Roman de la Rose*, still the differences between that didactic work and other romances are vast; he cannot legitimately be counted, even peripherally, among the writers of romance), he and his pilgrim would not have been personally implicated by an accusation intended only to condemn romances.

turn away from the temporality of reading, will lead their readers to damnation. Both the *Vita nuova* and the *Commedia* are literary works with moral ends, using literary themes and devices known to appeal to contemporary audiences in order to attract a public for the ideas that form their moral and spiritual foundation. In this sense both belong to the same literary category as the prose *Lancelot*. The pilgrim faints when he realizes that such works, despite the intentions of their authors, can be misread even in a sense that changes the meaning the authors intended into its opposite. Specifically, the pilgrim faints "from pity" for Paolo and Francesca; Dante depicts him as directing his attention toward them, not himself and his literary aspirations. Their situation is indeed extraordinarily pitiful: they have been lost just when an effort was being made to save them, or, in other terms, lost by receiving improperly what is endowed with salvific properties. There are few situations more pitiful than this.

The second aspect of their misreading consists in their mistaking a literary convention for something having special meaning for them. This second kind of misreading, which mirrors Lancelot's, is of greater interest to students of literature than the first. Dante shows that Francesca is familiar with the conventions of literary love by having her speak, as many of Dante's readers have noted, the language of the *dolce stil nuovo*. But instead of realizing that what she reads is literature and not life, a convention with no necessary and direct applicability to herself, Francesca tries to transform her life into literature.

Dante was doing the same thing: making himself, a poet, into a pilgrim, transforming his autobiography into a *speculum* of all human and divine history. This parallel explains the urgency with which Dante has the pilgrim interrogate Francesca, setting the stage for her to respond in terms that he will quote and reinterpret later in the poem, when he deals more directly with the relation between human time and interpretation and the temporal difference between human love and divine love.

The terms of her response are as follows: (1) Francesca's first speech returns repeatedly to the desire for repose, *pace* (v.92, 99). (2) Her second, as previously noted, is prefaced with a paraphrase of the opening lines of *Aeneid* II: "Nessun maggior dolore / che ricordarsi del tempo felice / ne la miseria" (v.121–23). (3) She interprets the pilgrim's request as a desire to learn "la prima radice / del nostro amor" (the first root of our love; v.124–25) and equates the "prima radice" of love with (4) "solo un punto": ". . . solo un punto fu quel che ci vinse" (one point alone it was that mastered us; v.132). The "punto" is the reading of the kiss, which, as noted above, is presented as a misreading; Dante could as readily have used the word 'passo had he not been looking ahead to developing, later in the poem, the image of the "punto" in a way relevant to Paolo and Francesca's sin. The phrase "prima radice" suggests the first sin not just of Paolo and Francesca, the first sinners the pilgrim interrogates, but of the first sinners in salvation history, Eve and Adam. (5) She concludes her reply by stating that their reading stopped at that "punto," the narration of the kiss, "più non vi leggemmo avante" (we read in it no farther; v.138).

All these terms represent motifs that are reintroduced, developed, and in fact turned upside-down in the *Paradiso*: the desire for a place of repose, the difficulty of remembering a joyful moment, the first root of love, the "solo . . . punto," and the interruption of reading. By means of their inversion, Dante develops the principal literary themes of the Paolo and Francesca episode into a sophisticated analysis of an important problem. The problem is that the meaning of the text constantly recedes. The pilgrim recognizes that readers (like Francesca) are unreliable and that authors (like those of the vulgate *Lancelot*) cannot control the meaning of their texts. This recognition, awakened early in the *Inferno*, becomes in the *Paradiso* an understanding of the nature and consequences of the complex temporality of reading.

From Discontinuous Temporal (Mis)reading to Continuous Eternal Reading

A major step in this reversal of the Paolo and Francesca motifs is accomplished in *Paradiso* XIII, where the pilgrim finds himself no longer among the damned victims of Eros, speaking with a daughter of Eve, but among the blessed spirits of wise men, speaking with Saint Thomas Aquinas. The heart of the canto is Thomas's lecture on the methods and perils of interpretation and it is important to note that the image within which this lecture is presented is the dominant image of the heaven of the sun, the circle and its center; the wise doctors form a circle around the pilgrim and Beatrice, "far di noi centro e di sé far corona" (make of us a center and of themselves a crown; *Paradiso* X.65). Dante describes this center, where the pilgrim and Beatrice stand as the doctors dance around them, as a "punto": he speaks of "la doppia danza / che circulava il punto dov'io era" (the double dance that circled round the point where I was; *Paradiso* XIII.20–21). This geometric image is again emphasized at the end of Thomas's lecture, as *Paradiso* xiv opens with a line—"Dal centro al cerchio, e sì dal cerchio al centro" (from center to rim, and again from rim to center)—that associates Beatrice and her next speech with the point at the center of the circle and Thomas and his concluded speech with its circumference.

Dante insists on this image because—like the state of the souls buffeted by wind in *Inferno* v—it represents something much more significant than the souls' physical situation or configuration. Thomas begins the explanation that will resolve the pilgrim's doubt by using the framing image of center and circle to describe the relation that will exist between the pilgrim's opinion and Thomas's own utterance when the explanation is concluded.

> Or apri li occhi a quel ch'io ti rispondo,
> e vedräi il tuo credere e 'l mio dire
> nel vero farsi *come centro in tondo*.

(Open now thine eyes to the answer I give thee, and thou shalt see that thy belief and my words meet in the truth as the center of the circle.)
[xiii.49–51; emphasis added]

The relation between center and circle thus suggests completeness, perfection, truth. In the body of his lecture Thomas uses the word "punto" in quite a different way, which nonetheless suggests perfection; with the phrase "Se fosse a punto la cera dedutta" (If the wax were moulded perfectly; xiii.73), he describes the unattainable case in which the earthly material ("cera") in which heaven stamps its imprint would be at such a state of perfection ("a punto") that the light of heaven would appear in that earthly material with no impairment or diminution. The perfection with which "punto" is associated is not attainable at the end of Thomas's lecture, or indeed at any time.

In this canto, the doubt that Thomas undertakes to resolve has arisen in the pilgrim's mind in response to a statement Thomas himself has made just a bit earlier, citing scriptural authority (x.113–14, based on 3 Reg. 3:12; that is, 1 Kings 3:12). The pilgrim's doubt is this: how can what Thomas and the Old Testament Jehovah have said about Salomon—that no one wiser than he lived before or after him—be true, since both Adam before the Fall and Christ must have been as wise or wiser? Thomas's resolution of the pilgrim's doubt has two parts. In the first (xiii.52–87) he argues that Adam and Christ, created directly by

God, are to be understood to be in a category entirely different from Salomon's. In the second (xiii.92–108) Thomas goes on (note the phrase "avanti piue," indicating a forceful and sustained interpretive effort, which contrasts with Paolo and Francesca's going no further: "non . . . più avante") to distinguish Salomon's wisdom as kingly from, for example, theological wisdom or dialectical wisdom.

But what is of particular interest is not Thomas's argument about Salomon itself, a mere illustration, but rather the imagery he uses in his argument and the lengthy peroration (xiii.112–42) on scriptural interpretation and misinterpretation with which he concludes. While the image of the center and the circle remains prominent, motifs suggesting the contrast betwen temporality and infinity also become very important.

In the first part of Thomas's argument, the most significant theme is the difference between mortal and immortal ("Ciò che non more e ciò che può morire"), between that which is eternally one ("etternalmente rimanendosi una") and that which is reflected ("specchiato") and contingent ("brevi contingenze"). Thomas also emphasizes that everything in the universe is generated by God's love (xiii.54), the source of divine light, reflected throughout the universe in various ways and in the mortal, temporal realm only to a diminished degree. He goes on to condemn those who distort scripture and "fish for truth without knowing the art" of fishing, remaining locked by emotion into a hurried judgment, not taking time to develop an interpretation properly.

His condemnation culminates in one central principle: skill in the art of interpretation depends upon a proper understanding of time. This principle is enunciated in a series of three images, involving the maturation of plants, the duration of a voyage, and the Resurrection and Last Judgment. In these images (which may also be taken to form a quasi-palinode or at least a qualifier with respect to Dante's own allocation of the sinners and the saved), Dante's Thomas makes clear that no interpretation of scripture or of human events may be accepted as final until time stops, at the Resurrection—until, to paraphrase Paul (1 Cor. 4:5), the Lord comes to throw light on shadows and to show forth the counsels of hearts. When Thomas warns the pilgrim always to move slowly in interpretation, he is advising slowness according to a divine rather than a merely human clock, thus recalling that, for God, one day and a thousand years are equal (2 Pet. 3:8). From this viewpoint, the reader understands that when Dante suggests that Paolo and Francesca's misreading was the result of a reading of insufficient duration, he does not mean merely that they should have read through to the end of the book before deciding to interpret. For him, all interpretation is provisional, pending the Second Coming.

In the last two cantos of Dante's poem, this basic correlation between temporal understanding and validity in interpretation is developed further. The images and problems associated with the very first sinners the pilgrim interrogates are resurrected and redeemed in the *Commedia*'s final verses. Here again, the seemingly banal word "punto" reappears, three times, finally demonstrating fully the nature of Paolo and Francesca's error in making what they saw as a single point in a text the "first root" of their love. In *Paradiso* XXXII.53 the word first appears as Saint Bernard of Clairvaux explains to the pilgrim that, in Paradise, all is fixed by eternal law (v. 55), and there is no room for the contingent or accidental: "casüal punto non puote aver sito" (nothing of chance can find a place). Here "punto" clearly falls within the category of the temporal rather than the eternal. The second appearance of the word in this canto begins with an allusion to time, though it goes on, startlingly, to the realm of tailoring:

> Ma perchè 'l tempo fugge che t'assonna
> qui farem punto, come buon sartore
> che com' elli ha del panno fa la gonna;
> e drizzeremo li occhi al primo amore.

(But since the time flies that holds thee sleeping we shall stop here, like a good tailor that cuts his coat according to his cloth; and we shall direct our eyes to the Primal Love.)

[XXXII.139–42]

Here "punto" is part of the idiom "fare punto," that is, "to stop." But since the idiom—indeed, the entire simile—is startling in Bernard's mouth, preceding his invitation to lift the eyes to the vision of God, it must be assumed that Dante used the word "punto" quite deliberately just here. The first line of the tercet indicates not merely that the poet is running out of time or out of cantos but that he is a mortal, one who must sleep and who must, in the image of sleep, die.

But it is only in the next and final canto that the word "punto" as used by Francesca ("ma *solo un punto* fu quel che ci vinse") is completely inverted:

> *Un punto solo* m'è maggior letargo
> che venticinque secoli a la 'mpresa
> che fé Nettuno ammirar l'ombra d'Argo.

(A single moment makes for me deeper oblivion than five and twenty
centuries upon the enterprise that made Neptune wonder at the shadow of the Argo.)

[XXXIII.94–96; emphasis added]

The speaker is the poet, as narrator; the "punto" he refers to is the
vision of God, conceived not only spatially, as the center and circumference of the circle (cf. XXXIII.127, 129, 134, 138, and especially the
last three lines of the poem), but also temporally; and the "maggior
letargo" is an obstacle, something that conquers the poet as the earlier
"punto" conquered Paolo and Francesca.

Indeed the association of "punto" with time in *Paradiso* XXXIII is
more prominent than any geometric meaning, because the "punto" is
described as creating a greater obstacle to memory than many centuries
have to the memory of the Argo. This "punto," the vision of God,
represents a temporal paradox; it indicates the smallest possible magni-
tude, which is nonetheless greater than the duration of many centuries.
Again, as he did with the allusions to Dido, Helen, and Tristan in
Inferno V, Dante cites an ancient literary tradition, but this time he does
so for the purpose of contrast rather than comparison. His "letargo"
(from *Lethe* with *argos*), an inability to remember, a kind of sleepy
ineffectiveness, confirms Bernard's observation in the previous canto
that time was making the pilgrim drowsy: "Ma perchè 'l tempo fugge
che t'assonna, / qui farem punto"(But since the time flies that holds
you sleeping, we shall stop here; XXXII.139–40).

In the final canto, Dante employs another motif from the episode of
Paolo and Francesca when he compares his divine vision to the reading
of a book, but a book of a kind that does not exist on earth or indeed
anywhere else in creation:

> Nel suo profondo vidi che s'interna,
> legato con amore in un volume,
> ciò che per l'universo si squaderna:
> sustanze e accidenti e lor costume
> quasi conflati insieme, per tal modo
> che ciò ch'i' dico è un semplice lume.

(In its depth I saw that it contained bound by love in one volume, that
which is scattered in leaves through the universe, substances and acci-
dents and their relations as it were fused together in such a way that
what I tell of is a simple light.)

[XXXIII.85–90]

The contrast is between the scattered pages that are of necessity the only reading material the created world provides, on the one hand, and, on the other, the unified volume, bound together with love, that is available only in God.

In other terms, reading in the created world is necessarily discontinuous; a complete, continuous text and interpretation is attainable only in union with God. This is only one of several places in the *Purgatorio* and the *Paradiso* in which insight into the divine is compared to reading in a divine book contrasted with earthly books. For example, in *Paradiso* xv. 50–51, learning God's purposes is described as "leggendo del magno volume / du' non si muta mai bianco né bruno" (reading the great volume where there is never change of black or white). The stress is on the mutability over a period of time of what is written in the "books" of the contingent world.

The "punto solo" conquers the poet, for it is easier to remember back through 2,500 years to the Argonauts than to "remember" what he saw in that divine point. In a different sense he shares the fate of Francesca, who had also been conquered by "solo un punto." She had read only interpretively, for the present, closed off from the meaning that had earlier been woven into the Lancelot text. The way in which the poet is conquered by "a single point" magnifies *her* failing, placing it in a much broader setting. The poet's mind is described as inadequate to the task of "remembering" his final vision, of calling it into the present from the past.

If one accepts the repeated injunctions of Vergil and Beatrice to gloss one part of the poem by another, and especially to gloss the earlier, dark passages by the doctrine expounded later when the pilgrim draws nearer to God, doing so confirms that Francesca's shaping of one "punto" in her book into the "prima radice" of a criminal love must be understood as a temporal flaw. Her complaint that it is painful to recall and recount the lost happiness of another time, then, is no casual prefatory remark, and her plight points to a temporal problem that is the very root and starting point of the *Commedia*. Just what temporal sin does she commit in reading? It must be more than the banal one of stopping her reading before the book is done.

What constitutes Francesca's act of temporal original sin as a reader becomes clear only after one has reflected on the theme of love, which is both the ostensible topic of *Inferno* v and, in a much broader sense, the central problem of the entire *Commedia*. The "first sin" in the long list the pilgrim will encounter on his journey is Paolo and Francesca's misdirected love; at the poem's very end this love is transformed into the final blessing the pilgrim receives, the vision of divine love. The transformation is encapsulated in the contrast between the terms of Francesca's bitter though clever explanation, "Amor condusse noi ad una morte" (Love led us to a single [shared] death), on the one hand, and, on the other, those of the final line of the *Commedia*, "l'amor che move il sole e l'altre stelle" (the Love which moves the sun and the other stars). When Francesca speaks of love, it is of a love not only profoundly mortal but actually fatal; it is equivalent to death (an equivalence brought out in the very form of the words: "un*a morte*"), a death that cannot even look forward to the Resurrection. When the narrator, by contrast, speaks of it at the end of the poem, "amor" is eternal life, the source of all life, guiding and moving everything in the universe.

The basis of this contrast between the two forms of love, temporal and eternal, is best explained in what is literally the center of the poem, the middle of the *Purgatorio*, where Marco Lombardo explains to the pilgrim the nature of love (XVII.91–139). Love, Marco says, is the source of all human action, whether good or ill. Every creature is born loving the "primo ben" (primal good), its Creator, but soon is distracted by other objects in which it thinks it sees love reflected and in which it hopes to find rest for the soul. Thus a contrast develops between properly directed love, the fruit and root of which is happiness, and misdirected love, which brings neither happiness nor peace but merely the never-fulfilled promise of them. Properly directed love has a future, in Paradise; misdirected love deludes by offering a future bliss it can never deliver.

Properly directed love arises as a response to God's love, the transmission of which Dante describes primarily through the image of light. For example, in *Paradiso* XVIII.1–2, he represents the pilgrim as delighting in the reflection of love in the "mirror" of Cacciaguida's soul and then, at Beatrice's command, turning to gaze at it in her eyes (XVIII.9), where it shines brightly because of her "proximity" to God. In *Paradiso* V.7–12, Beatrice describes the relationship of all objects of love to love's original source quite clearly, again using the image of light:

> già resplende
> ne l'intelletto tuo l'etterna luce,
> che, vista, sola e sempre amore accende;

> e s'altra cosa vostro amor seduce,
> non è se non di quella alcun vestigio,
> mal conosciuto, che quivi traluce.

(There shines now in thy mind the eternal light which, seen, alone and always kindles love: and if aught else beguile your love it is nothing but some trace of this, ill-understood, that shines through there.)

There is, then, in the *Commedia*'s terms, only one "point" of love, from which all its reflections radiate. The movement of the pilgrim's eyes, or of the soul, from one reflection to another is depicted as a successive process that occurs across time, the goal of which is its own cessation, the attainment of repose. The only point in which there is the "pace" (peace) for which Francesca longs is God: "E 'n la sua volontade è nostra pace" (And in His will is our peace; *Paradiso* III.85). It is Francesca's misapprehension of the "punto" of the kiss as the "prima radice" of "amore" that causes her downfall. Only eternal light can properly ignite the fire of love, creating a blessed *amoris ascensio:* "sola e *sempre amore accende.*" Francesca's allusion (*Inferno* v. 100, 103) to the stilnovistic touchstone, Guido Guinizzelli's "Al cor gentil ripara *sempre amore*" (*Love always* makes its way into the gentle heart), here finds its correction and fulfillment. It may seem outrageous, today, to make divine love and erotic love inversions of each other, but Dante's lifelong poetic quest was for an understanding of the soul that would be based on the continuity of these two. His best-known sinner, Francesca, is damned because she privileges a human "punto," reflective of love, in what is at its core an attempt to rebel against her own mortality and thus against the nature of mortal time.

By the endpoint of the poem the nature of her sin becomes clear, as Dante stresses that no human "punto" is static; every moment is one of change and process. To try to give the moment of reading a duration its nature does not permit by imitating an episode in a book is to try to falsify time: clearly, a form of rebellion against the workings of the divine. Yet Paolo and Francesca's form of rebellion against the temporal nature of human reading is not only familiar but necessary. Fundamentally, the root of their fall, constituting the state of readerly "original sin" from which there are no exemptions, lies not exclusively in themselves any more than in the book or the author. It is instead inherent in the nature of the temporal relationship among these three.

Geryon and the Temporality of Language

Dante's complex concern with reading and misreading is the practical expression of his reflection on the relation of human temporality to eternity and, concomitantly, on the relation of temporal to eternal language. He views language on earth as bringing those who use it both profit and peril. But the intimate and necessary relation of peril and profit which for Dante is intrinsic only to finite, fallen, earthly language will come to be seen by later thinkers as inherent in all language, understood to exist in only one temporal context, human rather than divine. Dante's thinking about mortal language may thus be seen as marking the beginning of a secular approach to the problem of the temporality of reading.[13]

The concept that will make possible such a transition from a problem in the theology of language to one entirely secular—literary and linguistic only—emerges forcefully in the episode in *Inferno* XVI-XVII in which the monster Geryon appears. This episode plays a crucial role in the overall structure of the *Inferno*. In this first of the poem's three *cantiche*, Dante divides sins (and thus the souls of sinners) into three categories, each worse than the one before and each therefore punished deeper in Hell. As the Geryon episode opens, the pilgrim has left far behind sinners guilty of mere "incontinence," like Paolo and Francesca, and is about to leave the realm of violent sinners also; he is preparing to enter the last and worst part of Hell, the realm of fraud. It is Geryon who transports the pilgrim and his guide into this most hellish of hells and who serves as the introductory symbol of the vilest of the three categories of sin.

Dante emphasizes the importance of this episode in a singular way later in the poem, when Vergil recalls it to the pilgrim's mind as both the measure of the extremity of the perils they faced together in Hell and the witness of the reliability of the Mantuan "master's" ability to protect his charge, no matter how fearful the situation:

> Ricorditi, ricorditi! E se io
> sovresso Gerïon ti guidai salvo,
> che farò ora presso più a Dio?

---

13. The reading of Dante and especially of *Inferno* XVI-XVII presented here complements Eugene Vance's study of *Inferno* XV in *Mervelous Signals: Poetics and Sign Theory in the Middle Ages* (Lincoln: University of Nebraska Press, 1986), chap. 8. Vance presents Dante as "a poet whose art is constantly both asserting and calling into question the

(Remember, remember; and if even on Geryon I brought thee safely,
what shall I do now nearer to God?)

[*Purgatorio* XXVII.22–24)

In retrospect, then, the episode is strongly associated with extremes,
two opposite experiences the pilgrim has had so far on his journey:
peril and protection. It serves as a touchstone for Vergil, who is at this
point in Purgatory about to abandon the pilgrim to another guide,
Beatrice. It enables Vergil to sum up the experiences he and the pilgrim
have shared in Hell and Purgatory. The surprisingly safe ride the pilgrim is granted on the back of the terrifying Geryon serves as a kind of
synecdoche, representing all those experiences.

As crucial as the episode is, however, it is hardly so well known as
that of Paolo and Francesca, so a brief summary may be useful. At the
edge of a steep bank above turbulent dark water, the pilgrim, at Vergil's bidding, removes a cord ("corda") that he has worn as a belt and
hands it to Vergil, coiled and knotted (*Inferno* XVI.106–11). Vergil then
flings it into the abyss, and the pilgrim thinks to himself that something very strange must arise as a response to this strange signal
(XVI.112–17). At this point the poet interrupts his narrative to state his
embarrassment at what he has to report next, since it will seem to be a
lie. He swears to the reader that the strange thing that answered Vergil's strange signal was a figure swimming up through the air toward
the travelers, like a diver returning from the bottom of the sea
(XVI.124–36). Vergil identifies the figure as "the beast with the pointed
tail . . . that infects all the world" and "that foul image of fraud"
XVII.1–3, 7). The head and chest of the beast come to rest on the bank,
but he leaves his tail below. The face is that of a just man, the body that
of a serpent, painted with knots and circles rivaling in their color and
intricacy the greatest achievements of weavers; the tail (*coda*) waves in
the air, its poisonous fork suggesting a scorpion's (XVII.10–18, 25–27).
Vergil then sends the pilgrim off to interrogate the usurers, while he
persuades the beast to lend the travelers his "strong shoulders"
(XVII.37–42). When the pilgrim returns, he finds Vergil already
mounted on Geryon's back, and Vergil tells him that their descent will
henceforth be "by such stairs as this" (XVII.79–82). Following Vergil's
instructions, the trembling pilgrim mounts in front of his guide, so as

legitimacy of poetic signs" (p. 233). Also relevant is Vance's second chapter, which
treats Augustine's conception of the processes of language as reflective of temporality.

to be protected from the beast's tail, and Geryon descends into the abyss in wide, slow circles, swimming like an eel (xvii.83–105). Having terrified the pilgrim, Geryon at last sets the travelers down at the bottom of the pit and immediately takes off again like an arrow shot from a bowstring: that is, once again, a "corda" (xvii.106–36).

Heavy with dramatic tension, this episode is also extremely complex in its language, filled with classical allusion and dense with tropes. Far from fortuitous, the striking verbal complexity points to language as one of the passage's most important themes. There is hardly a word in it which, if explicated, would not reveal the depth of Dante's reflection on the nature of secular rhetoric (including the name Geryon, from the same root as *garrulous*: Greek *gerys*, "voice," in participial form, "speaking"). One can begin to understand the deeper connections, not just the contrasts, between Dante's view of the reader and Baudelaire's despised but necessary "hypocrite lecteur" by analyzing Dante's "personification" of hypocrisy and specifically its most typical vehicle, speech.

Three features of the Geryon episode, above all, combine to articulate Dante's conception of the complex temporality of reading: (1) the metonymic, and paradoxical, relation between the pilgrim and the beast ("mon semblable, mon frère"); (2) the narrative structure that compels Geryon's presence at this point in the poem rather than another; (3) Dante's insistent use of a particular figure of speech, paronomasia, in the Geryon episode.[14]

(1) The very opening of the passage begins to set up a symmetry between the pilgrim and the beast. Without any transition from his narrative of the climb down the steep bank (xvi.91–105) or any introduction to what is to come, the poet describes the unwrapping of the cord with which the pilgrim has been girt and mentions that he formerly thought of using it to capture a menacing, painted beast (xvi.106–8), the leopard of *Inferno* i. What is important to an understanding of what the cord represents is not so much the symbolism associated with the leopard—Dante classifies the idea of a functional connection between cord and leopard as something abandoned, associated with the past—but that the cord is the right kind for capturing a beast, and especially a painted one.

---

14. For a suggestive account of paronomasia, see Paolo Valesio, *Novantiqua: Rhetorics as a Contemporary Theory* (Bloomington: Indiana University Press, 1980), chap. 4, esp. pp. 189–92.

The cord, which has been intimately wrapped about the pilgrim's body, is, he has thought, suitable to the conquest of such a beast, though he has not so far succeeded in using it for this purpose. A reciprocal relation between the beast and the cord is suggested, first of all, by two of the verbs the poet uses to describe the advent of Geryon, even before Vergil has identified the beast. First, he writes that Vergil "la gittò giuso in quell' alto burrato" (flung it . . . down into the depth of the abyss) and mentions that the pilgrim then thought: "E' pur convien che novità risponda" (Surely. . . something strange must answer; XVI.114–15). The pilgrim expects the strange something to answer the cord as if the cord were a question or request which the "novità" is tailored to suit. Second, in the simile that closes the canto, the poet describes the beast as resembling a swimmer who returns after having dived to the bottom of the sea: "sì come torna colui che va giuso" (even as he returns who goes down; XVI.133). That the beast is like something that returns makes it different from something that simply emerges from the abyss; what returns from the depths must first have descended into them, and what has descended here is the cord. The repetition of the form "giuso" (down), said of both the cord and the swimmer that stands for the beast (XVI.114, 134), further emphasizes the symmetry whereby something goes *down* as cord and returns *up* in a form that is new and strange: a monster with a long tail.

The transformation that occurs here is well known to Dante and his readers: it is a metamorphosis. Rather than in Ovid or Lucan, whom Dante challenges explicitly in the *Inferno*'s most famous instance of metamorphosis (cf.XXV.94–102), the literary precedents for this particular instance are to be found in two sources much more heavily used by Dante—probably his two favorites: the Bible and the *Aeneid*. Both include episodes in which an object shaped approximately like a snake is transformed, by divine intervention, into a snake; furthermore, thematic and/or verbal parallels with the Geryon episode in each case attest that Dante had them in mind.

The story of Aaron's rod in the book of Exodus relates the first in a series of what might be called "rhetorical miracles" that Yahweh instructs Moses and Aaron to perform before Pharoah as support for the request to "let my people go." As usual, Yahweh's purposes are not really so straightforward as this. He tells Moses and Aaron at the outset (Exodus 7:3–5) that he will harden Pharoah's heart so that he will refuse to be persuaded by the miracles and by the rhetoric of Yahweh's power which they support, giving the Lord the opportunity to punish

Egypt repeatedly and severely. Thus, the particular rhetorical metamorphosis Dante takes as his model in this first instance has a dual
purpose, the second of which depends on the reader's—in this case,
Pharoah's—thwarting of the first.

Yahweh tells Moses and Aaron (v. 9) that Pharoah will order them
to show him a sign ("ostendite signa": the word suggests Dante's
"novità," v. 115, "novo cenno," v. 116, and "figura," v. 131) and tells
Aaron to respond by casting ("proiice") his rod before Pharoah, who
will see it turned into a serpent ("colubrum"). The metamorphosis
takes place as Yahweh has foretold, but Pharoah hardens his heart
against its message when a repetition of the metamorphosis is performed by Egyptian magicians working (so it seems) against the divine
message. The sorcerers throw down their rods and, with incantations,
turn them into serpents, too ("dracones," v. 12, suggesting Geryon's
dragonlike features, such as feet). Good magic, or divinely sanctioned
metamorphosis, is thus opposed to bad magic, and Pharoah is the
model of the interpreter who does not know how to distinguish the
two.

The story from Exodus thus establishes a visual link between rod
and serpent and assigns them both a role in two matters that will be of
concern to Dante in the Geryon episode. The first (a parallel that will
readily occur to anyone familiar with Charles Singleton's treatment of
the pilgrim's journey as an echo of the Exodus[15]) is "departure on a
journey" ("Omai si scende per sì fatte scale"; XVII.82) that will lead
through many trials and terrors before arriving at a blessed destination.
The second is the discrimination of what is truly fraud from what is
really truth but nonetheless appears to be in the same category as fraud
(XVI.124–26). Aaron's rod and its divine metamorphosis, which *seems*
to be just like the metamorphosis produced by Pharoah's magicians,
are the first of several means of bringing about the Exodus itself, just as
the pilgrim's cord and its metamorphosis, which seems a fraud, are the
means of beginning a journey into the last and worst section of Hell, a
desert that must be traversed before there is any hope of entering the
Promised Land.

The second literary precedent for the metamorphosis of Dante's
cord into the serpent Geryon occurs in, once again, the second book of

---

15. See esp. Charles S. Singleton, "In Exitu Israel de Aegypto," *Annual Report of the
Dante Society of America* 78 (1960), 1–24, reprinted in John Freccero, ed., *Dante: A
Collection of Critical Essays* (Englewood Cliffs, NJ: Prentice-Hall, 1965), pp. 102–21.

the *Aeneid*. Here the mode of creation of Dante's emblem of fraud finds its root in the archetypical story of fraud, the narrative of the Trojan horse—more specifically, in the subplot of Laocoön's death, the two parts of which frame the introduction of the fatal horse into Troy's walls. It is the priest Laocoön who tells his fellow Trojans the truth about the fraudulent horse: it cannot really be what it seems, an offering to Athena; if it comes from the Greeks, he says, it must hide Greeks in its belly or in some other way be a tool of warfare (*Aeneid* II.45–47). He concludes his speech with the famous line "timeo Danaos et dona ferentis" (I dread the Greeks, even when they bring gifts; II.49) and then performs an action that will cost him his life: he hurls his spear against the belly of the beast (II.50–52). The response to what appears to be Laocoön's blasphemous attack on an offering to a goddess is not immediate. As the spear stands quivering in the beast's side, shepherds bring to Priam a man who seems to be an unfortunate Greek captive. As B. M. W. Knox has indicated in a powerful essay,[16] Sinon's very name suggests to the Latin reader his connection to that traditional image of fraud, the snake. Vergil focuses again and again not merely on Sinon's hypocrisy but on its verbal character: Sinon insists repeatedly that he will speak nothing but the truth, no matter what its consequences for him (II.77–78), but of course everything he says is a lie. He claims to break his oath of loyalty to the Greeks in order to bring to light all the things the Greeks conceal (II.158–59). He speaks movingly of Ulysses' ambiguous and treacherous words (II.99, 125) in words that are themselves, as Aeneas repeatedly stresses, false (II.107). Yet Sinon's false words have power to do what the most famous of Greece's warriors and its immense fleet could not accomplish in ten years of siege (II.195–98).

Aeneas then turns from his sorrowful tale of Sinon's treacherous words back to Laocoön. Out of the depths of the sea there emerge suddenly twin snakes with immense coils, who strangle and devour first his sons and then Laocoön himself. These are no ordinary serpents: Aeneas repeatedly stresses the "immensity" of their coils and mentions the knots with which they tie themselves about Laocoön (II.204, 208, 220). When the deed is done and they flee to the goddess's temple, they are no longer called snakes but dragons (II.225: "dracones"), like Geryon.

16. B. M. W. Knox, "The Serpent and the Flame," *American Journal of Philology* 71 (1950), 379–400.

It is the Trojans who read this episode as a metamorphosis, inter-preting the snakes as the answer to Laocoön's blasphemous spear (II.229–31). The way having been prepared by the words of the serpen-tine Sinon, the terror which "in*sinu*ates" (II.229) itself into the hearts of the Trojans as a result of this apparent metamorphosis brought about by an offended Athena is the direct cause of their breaking down their own walls to bring the horse (itself also imagistically linked to the snakes) into the city. The immediate consequence, of course, is the downfall of Troy.

In the longer view, however—that is, from a Roman and especially a medieval viewpoint—Sinon's fraud and the "metamorphosis" that terrorizes the Trojans into destroying their own fortifications have a salutary outcome. They lead to Aeneas's journey and ultimately to the founding of Rome, seat of Empire and Church. Immediately after recounting the piercing of the horse's side by Laocoön's spear, Aeneas notes that Laocoön's insight could not forestall Troy's destruction be-cause it was fated (II.54); like Pharaoh, the Trojans are fulfilling a divine purpose when they ignore the priest's warning. The notion that the episode of the horse leads eventually to a divinely willed outcome is further emphasized by its closing scene: the same night, Hector appears to his brother in sleep, warns him to flee the now burning city, and foretells that after wandering over the sea, Aeneas will found another great city (II.294–95).

In the context created by these two well-known sources, then, it is not surprising that the pilgrim's "corda," coiled and knotted like Ver-gil's snakes (*Inferno* XVI.106–11) and cast down into the abyss by the character Vergil, should return metamorphosed into a serpent with a "coda," painted all over with knots and circles (XVII.1–3, 15). The "corda," part of the pilgrim's garb, represents him metonymically; through metaphor, it is metamorphosed into Geryon. The physical connection thus established between Dante and the beast is further emphasized on the level of moral allegory. The poet has identified himself (XVI.124–26) as one compelled to speak truth that seems to be a lie, while Geryon, whose very name means "speaking," is a lie with the face of truth (XVII.7–12): "faccia d'uom giusto . . . d'un serpente tutto l'altro fusto" (the face of a just man . . . all the rest was a serpent's trunk).

(2) This is a disquieting symmetry but one extremely well suited to the position in Dante's narrative which the Geryon episode occupies. The intimate and paradoxical relation of Dante and Geryon suggests a

notion that develops directly out of the Paolo and Francesca episode: an author with good intentions may see his work metamorphosed into a fraud, a deceiver, a Galeotto; the transformation of what an author "casts forth" into something entirely different is indeed present not as a mere possibility but as a necessity. The pilgrim *must* climb on Geryon's back if he is to continue his journey; as Vergil tells him, "the descent henceforth is by such stairs as this" (xvii.79–82). Geryon is a kind of Trojan horse the pilgrim must mount in order to reach his goal, as the Trojans had to embrace the horse so that one of their number could found Rome. What this means for Dante the poet is that his poem can continue only through the use of fraudulent language. Geryon not only represents the kind of morally repulsive language on which Dante must depend; he is indeed fabricated from it.

(3) The most prominent feature of Dante's rhetoric in the Geryon episode is his use of paronomasia, the figure that plays on pairs of words with different histories and meanings but similar forms. The *Aeneid*'s Trojan-horse episode is itself rife with examples, all focusing the reader's attention (as Knox has shown) on the sinuosity of Sinon, of the snakes, and of the flames which finally engulf Troy. Dante reinforces the connection between the pilgrim and Geryon with two instances of this trope.

The first pair of words, already mentioned, is *corda/coda*. The flinging of the *corda* opens the Geryon episode, which is then punctuated by repeated references to Geryon's *coda*. Finally the word *corda* returns as Dante closes the episode: after depositing his passengers in the eighth circle of hell, Geryon "si dileguò come da corda cocca" (vanished like an arrow from the string; xvii.136).

The second paronomasia pairs *note/notando*. This pair, more peculiar semantically and orthographically than the other, perhaps more daring, does not just illustrate the kind of fraudulent rhetoric to which Dante is here confessing but inherently provides something of an analysis of that rhetoric and its moral justification. Dante introduces and attests to the veracity of the appearance of Geryon with a vow whose terms are unusual:

> Sempre a quel ver c'ha faccia di menzogna
> de' l'uom chiuder le labbra fin ch'el puote,
> però che sanza colpa fa vergogna;
>   ma qui tacer nol posso; e per le *note*
> di questa comedìa, lettor, ti giuro,
> s'elle non sien di lunga grazia vòte,

> ch'i vidi per quell'aere grosso e scuro
> venir *notando* una figura in suso,
> marvigliosa ad ogni cor sicuro.

(A man should always close his lips, as far as he can, to the truth that has the face of a lie, since without fault it brings him shame, but here I cannot be silent; and by the "notes" of this Commedia, reader, I swear to you if they be not empty of long grace, that I saw through that heavy and dark air come swimming upward, a figure amazing to every stout heart.)

[XVI.124–32; emphasis added]

Whereas traditionally a vow is made by or on something eternal (showing the abiding nature of the vow), as well as something true, not illusory (for example, the Bible), here Dante swears on the physical aspect of the poem itself. All the early commentators gloss *note* in *Inferno* XVI.127 as referring to some concrete aspect of the poem: Ottimo to the "versi," Buti to the "Canti," Anonimo to the "rime," and Benvenuto to the "literas."[17] Their inability to agree on precisely what aspect of the general category of physical marks Dante had in mind is of little concern. What does matter is the rather technical resonance of the word: it refers to one of the tools of the poet's trade. In the twelfth century, glossators and commentators affected by the new techniques of scholasticism had begun to use the equivalent verbal form *notare* to describe the act of writing, composition.[18] Thus *note* are letters and the structures built from them, and *notando* is the inscription of such letters and letter structures: writing.

Several early commentators were struck by Dante's choice of this precise moment to give his poem a title: "questa *comedìa*," (emphasis added).[19] The poet's swearing "per le note / di questa comedìa" means that the veracity of his witness is to be proved by the very physical existence of the components of his poem. The monster Geryon is as real as the sounds or letters of the words that call him forth, a reality that is indisputable for anyone reading them.

It is just at the point at which Dante names his poem and swears by the tools of his craft, then, that he asserts that poetry is a kind of fraud in reverse and pairs the terms *note* and *notando* in a singularly appropri-

17. Guido Biagi, ed., *La Divina Commedia nella figurazione artistica e nel secolare commento* (Turin: Unione Tipografico-editrice Torinese, 1924).
18. Saenger, "Silent Reading," p. 385.
19. Cf. Franco Ferrucci, "Comedìa," *Yearbook of Italian Studies* 1 (1971), 29–52; and Pio Rajna, "Il titolo del poema dantesco," *Studi Danteschi* 4 (1921), 1–37.

ate instance of paronomasia. *Notando* here means "swimming"—in modern Italian, *nuotando*. But it is to the characters, the *note*, precisely as they are written, that one must pay attention, rather than translating them too quickly into another form. The alternative spelling for the equivalent of "swimming" was available to Dante;[20] he could have described Geryon as *nuotando*, the diphthongized form he did use in the only other reference to swimming in the poem (*Inferno* XXI.49). But no extant manuscript attests the spelling *nuotare* in reference to Geryon, even though it appears in midline (the pure "o" usually being reserved for words in rhyme position).[21] Early copyists left *notando* in a form that echoes the *note* four lines above, making no effort to differentiate two roots, so different in etymology, which the context appears to make so different in meaning. Later, when Geryon swims through the air with the two poets on his back, his movement is again designated by the same word: "Ella sen va notando lenta lenta" (XVII.115). A translation of this line as "[The beast] goes along swimming slowly, slowly" would be overliteral; it means also "The beast [with the name which means "speaking"] goes along by writing slowly, slowly." The evolving state of Tuscan pronunciation and orthography thus put at Dante's disposal the possibility of a play between *note* and *notando/nuotando* which he used to enhance the resemblance between the poet and his monstrous creation: the poet is one who creates *note*, products of his craft so important that he can make a vow on them, and the emblem of the fraud that results proceeds by *notando*.

These prominent instances indicate that paronomasia is the trope that best exemplifies the kind of inversely fraudulent poetic language with which Dante wishes to identify himself by establishing an inverse relation between pilgrim and beast. Indeed, it is a trope that reveals especially well the temporal nature of all words, not only those that have homonyms but also those that do not. Word-pairs like *corda/coda* and *note/n(u)otare* show that authorial control of language is very limited indeed. Once set down in a text, words establish resonances with one another whether their putative author wishes them to or not—

20. E.g., Bartolommeo da San Concordio (1262–1347) used the diphthongized spelling of *nuotare*; see Nicolò Tommaseo and Bernardo Bellini, *Dizionario della lingua italiana* (Turin: Unione Tipografico-editrice Torinese, 1915), s.v. "nuotare e notare." The form *notare* appears through the sixteenth century.

21. On the pattern of oscillation between "o" and "uo," see Petrocchi, "Introduzione," in *La Commedia* 1:426, 96, 296, 336; see also the editor's comments, 2:275, 291, 350.

indeed, whether the author has heard their resonances or not. An author who deliberately selects such pairs from the lexicon available is not creating meanings and structures with them so much as making use of the meanings and structures they already have. It is time that shapes the meanings of words, as well as their forms (orthographic and phonic) and their potential relations with other words (in semantic, syntactic, phonic groupings, and so on). For Dante, who reflected long and seriously on the meaning of the evolution of the vernaculars from Latin, words are not what they would seem to neoclassical theorists: pieces of uncut marble that the poet chisels to fit a preconceived idea. Rather, they are like objects found here and there which a modern sculptor might assemble into a construction, building an overall form whose elements would nonetheless continue to have an independent identity of their own.

Dante's image for this temporal aspect of language comes not from visual art but from classical rhetoric and New Testament theology: "le note di questa comedìa . . . s'elle non sien di lunga grazia vòte" (the "notes" of this comedy . . . if they be not of long grace empty; XVI. 127–29). With the curious phrase, "non . . . di lunga grazia vòte," Dante expresses his hope for his *note*. He would see them connected with grace, but "grace" itself is, he is aware, a word whose meaning has changed. He marks his awareness of the two different connotations time has brought to it by the two adjectives with which he juxtaposes it. The phrase "lunga grazia" directly translates a Latin phrase used by such writers as Propertius to describe elegant words, "enduringly graceful" in the modern sense. The phrase "di grazia vòte" inverts, no doubt for modesty's sake, the formula "di grazia piena" with which Gabriel describes the Virgin at the Annunciation: "Ave Maria, gratia plena." The angel is not, of course, merely telling Mary that she is a graceful young woman, although this is how Boccaccio's Donna Lisetta would "read" the Annunciation.[22] There is a kind of double-entendre in the angel's speech in that, from this the moment of Incarnation, "grace" means not just grace of form, a gift from the Muses, but a gift of salvation. The "grace" with which the pregnant Mary is filled is her son Jesus, Logos. Dante, as a Christian writer, expresses the hope that Logos may fill his *note* as well; he realizes, however, that the power to make this happen is not his.

Words filled with enduring grace and a grace that is not only the

22. Giovanni Boccaccio, *Decameron* IV. 2.

external beauty of classical rhetoric but also the inner beauty of a power that brings salvation: these are what Dante wishes to write in his *comedìa*. He is aware that, if "his" words endure, they can and will be read in ways other than the ones he intends: Paolo and Francesca's misreading of the Lancelot romance shows this clearly. He has called these words from their lives elsewhere to a metamorphosis in his text, and there they have taken on new meanings. These found objects, constantly changing, have been the only "steps" available to him in his poetic journey. Yet the words themselves, if Dante gets his wish, will endure, even if time changes their meaning.

Words, then, are not only a reminder of the change time brings but also a refuge against that change. For a Christian writer the longevity of language holds out the promise that when time or, more concretely, readers of other times transform an author's meaning, they will not necessarily always change it for ill (as Paolo and Francesca do) but may instead change it for the better (as, for example, Dante's Christian Statius does in his surprisingly salvific reading of the pagan Vergil's words in *Purgatorio* XXII). Such a theological context makes it possible for an author (certainly not an eccentric but one indeed centered in the Christian tradition) to say without distress not only that his words "now" mean something different from what they did "then" but also that they will in future mean something else again.

This, then, is Dante's solution to the problem of the temporality of reading. He can accept what time, and the new readers time brings, will do to his words because he sees them all—time, words, and read-ers—as in the hands of God. As noted earlier, he depicts himself as learning from Saint Thomas that all readings are provisional, pending the Second Coming.

Dante's solution, however, would not suit later writers.[23] In the very next generation it proved troubling to a writer more prolific than Dante, one who thus had even more books to leave behind: his fellow Tuscan, born in Dante's last years, Giovanni Boccaccio.

---

23. Relevant here is the gradual crumbling of the *certitudo salutis*, which, Wolfgang Iser shows, has considerable impact on literature: *The Implied Reader* (Baltimore, Md.: Johns Hopkins University Press, 1974), chap. 1.

Chapter 3

From Dante to Boccaccio: Blurring the Margin

> Of all sciences . . . is our poet the monarch. For he doth not
> only show the way, but giveth so sweet a prospect into the
> way, as will entice any man to enter into it . . . He beginneth
> not with obscure definitions, which must blur the margent
> with interpretations . . .
>
> PHILIP SIDNEY, *The Defense of Poesie*

Dante's solution to the problem of the temporality of reading was hard won, reached only late in a long writing career that had been at every stage urged forward by his desire to locate a new audience.[1] Indeed, insofar as the pilgrim's journey in the *Commedia* figures, among other things, the succession of disillusionments and insights about writing which marked that career (as in the episodes of Paolo and Francesca and of Geryon), it presents not just the last but rather a range of successive perspectives on the temporality of reading identifiable with stages in Dante's poetic development.

This fact fundamentally qualifies the contrast between Dante and Baudelaire with which my analysis began. It makes clear that reducing Dante's attitude toward his reader to one formulation alone is an oversimplification. The reader Dante addresses as studying at his desk is the poet's intellectual inferior. This is the reader whom Dante most often invokes in the *Commedia*, the one associated earlier in this study with such lay readers as were being educated in the time of Saint Louis. It is

---

1. See Andrea Battistini and Ezio Raimondi, "Retoriche e poetiche dominanti," in *Letteratura italiana*, ed. Alberto Asor Rosa (Turin: Einaudi, 1984), 3 (pt. 1):33–34; and Domenico De Robertis, *Il libro della 'Vita nuova'* (Florence: Sansoni, 1961), p. 16.

presumably not the reader to whom Dante would have been willing to pass on control over the meaning of his words.

If it is possible to identify a moment of transition in which Dante is truly ready to envision a reader who is his equal, fulfilling the ideal relationship suggested by the *Commedia*'s first line ("in the middle of the journey of *our* life, I found myself . . ."), that moment coincides with the radical opening to the temporality of language depicted near the end of the *Purgatorio* when Vergil, reminding the pilgrim that he has so far traveled safely even on the back of Geryon, hands him over to a new guide. Beatrice is, at an even more fundamental level than Vergil, a representation of a text, going back to the time of her appearance in the *Vita nuova* (New Life). A new attitude toward the temporal relation of reader and sacred text is first signaled by Dante's allegorical representation of the entire Bible in *Purgatorio* xxix, which explicitly uses the authority of the (later) Saint John to correct the (earlier) book of Ezekiel (xxix.100–105). More important, however, is the fact that the *Commedia* indeed goes on even after the representation of the last book of the Bible, thus suggesting that the *Paradiso*, the last section of what Dante calls a "sacred poem to which both heaven and earth have put their hands," is a continuation of the Bible by one of its latter-day readers. Even the Bible is not regarded as unchanging, then.[2]

It is hardly surprising that such a moment of transition to an understanding of all books as open to later readings comes just as the pilgrim is entrusted to Beatrice. The poems Dante dedicated to her early in his career are associated with his earliest recorded reflections on the temporality of reading, in the *Vita nuova*. His first major work, it draws together with some new poems a number of his earlier lyrics and provides them with "divisions" (a kind of structural explication ori-

---

2. Whether such a new attitude toward the reader marks a step toward the Reformation is a question too complex to be competently addressed here. It must be remembered that the ground for reformation was prepared less by a free attitude toward biblical interpretation than by a new rigor in biblical exegesis. When Newman pointed in 1837 to "the popular feeling of the sixteenth century" as explaining a new attitude toward the reading of the Bible (see Introduction, above), he was guessing at something the history of reading still needs to work out, going back well before the sixteenth century. For a summary of recent studies of the peculiar status Dante attributes to the language of *Paradiso* and a detailed analysis of its linguistic forms, see Joan M. Ferrante, "Words and Images in the *Paradiso*: Reflections on the Divine," in *Dante, Petrarch, and Boccaccio: Studies in the Italian Trecento in Honor of Charles Singleton*, ed. A. S. Bernardo and A. L. Pellegrini (Binghamton, N.Y.: Medieval and Renaissance Texts and Studies, 1983), pp. 115–32.

ginating in prescholastic scholarship). It also places these lyrics within a highly allegorical prose narrative recounting the circumstances in which they were written.

These retrospective glosses on the poems make of the *Vita nuova* a capital example of an author's rereading of earlier work. As Domenico De Robertis points out, there is a dialogue between the lyrics and the prose which takes on "the character of dialogue . . . between poetry of yesterday and poetry of today . . . .The anteriority of the poetry with respect to the prose is explicitly declared, the two time periods are kept quite distinct; and from the first instant emphasis is placed upon this character of return to one's own experience, of a glance turned to the past (even if to lift it up again into a new light, to its truer meaning)."[3]

In the *Vita nuova* the relation of poetic text to prose gloss is, then, a figure for the temporality of reading. The poet publicly reads the works of an earlier period of his youth expressly because they mean more "now" than they did "then." This awareness of the change between the time of writing and that of reading does not as yet, to be sure, suggest that Dante is prepared to hand his work over to an endless succession of readers who may interpret his words as God, not the poet, directs; this is an attitude Dante attained only in his maturity. In the *Vita nuova* he seeks to have his poems read by a quite specific audience, the elite circle of those who are faithful to and well read in a certain ideal of love: the "fedeli d'amore" (devotees of love). It is indicative of the attitude toward his readers suggested at the very end of the *Paradiso*, however, that at this early point he does not describe the readers he seeks as inferior to him. If anything, it is he who is cast in the inferior role at the beginning of this early work; he wishes to join as an equal in a circle to which he has not yet been admitted and hopes to gain the friendship and respect of its members by his writing.

Boccaccio at times displayed a very different attitude toward the temporality of reading. This difference is manifested, once again, in his approach to the relation of text and gloss. The new attitude emerges above all in two relatively little-known parts of Boccaccio's work. The first is his editorial intervention in the text and gloss of Dante's *Vita*

---

3. De Robertis, *Il libro della 'Vita nuova'*, pp. 7, 11. Dante's form has an important French predecessor in the *chantefable* (e.g., *Aucassin et Nicolette*) and a fourteenth-century analogue in Guillaume de Machaut's *Le Voir dit*, which uses the alternation of verse and prose to dramatize the separation of past and present selves.

nuova, of which he was perhaps the first influential editor. The second is the gloss he prepared for one of his own texts, for which he too envisions new readers. Like dramatists writing parts for characters, both Dante and Boccaccio in their self-glosses write scripts for the readers they hope to find. But Boccaccio's purpose as a glossator differs somewhat from Dante's. At no moment does he place himself on an equal footing with his readers, much less a step below them. Moreover, although his glosses arise from a recognition of the temporal discrepancy between text and reader, Boccaccio sometimes turns away from the recognition and tries to use some glosses to suppress this temporality.

Boccaccio's marginal commentaries on his epic *Teseida* play a role in his effort to raise the secular, vernacular poet to the level of a "monarch," as Philip Sidney would call him much later in the Renaissance,[4] and even perhaps somewhat higher than that; for the power to make a work timeless, which Dante finally recognizes as God's, Boccaccio sometimes seems to want to keep for himself. In the terms suggested by Dante at the end of the *Commedia*, a timeless text—one "not empty of long grace"—would take on new and blessed meanings over time. In the view of such an early humanist as Boccaccio, on the contrary, a timeless text was one that did not change. Among the most indefatigable and fervent of those who sought to retrieve the works of antiquity in the form in which they had been written and to reconstruct, with all the tools of erudition, their original meaning, Boccaccio (as one might expect) sought also to hand down his own work to posterity not merely in the exact form he had created but with the meaning he wished to find in it, and no other.

To be sure, just as it would be simplistic to reduce Dante's attitude toward his reader to one formulation alone, it would be misleading to conceive of the attitude Boccaccio displays in his editorial work on Dante's *Vita nuova* and in his preparation of his *Teseida* self-gloss as typical of his entire career as a writer and reader. Reading is far too complex an activity to permit anyone who engages in it intensively and reflectively to understand it in only one way. Boccaccio was perhaps the most sophisticated literary theorist of the late Middle Ages. He devoted an extremely long and productive career to working out an

---

4. Philip Sidney, *The Defense of Poesie*, in *Literary Criticism: Plato to Dryden*, ed. Allan H. Gilbert (1940; rpt. Detroit: Wayne State University Press, 1962), p. 427.

understanding of the relation of literature to society.[5] At times, he embraced an idealistic vision of the text as capable of achieving a timeless status through the labors of its author. This vision was formulated under the influence of what I have identified as the exegetical model of reading, which presupposes a timely text for the exegete to recover. At other times, however, Boccaccio's view of reading was much more pragmatic. At such moments, recognizing the power of the interpretive model, he turned his attention to what readers could and would do with the words they read.

The frequent shifting to and fro between the vision of an exegetical ideal and the recognition of a pragmatic interpretive limit to that vision is typical not only of Boccaccio but of many of his best-known humanist heirs. Their herculean efforts to recover the original state of biblical and classical texts were in fact motivated by an underlying distrust of the historical character of the version of these texts that generations of scribes had handed down to them. This distrust developed gradually, and certainly by the time of Lorenzo Valla, into a model of the text's radical instability. Valla's *De Elegantia* showed clearly that the sentence structure and very words of ancient Latin had conveyed meanings markedly different from those of medieval Latin. A haunting consciousness of the fundamental mutability of the meaning of written language went hand in hand with the better-remembered humanist quest after the exegetical ideal. Thus, my exploration of those instances in Boccaccio's work in which he pursued the ideal of a timeless rather than a timebound text must be understood as representing only one extreme position in the thought of a complex figure who helped shape the foundations of a very complex period in the history of reading.

Before I proceed to discuss Boccaccio's editorial alteration of Dante's *Vita nuova* glosses, his glosses for his own *Teseida*, and the attitude toward the temporality of reading which they manifest, a word of explanation about my choice of texts is surely in order. One might well ask why, if Boccaccio had a different attitude from Dante's toward the temporality of reading, I do not explain this new attitude by reference to the *Decameron*. If I want this book to interest readers who

---

5. Both Joy Hambuechen Potter, *Five Frames for the "Decameron": Communication and Social Systems in the Cornice* (Princeton, N.J.: Princeton University Press, 1982), and Giuseppe Mazzotta, *The World at Play in Boccaccio's "Decameron"* (Princeton, NJ: Princeton University Press, 1986), may be read as presenting Boccaccio in this light. This issue is the central concern of Millicent J. Marcus, *An Allegory of Form: Literary Self-Consciousness in the "Decameron"* (Saratoga, Calif.: Anma Libri, 1979).

are not literary specialists, why do I devote most of this chapter (and the next one as well) to minor texts almost no one in my audience is likely to read, even basing part of my argument on observation of one-of-a-kind manuscripts housed in European libraries, which few in my audience are likely to visit? How can I prove that my point is of major importance if I base it partly on minor texts?

First of all, it is essential to the historical trajectory I am tracing to deal with the work Boccaccio did while consciously following in Dante's wake. Dante was the very first to envision and write serious literature for a new reader who would not know how to play by the old rules of clerical reading and would thus need to learn new ones. We know from scattered historical information that his *Commedia* almost immediately began to find some nonclerical readers but was also quickly appropriated by scholars. Trying as best he could to follow in the footsteps of his much older contemporary, Boccaccio sought in the next generation to locate and satisfy the audience Dante had envisioned, an audience whose reality was still at least as much rhetorical as historical.

But he did not keep to this goal consistently. The *Decameron*, especially, has little in common with the *Commedia*. The elegance of its language did make it of interest to those who shared Dante's interest in eloquence in the vernacular, and its seriously witty way of addressing complex ethical problems gave it appeal to those sophisticated readers ready to consider from a more secular viewpoint the ethical issues that Dante sees theologically. Yet even the most adventurous critic would scarcely argue that the *Decameron* represents a conscious attempt on Boccaccio's part to continue the project begun in the *Commedia*. Instead, one must look elsewhere for Boccaccio's deliberate efforts to respond to Dante's proposals about the nature of the new, serious, vernacular readership and the books needed to serve its ends.

Second, the evolution in the attitude toward the peculiar timeliness of reading which took place in Dante's and Boccaccio's lifetimes stands out with greater sharpness in interpolated and marginal glosses than in the main texts. One reason for this should be evident to anyone who has ever tackled a conceptually difficult or markedly unfamiliar text by relying heavily on the aid of explanatory footnotes, those modern descendants of the late medieval vernacular gloss. Glosses are a witness to the fact that readers do not read effortlessly, that there is some sort of gap to be bridged between reader and text. If later centuries found more sophisticated ways to deal with this gap, ways that have tended to cover it over rather than calling attention to it by leaving it awk-wardly visible in the margin, then it is especially important to dig out from the dusty manuscripts of early, serious vernacular texts these first attempts that form an essential episode in the history of reading. To adopt the deprecatory attitude toward the gloss that Sidney was al-ready expressing in the sixteenth century is to do a disservice to the study of the fourteenth and fifteenth centuries and, more important, to miss the chance to understand something basic to the nature of reading which is often forgotten.

Third, my own exegetical efforts in excavating certain details about these glosses, not merely from the apparatus of little-read printed edi-tions but also from literally decaying manuscripts, is necessarily em-blematic when placed in the context of the present book's argument. Although certain concepts of "margin" and "gloss" have enjoyed cur-rency in literary theory since the early 1970's—most notably in the wake of the publication of Jacques Derrida's *Marges*—arguments founded on the study of actual historical glosses have been absent from the mainstream of critical discourse. Similarly, while those who follow literary theory were not long ago interested in what Jean Starobinski and Roland Barthes had to say about some of the manuscripts of Ferdinand de Saussure, the study of manuscripts rarely comes to the fore in discussions of problems of literary theory. Analysis of such things as old glosses and old manuscripts is, in fact, unfashionable, even regarded as quaint. When literary theory and philology are thus divorced and not even on speaking terms, both are, I submit, deeply disabled. My argument in this chapter and the next is made on the basis of readings that go much further in the direction of exegesis than do those that generate much recent theoretical discourse. What may ap-pear to some a degree of exegetical extremism is meant to provide a marker of one of the two points between which reading continues to oscillate, a point seldom seen by those who may (mistakenly) think their readings are wholly interpretive.

Dante's Early Self-Glosses

In the *Convivio* (Banquet)—a somewhat later work than the *Vita nuova* which also combines text and gloss—Dante compares verse *canzone* (song) and commentary to two foods taken together at the same meal. The poems are the *vivanda* (main course), while the glosses are the *pane* (bread) that is to be eaten with it. Many, he says, will fill themselves with the bread of the commentary alone; these are the readers not able to penetrate the deeper levels of the poems without assistance.

It is essential to note Dante's emphasis here. In adopting the gloss (and especially the "division") from scholarly writing, Dante does something relatively new by employing it in works for a nonclerical audience. The projected presence of this new, inexperienced audience impels him to stress that text and gloss are to be read together. The bread is not to be taken alone but only as an accompaniment and help in eating the "meat and potatoes."

The integral relation between poem and gloss which Dante shapes in the *Vita nuova* is emphasized by Michele Barbi, whose modern critical edition of the work constitutes a landmark in the history of Italian philology. His observation is an implicit criticism of Boccaccio's procedure in editing the *Vita nuova*:

> It is more important to clear up a doubt about the organism of the work which may arise from examination of the various editions and even from the very manuscripts themselves, because in both [printed editions and manuscripts] the divisions or glosses of the various poems in some instances are included in the text of the work, in others are placed in the margins, and in still others are lacking entirely. It is certain that the author intended the divisions to be an integral part of the work, so that one might, without any discontinuity, go on to them from the narratives and from the poems.[6]

Both the *Convivio* and the *Vita nuova* are highly self-conscious about the integration of gloss and text, drawing attention to the purpose behind their incorporation of two different kinds of material. The better part of the first Trattato (Treatise) of the *Convivio* is thus devoted to a defense and description of the purposes of the vernacular commentary. In the *Vita nuova* the theme of the defense of poetry arises from Dante's anticipation of the reader's doubts about poetic personification (expressed as early as chapter 12, but becoming acute in chapter 25). Such anticipation leads Dante to stress the necessity of prose explana-

---

6. Michele Barbi, ed., *La vita nuova* (Florence: M. Bemporad e Figlio, 1932), p. xvi. A useful perspective on the legitimacy of Boccaccio's textual intervention in medieval terms is provided by Gerald Bruns's distinction between "the open text of a manuscript culture" and "the closed text of a print culture"; see *Inventions: Writing, Textuality, and Understanding in Literary History* (New Haven, Conn.: Yale University Press, 1982), chap. 2.

tion of difficult or unbelievable elements in a poem, as an aspect of this defense of poetry. He discusses the fact that poets sometimes write things that are patently false (in this case the falsehood is the personification of Love) and explains how readers are to regard this fact:

> E acciò che non ne pigli alcuna baldanza persona grossa, dico che nè li poeti parlavano così sanza ragione, nè quelli che rimano deono parlare così non avendo alcuno ragionamento in loro di quello che dicono; però che grande vergogna sarebbe a colui che rimasse cose sotto vesta di figura o di colore rettorico, e poscia, domandato, non sapesse denudare le sue parole da cotale vesta, in guisa che avessero verace intendimento. E questo mio primo amico e io ne sapemo bene di quelli che così rimano stoltamente.

> (And lest any uneducated person should assume too much, I will add that the Latin poets did not write in this manner without good reason, nor should those who compose vernacular verse, if they cannot justify what they say; for it would be a disgrace if someone composing in the vernacular introduced a figure of speech or rhetorical ornament, and then on being asked could not divest his words of such covering so as to reveal a true meaning. My most intimate friend [Guido Cavalcanti] and I know quite a number who write vernacular verse in this stupid manner.)

> [*Vita nuova*, chap. 25][7]

According to Dante at this time, the poet is responsible for making sure readers understand what lies beneath the surface of words and do not fall into traps of misinterpretation. Only later (as illustrated in the Paolo and Francesca episode) does he come to realize that such protection of the reader exceeds the author's powers.

It is especially interesting that Dante at the period of the *Vita nuova* is so concerned with the relation between poem and gloss that at one point he even gives specific instructions about their respective positions on the page. In chapter 31 and the chapters which follow it, he says that after his announcement of the death of Beatrice, the lady who is the subject of the book, the positions of poem and gloss are to be reversed. Whereas until this crucial moment the glosses have followed the poems, after her death the glosses must precede them: "E acciò che questa canzone paia rimanere più vedova dopo lo suo fine, la

7. All citations to the *Vita nuova* are to the Barbi edition cited in n. 6. English translations of Dante's text are from Barbara Reynolds, trans., *La Vita Nuova* (Harmondsworth: Penguin Books, 1969); those of Barbi's text are my own.

dividerò prima che io la scriva; e cotale modo terrò da qui innanzi" (So that this *canzone* may seem the more widowed after its conclusion, I will divide it now before I transcribe it, and this method I shall adopt from now on).

Dante here displays an acute awareness of the temporal discrepancy between the time of composition and the time(s) of reading, even to the point of considering the effects of physical order on the page upon the temporal process of reading the text and consequently upon the reader's emotional response. His concept of the way a defective ordering of poem and gloss might disrupt the reader's understanding of and response to the text is akin to that of the theatrical director alert to the problems of pacing a stage play.

When juxtaposing in any order a poem and self-gloss, an author-glossator necessarily creates a temporal split, a state of spatial non-coincidence or non-identity that represents temporal non-identity. The split is itself a signifying or semiotic structure that becomes an element in the text, just as a word is an element. The placement of this split must therefore be weighed as carefully as if it were indeed a word. Such a figure of temporal discrepancy in general (and certainly in the *Vita nuova*) takes a particular form that has a particular meaning. The movement from poem to gloss is from past to present, the present being the time of reading or encounter with the book. The relation between poem and gloss is thus a mnemonic device for the temporal split that marks the relation of the author's words to the reader.

In the *Vita nuova* the time of reading is double: it is both the "present" in which the reader reads the *canzoni* and approaches an understanding of them, and the "present" in which the author's persona reads the book of his memory and approaches an understanding of the experiences written there. Thus Dante is already suggesting at this early moment in his career that the "present" time of "his" reading is merely a figure for a potential series of "present" moments. The constituents of this series are only metaphorically "present"; they could be more correctly described as "later," a word that designates their temporality as relative rather than absolute.

Dante accomplishes the multiplication of the moment of reading by emphasizing in the first two sentences the metaphor that makes the *Vita nuova* an excerpt from another book:

> In quella parte del libro de la mia memoria dinanzi a la quale poco si potrebbe leggere, si trova una rubrica la quale dice: *Incipit vita nova.*

Sotto la quale rubrica io trovo scritte le parole le quali è mio intendi-
mento d'assemplare in questo libello; e se non tutte, almeno la loro
sentenzia.

(In the book of my memory, after the first pages, which are almost
blank, there is a section headed *Incipit vita nova*. Beneath this heading I
find the words which it is my intention to copy into this smaller book,
or if not all, at least their meaning.)

The volume that the *Vita nuova*'s actual reader physically holds is thus
metaphorically doubled in its first lines. This is accomplished by means
of three details that evoke the book's physicality. First, Dante specifies
the part of the book of memory where the *Vita nuova* starts by reference to the quantity of material in the book which is to be read before
that part, making the *Vita nuova* an excerpt from a larger volume. This
specification, close in form to a citation in a footnote, anticipates the
description in *Inferno* XI.101–2:

> se tu ben la tua Fisica note,
> tu troverai, non dopo molte carte . . .

(If you look carefully at your [copy of the] *Physics*, you will find, after
not many pages . . .)

Second, Dante twice refers to a heading in the larger book which
becomes the "incipit" or title of the extracted book. Third, he qualifies
the extracted book as a "libello," implicitly contrasting it to the "libro"
by stressing its smaller physical size. This evocation of the encounter
with the book of memory as if it were a physical object in turn emphasizes the reader's encounter with the excerpted book as physical object
and designates both encounters as taking place in distinct time periods
that are nonetheless parallel.

It is in this double sense that the *Vita nuova* glosses come to constitute what Michelangelo Picone calls the "intermediate passage between past illumination (poetry) and present interpretation (prose)."[8]
The creation of glosses and their placement on the page with the poems
engenders a visibility for the split between the moment of past understanding and the moment of "present" (later) understanding. In other

8. Michelangelo Picone, "Strutture poetiche e strutture prosastiche nella *Vita
nuova*," *MLN* 92 (1977), 125.

words, it makes visible an inherent feature of reading from which authors and readers regularly turn away.

Dante's acute self-consciousness about the integration of gloss and text, extending even to concern with page layout and its effect on the reading process, and especially on its pacing, derives from the complexity of the purpose his self-glosses are conceived to serve: they go beyond mere explanation to make visible to the reader a temporal ordering. In providing his own glosses in the *Vita nuova* and the *Convivio*, the most notable champion of the vernacular is no doubt participating in the contemporary movement to make vernacular works serious objects of study—yet Dante's self-glosses do much more than simply make the poems "illustrious" by an erudite explanation of their meaning. As part of their explanation and defense they indicate explicitly the internal order of the poems, and by unfolding this order they focus attention on the act of reading and on the reader.

Whereas later (and already to a large extent for Boccaccio) glossing would generally be associated with philological explanation as an end in itself, for Dante it arises from the need to defend vernacular poetry, a need that explanation serves but does not in itself fulfill. The defense is constituted not by the explanations but by the demonstration that the vernacular work possesses a "veiled" meaning, which its author is capable of "unveiling" for the reader. The defense, which is the *raison d'être* of the gloss, is a reading of hidden meaning in the text. It depends on the notion that there is in the text an internal order, a "ragione" (reason), which in neo-Platonic and Augustinian terms is a hidden divine "footprint" that must find a corresponding imprint in the interpreter's soul. The glosses to the *Vita nuova* are thus no mere explanations but rather indications of essential order by means of the divisions of the poems.

The divisions begin with such sentences as, "Questo sonetto si divide in due parti" (This sonnet is divided into two parts; chap. 3). In the *Vita nuova* as in the late medieval schoolroom, *divisio* is the primary tool for the understanding of a text, an important intermediary between the text on the page and the divinely formed text that is the reader's soul. The glosses in the *Convivio* also divide the poems into parts according to units of meaning or, in contemporary terms, *materie* (subject matter; II.6ff.); some parts comprise only one stanza, others several. Such division into parts is not a sterile academic exercise but rather aims to make the inner "reason" of poems clearer and thus to show that they are "vera poesia" (true poetry).

For Dante, the notion of an integral relation between text and commentary is so basic that he incorporates self-glosses into a text that appears to have none—the *Commedia*, as Tibor Wlassics has shown in his extensive study of what he calls Dante's "postillating" narrative technique.[9] While some of the nonmarginal "glosses" in the *Commedia* serve to explain words or phrases, many others are, from the perspective of understanding, superfluous embroideries on the fabric of the text proper. These become a part of Dante's style, helping him once again to manipulate the pace of his narrative; in fact, they give the poet a way to create minute changes in syntactic order.

The relation between text proper and internal gloss is not unlike that between the *Commedia*'s narrative and dialogue sections and its addresses to the reader. While the addresses may disrupt the drama of the pilgrim's journey and the reader's imaginative engagement with it, they facilitate the reader's cognitive engagement with the text. Similarly, while the internal glosses cause discontinuity in the reading of the narrative, they urge a more reflective and less mystified relation to the unfolding of the text in which the narrative is only one element.

Boccaccio as Editor of the *Vita nuova* Glosses

Like Dante, Boccaccio saw the gloss as playing an important role in the defense of poetry. The fifteenth book of the *Genealogie deorum gentilium libri* (Genealogy of the Pagan Gods), the crowning work of his long scholarly career, defends the preceding books against the charge that they are filled with citations from little-known ancient writers and unimportant modern ones; it includes a lengthy peroration on the gloss which contrasts the situation of poetic texts (both Latin and vernacular) that are sorely in need of defense to that of other kinds of texts:

> Habent enim civiles et canonice leges preter textus multiplices, hominum nequitia semper auctos, apparatus suos a multis hactenus doctoribus editos. Habent phylosophorum volumina diligentissime commenta composita. Habent et medicinales libri plurimorum scripta, omne dubium enodantia. Sic et sacre lictere multos habent interpretes; nec non et facultates et artes relique glosatores proprios habuere, ad quos, si oportunum sit, volens habet, ubi recurrat, et quos velit, ex multis eligat. Sola poesis, quoniam perpaucorum semper domestica

9. Tibor Wlassics, *Dante narratore* (Florence: L. S. Olschki, 1975).

fuit, nec aliquid afferre lucri avaris visa sit, non solum per secula multa neglecta atque deiecta, sed etiam variis lacerata persecutionibus a se narrata non habet!

(The great text of both civil and canon law has grown in bulk throughout generations of human failing, by editorial apparatus from many a doctor. The books of the philosophers also carry with them their commentaries compiled with great care and zeal. The books of medicine are filled with marginal notes from countless pens that resolve every doubt, and so with sacred writings, and their numerous expositors; so also with the liberal and the technical arts—each has its own commentary, from which anyone may select on occasion according to his preference. Poetry alone is without such honor. Few—very few— are they with whom it has dwelt continuously. Money-getters have found it unprofitable. It has therefore been neglected and scorned for many centuries, nay even torn by many persecutions and stripped of the aids given to the other arts.) [10]

Boccaccio's list of the kinds of glossed texts, carefully structured for maximum rhetorical effect ("Habent . . . habent . . . habent . . . multos habent . . . . Sola poesis . . . non habet"), makes it appear that poetry without glosses is bereft and abandoned. The series "neglecta . . . deiecta . . . lacerata" would seem more applicable to the situation of the bride of the *Song of Songs* (5:6–7) than to that of a poem without a gloss. Yet though Boccaccio, like Dante, is led to look to the gloss by his desire to defend poetry, his attitude toward poetic commentary is subtly different.

In the final books of the *Genealogy*, which present Boccaccio's most mature statement on poetic theory, he is concerned to show that poetry is in essence theological, that it is not merely a servant art illustrating the truths of philosophy but rather a different kind of vehicle permitting a different means of access to and apprehension of truth. Such a view makes of the poet a prophet whose office it is to veil truth from the vulgar and lift the veil to reveal it to initiates.

Not yet identical with Sidney's view of the poet as monarch of all sciences, Boccaccio's perspective in this late work nonetheless differs from Dante's in that it is the poet and not the reader who stands at its center. This is a small nuance whose effects are enormous. Dante's

10. Vincenzo Romano, ed., *Genealogie deorum gentilium libri*, 2 vols. (Bari: Laterza, 1951), 794; translations are those of Charles Osgood, *Boccaccio on Poetry* (New York: Library of Liberal Arts, 1930; rpt., 1956), 117. Citations in the text refer to these two editions.   ·

glosses are the result of his thinking about the reader: the reader's background, the reader's impulses, the reader's needs. Boccaccio, in this passage from the *Genealogy*, makes no mention of the reader. For him, the gloss is something of which "poesis . . . deiecta" has need. Moreover, it is not difficult to see in his rhetoric that it is not really the persecution (lack of glosses) of the text that so incenses Boccaccio but rather the persecution of the poet—in this instance, Boccaccio himself, purportedly under attack for writing in the *Genealogy* a lengthy gloss on ancient poetry.

Boccaccio also had occasion to reflect on the poetic gloss and Dante's self-glosses in the course of his work as copyist and influential editor of the *Vita nuova*. Now the thrust of his scholarly work would seem to indicate that he wished to facilitate exegetical, historically informed reading of ancient works, aiming at the reconstruction of what the works meant to their authors at the time of composition. He seems not to have read the *Vita nuova* according to this strict exegetical model, however, as his own first gloss in the margin of a manuscript of the work that he himself copied indicates. Boccaccio here explains why he will (dis)place into the margins the glosses or "divisioni" that Dante had incorporated into his text:

> Maraviglierannosi molti, per quello ch'io advisi, perchè io le divisioni de' sonetti non ho nel testo poste, come l'autore del presente libretto le puose; ma a ciò rispondo due essere state le cagioni. La prima, per ciò che le divisioni de' sonetti manifestamente sono dichiarazioni di quegli: per che più tosto chiosa appaiono dovere essere che testo; e però chiosa l'ho poste, non testo, non stando l'uno con l'altre ben mescolato. Se qui forse dicesse alcuno—e le teme de' sonetti e canzoni scritte da lui similmente si potrebbero dire chiosa, con ciò sia cosa che esse sieno non minore dichiarazione di quegli che le divisioni—dico che, quantunque sieno dichiarazioni, non sono dichiarazioni per dichiarare, ma dimostrazioni delle cagioni che a fare lo 'ndussero i sonetti e le canzoni. E appare ancora queste dimostrazioni essere dello intento principale; per che meritamente testo sono, e non chiose. La seconda ragione è che, secondo che io già più volte udito ragionare a persone degne di fede, avendo Dante nella sua giovanezza composto questo libello, e poi essendo col tempo nella scienza e nelle operazioni cresciuto, si vergognava avere fatto questo, parendogli opera troppo puerile; e tra l'altre cose di che si dolea d'averlo fatto, si ramaricava d'avere inchiuse le divisioni nel testo, forse per quella medesima ragione che muove me; là onde io non potendolo negli altri emendare, in questo che scritto ho, n'ho voluto sodisfare l'appetito de l'autore.

(Many will be astonished, I think, that I have not placed the divisions of the sonnets into the text, as the author of the present little book did; but to this I answer that my reasons have been two. The first is that the divisions of the sonnets are clearly declarations of them; and thus I have placed them as gloss, not as text, since text does not properly stand mixed together with glosses. If at this point someone were to say that the explications of the sonnets and *canzoni* he wrote could similarly be called glosses, in that they are no less declarations of them than are the divisions—I say that, insofar as they are declarations, they are not declarations made to declare, but rather expositions of the reasons which led him to write the sonnets and *canzoni*. And these expositions still seem to belong to the principal intention, so that they deserve to be called text and not glosses. The second reason is that, according to what I have several times heard recounted by persons worthy of credit, Dante, having written this little book in his youth, and then having with time grown in knowledge and practical experience, became ashamed of having done this, for it seemed to him too childish a work; and, among the other things he lamented having done, he regretted having included the divisions in the text, perhaps for the same reason that motivates me; whereas I, not being able to remedy the other [things Dante lamented], in this [copy] which I have written have wished to satisfy the author's desire.)[11]

The most striking thing about this passage to anyone who already knows the *Vita nuova* "divisions" under discussion must be Boccaccio's omission of any mention of the reader. Whereas Dante's own statements about the function of the divisions are entirely focused on the reader and the reader's efforts to understand the poems, Boccaccio overlooks the reader to focus exclusively on author and text: specifically, the author's "appetito" (desire) and the text's definition and properties seen from the viewpoint of contemporary Aristotelian analysis.

Of the two reasons Boccaccio gives for altering the layout of the *Vita nuova*, the second is familiar in editorial practice even in this century: the text should be made to conform to the author's "final" intentions rather than to those of the earlier time when the work was first published or, in the case of a manuscript book, put into circulation. This editorial principle represents an important variation on the one Dante enunciates through the words of the character Thomas Aquinas in the *Paradiso*. Whereas Dante there argues that all earthly readings must be

---

11. Barbi, *La vita nuova*, pp. xvi–xvii n.1.

considered provisional because all books, as reflections of God's book, are in a state of constant metamorphosis until the Second Coming of Logos, Boccaccio claims to make the "last judgment" on a text's form and meaning that of its earthly author.

His assertion that Dante came to regret the inclusion of the divisions in the text proper, as well as other aspects of the *Vita nuova*, possibly originated in the observation that the *Commedia* is indeed a mature reworking of many ideas and forms from the earlier book. It must nonetheless be classed with the other Dantean anecdotes invented by Boccaccio and has the air of something in Boccaccio's own personality read retrospectively into Dante's. Whereas Dante tended constantly to "recycle" his works (as the *Vita nuova* and the *Commedia* especially attest), Boccaccio was more likely to reject or feel embarrassed by his juvenilia. His biographical assertion here is, more than anything else, a way to create a fictive Dante who, at the opening point of Boccaccio's *Vita nuova* edition, classes his own work as puerile, a work he was ashamed of having written.

The first reason Boccaccio gives for altering the structure of the *Vita nuova* is more interesting than the second in that it delineates a typology of text and gloss. This typology differs markedly from Dante's in moving toward a view of textual autonomy which declines to admit the reader as a partner in the generation of meaning. Boccaccio may well have disliked the divisions because they were old-fashioned. Though even Aquinas, in his *enseignement de bachelier* (a kind of bachelor's thesis), had felt obliged to provide the analysis of his text by the divisions favored by prescholastic writers, together with the modern "questions,"[12] by the latter half of the fourteenth century this method may well have seemed dated. Yet the end to which Dante used the divisions is an important one: to give the reader a kind of map for navigating the poems with some degree of independence or, to use a different metaphor, to keep the reader from being completely dependent on the "bread" of the narrative prose with no access to the "meat and potatoes" of the poems. Choosing to include the divisions within the main body of the *Vita nuova* meant giving the reader an essential tool to encourage direct study of the poems rather than immediate and exclusive reliance on the prose commentary.

Boccaccio creates a new typology of text and gloss based on a liter-

12. Marie-Dominique Chenu, *Introduction à l'étude de St. Thomas d'Aquin*, 2d ed. (Montreal: Institut d'études mediévales, 1954), p. 82.

ary hierarchy not present in Dante and, in so doing, softens the crisis of chapter 31 (following Beatrice's death) by eliminating the effect of Dante's deliberate displacement of the divisions there. Boccaccio's new typology, designating "text" in the singular form ("test*o*") and "gloss" in the plural ("chios*e*") idealizes "text" as something independent of readers and readings, in conformity with humanist aspirations. Boccaccio makes "chiosa" synonymous with "dichiarazione" (declaration) but then distinguishes between two types of "dichiarazione." The first is tautologically defined as "dichiarazione per dichiarare," exemplified by the divisions, the glosses that explain the structure of the poems; the second is the "dichiarazione" that sets forth the author's reasons for writing the poems ("cagioni che a fare lo 'ndussero i sonetti"). This type of "dichiarazione" deserves to be called "testo" because it belongs to the "intento principale," Boccaccio argues.

"Intento" (Latin *intentio*) and "cagione" (cause) are technical terms here. "Cause" implies *causa efficiens* and derives from the Aristotelian tradition of textual analysis most prominently used in the Trecento in the *Letter to Can Grande* explicating the *Commedia*. "Intento" does not indicate, in the modern sense, authorial intention but rather what would today be called intentionality.[13] It connotes all the truth that resides in a text, which may be more than the truth willed by the author. The notion is similar to that employed by Newman in his 1870 rereading of what he had written decades earlier.

In his most mature statement on literary theory, the fourteenth book of the *Genealogy*, Boccaccio describes "intentio" as affecting the will and understanding of the author but not controlled by it. This is shown in the limit case he presents in the last sentence of chapter 10. The little old woman telling stories at the hearth senses ("sentiat") meaning ("sensum") in the fables she is narrating and performing ("fingentem atque recitantem"), meaning already present in the basic content of the narratives of Hell, the Fates, and ghosts which she wishes to shape to her ends. She does not *make* the meaning in her stories; she *finds* it there and tries, sometimes in a ridiculous way, to make use of it. "Intentio" is thus meaning that is temporally prior to the author; the author, a relative latecomer, may or may not find it there. The author-figure—in this case actually an authoress—has little dignity, being in a position similar to that of the crudest class of readers. It is the "text" and its intentionality that are important.

13. Ibid., p. 87.

Boccaccio is once more emphasizing an aspect of intentionality different from the one that interests Dante. The notion of "intentio" rests on certain premises about the dispositions of the soul, premises that are also the foundation of Boccaccio's argument that one is more likely to discover the truth through poems than through syllogisms. First, it is assumed that it is not the poet himself (or the crone herself) as an individual who creates poetry; poetry is, rather, created by the disposition toward it within him (her). The poetry is thus ordered in response not to the vagaries of the author's personality and age but rather to this disposition of the soul toward poetry. Second, it is assumed that the order with which the poet thus invests the poem is analogous to the order with which God eternally invests the world.

Again, Boccaccio's emphasis at this point in his career differs from that of Dante in the *Paradiso*. For Dante, the order with which God invests the world can be perceived as unitary, continuous, and stable only by God; mortals inevitably see only pieces of that order, appearing and disappearing and thereby creating relationships to one another that change ceaselessly. To use the terms of the final image of the *Paradiso*, what mortals read in scattered fascicles, God possesses bound in a single volume. Mortal reading, unavoidably tied to a particular moment in history, is most likely to approach God's precisely when the reader keeps him- or herself most fully open both to the moment in which God has provided the occasion to read and to the grace dispensed by God in that moment. Thus it is that, as Erich Auerbach has explained,[14] Dante is at his most political and polemical just when he is closest to the sacred, for he believes that the most earthly of his concerns are the most likely to give him a living glimpse of divine purpose.

At the time of composition of the fourteenth book of the *Genealogy*, by contrast, Boccaccio not only sees *divine* order as one; he also sees it as wearing just one face on *earth*. Recovery of that single face is reached not by many shifting paths but by one path. This view leads Boccaccio away from Dante's concern with the reader and may stem from an acute consciousness of textual order per se: the relation of a poem's words, lines, and stanzas to a timeless understanding, higher than that of mortals.[15] A close connection between divine and compositional

14. Erich Auerbach, *Dante, Poet of the Secular World*, trans. Ralph Manheim (Chicago: University of Chicago Press, 1961).

15. It may appear that I am here using "order" ambiguously, to indicate both a temporal and an atemporal (that is, compositional) dimension. The ambiguity exists

order (in contemporary terms, "narratio") will mean that the soul will be better able to contain the parts and levels of a narrative. To find such a link, the author will have to know how to divide an inherited plot into segments that retain meaning when separated and that can be reordered to make new plots—whether the segments be stock characters, interactions between characters, sequences of events, or clichéd phrases. To retain meaning when separated and reordered, such segments must continue to find a response in the poetic disposition of the soul. A lack of clarity in composition could mean that the underlying spiritual order would not be clear.

Boccaccio's Self-Glosses for the *Teseida*

Boccaccio's concern with compositional order as revelation of divine order—although shaped by a notion of text that emphasized its autonomy rather than its synthetic relationship with the reader, and despite the impulse this concern gave him to remove Dante's divisions to the margins of the *Vita nuova*—did not prevent him from writing glosses for one of his own works, disrupt the reading process though they might. His epic poem, the *Teseida delle Nozze d'Emilia*, is best known to English-speaking readers as the source of Chaucer's "Knight's Tale"; in its own country, however, it can claim the more important position of first vernacular epic.

Boccaccio, highly conscious of his poem's claim to such originary status, insists on it in the *Teseida*'s antepenultimate octave:

> Poi che le Muse nude cominciaro
> nel cospetto degli uomini ad andare,
> già fur di quelli i quai l'esercitaro
> con bello stilo in onesto parlare,
> e altri in amoroso l'operaro;
> ma tu, o libro, primo a lor cantare
> di Marte fai gli affanni sostenuti,
> nel volgar lazio più mai non veduti.

(Since the Muses began to walk unclothed before men's eyes, there have been those who employed them with graceful style in virtuous

---

only from a modern viewpoint, which sees compositional structure as atemporal. Boccaccio's struggle to articulate the connections among temporal, compositional, and spiritual order drew importantly, I am convinced, on his study of speculative grammar. I plan to trace this struggle in a future publication.

discourse, while others used them for the language of love. But you, my book, are the first to bid them sing in the vernacular of Latium what has never been seen thus before: the toils endured for Mars.)[16]

More clearly than in any of his other works, Boccaccio is in the *Teseida* consciously following in Dante's wake. He indicates that he conceives of himself as filling the last slot in the three-part literary program mapped out by Dante's *De vulgari eloquentia* for what both authors call the Latian, or unified Italian, language.[17] He therefore had to be concerned about whether his martial epic would be seen as a work of elevated style and purpose, clearly different from *cantari* (the vernacular chivalric romances, made to be performed in the piazzas before popular audiences), which were its only precedents in the Italian language. Whereas the *cantari* neither laid claim to theological or philosophical truth nor implied prophetic powers in the minstrels who composed them, Boccaccio wanted both these attributes for the *Teseida* and for himself as its author.

He thus composed both marginal and interlinear glosses for a copy of the *Teseida* that he made himself, seemingly for his own use (now Biblioteca Medicea Laurenziana MS. Acq. e Doni 325). But this manuscript soon had a life beyond Boccaccio's study, in manuscript copies and then printed editions. Giuseppe Vandelli, who was the first to identify this glossed manuscript as being in Boccaccio's hand, in fact paraphrases the very next (penultimate) stanza—emphasizing the words that quote it directly—in asserting that Boccaccio's primary goal in creating the gloss was to elevate the *Teseida* to the status of classical epic:

> The new heroic poem—so Boccaccio must have thought—ought not and could not lack such outfitting and ornament, which, extremely useful to its readers, would make the *book* still more like *its ancestors* and more deserving *to come* among them and appear *worthy of some honor*. Above all for this reason Messer Giovanni, I believe, made up his mind to make a commentary on his own work, from which he clearly took

16. Citations from the *Teseida* refer to the edition of A. Limentani in *Giovanni Boccaccio: Tutte le opere*, ed. V. Branca (Verona: Mondadori, 1964), vol. 2. The translations are by Bernadette Marie McCoy, *The Book of Theseus* (New York: Medieval Text Association, 1974).

17. The other two kinds of literary achievement that the quoted passage alludes to are didactic poetry (such as the *Commedia*) and love poetry.

much satisfaction, as from another good service [a commentary as well as an epic] bestowed upon Italian letters.[18]

Yet, scholars have more recently noted that Boccaccio's gloss only superficially resembles the specific classical gloss (Lactantius Placidus's gloss to Statius's *Thebaid*) that Vandelli took Boccaccio to be imitating; they have failed to discover confirmation of Boccaccio's dependence upon it. Robert Hollander has even found some of Boccaccio's glosses so aberrant from the function of allegorical explanation, which one might expect an imitation of a classical gloss to serve, that he has been led to "wonder whether or not Boccaccio might have been pulling our collective leg."[19]

The oddity of certain of the *Teseida* glosses, however, stems not from irony but rather from a different kind of doubling: a tension between two different positions with respect to the temporality of reading, the exegetical and the interpretive. Although those glosses that Boccaccio composed earliest are indeed modeled on the classical gloss and are therefore exegetical in function, many of them—especially the later ones—may be said to be more Dantesque than classical in that they are, like the *Vita nuova* glosses, interpretive.[20] Again, this progression may be seen as an element in the constant oscillation between exegesis and interpretation to which I have already alluded.

Set among the more conventional exegetical glosses, the interpretive glosses are, so to speak, masked as exegetical. They are therefore figures of an approach to the temporality of reading which is uneasy, even self-deluding (as the oscillation between exegesis and interpretation must often, and perhaps always, be). Yet this very quality of uneasiness makes the *Teseida* glosses tools that Boccaccio uses in order to experiment with the influential new narrative techniques he will display in the *Decameron*.

18. Giuseppe Vandelli, "Un autografo della *Teseida*," *Studi di filologia italiana* 2 (1929), 1–76; material cited in the text is from p. 76.

19. Robert Hollander, "The Validity of Boccaccio's Self-Exegesis in His *Teseida*," *Medievalia et Humanistica*, n.s., 8 (1977), 167–68. See also Victoria Kirkham, "'Chiuso Parlare' in Boccaccio's *Teseida*," in Bernardo and Pellegrini, *Dante, Petrarch, and Boccaccio*, pp. 305–51, esp. 324–28.

20. My assertion that the glosses were produced over a long period of time is based on paleographic observations that I plan to present elsewhere. I am grateful to students in my "Boccaccio and Chaucer" class at the University of Chicago who offered helpful suggestions when I first formulated my ideas on the *Teseida* glosses, and to Chicago colleagues who provided feedback when this material was presented as a public lecture in 1975.

To locate the glosses that are the product of such tension, one must put aside all those that actually provide necessary lexical, mythological, or allegorical explanation. The latter category includes three groups. The first is made up of glosses that give ordinary vernacular synonyms or definitions for latinizing or particularly literary words: for example, *are/altare* (altar); *perso/nero* (black). This group is quite large, for the vocabulary of the *Teseida* is notably rich. The second group is composed of glosses that give brief explanations of the names of pagan divinities and localities (who Pallas is, what an Argive is) and even brief mythological tales (up to about fifty words) that are introduced by the mention of a name from mythology but are not otherwise pertinent to the *Teseida*. The third group includes glosses that provide simple explanations of poetic expressions, such as "il fior di tutte le donne amazone" (the flower of all the Amazon women)—"cioè Emilia" (that is, Emilia; III.37.6). These three groups together, constituting nearly 70 percent of Boccaccio's glosses, are exegetical in function. They arise from a view of the text as removed from the reader, who needs information to decipher it.

The approximately three hundred remaining glosses function quite differently: while they, too, have exegetical form, their effect is not to explain; rather, they re-order the temporal structure of the text by imposing an order on the temporal relation between the text itself and the "fictive reader" envisioned by the gloss. This movement toward an interpretive reading of the epic serves, in contemporary terms, the purposes of the defense of poetry, for by re-ordering narrative sequences established in his text, Boccaccio demonstrates that the meaning of the *Teseida* is not limited to the elaboration of its plot. The linear temporal sequence that constitutes the plot, these glosses imply, is less important than the order that the glosses "unveil" in the text. Because this "unveiled" order reflects divine order, it transcends mere mortal temporality. Thus, to a text written by a mortal—a poem bound to the period and place of its conception—is attributed a timeless meaning.

Some of the glosses in question, for example, add transitions that the text lacks in its autonomous, "unglossed" form—either transitions between one narrative episode and the next or between one level of meaning and another. Some of them clarify an already existing transition, to assure that the relation between one scene and the next is clear to the reader. In certain instances the position of the transition in the margins (as contrasted to its insertion in the text through revision) is, from the viewpoint of narrative structure, advantageous.

An example appears in Book I, in which, up to the thirteenth octave, the focus of attention has been on Theseus, duke of Athens, and the wrongs the Amazons have inflicted on his people. The octave closes with a description of Theseus's increasing but withheld rage and his decision to take revenge. With the next line, suddenly, attention turns to a new "character," the only transition being the adverb *allora* (then): "Marte tornava allora sanguinoso / dal bosco" (Mars returned, then, bloody / from the wood . . .)." Mars is a "character" in the sense that the text does not qualify him as a divinity and instead treats him just as it treats Theseus; in fact, the two become almost doubles, the abruptness of their juxtaposition in this passage in which Mars first appears reinforcing the similarity. Much of the effectiveness of the passage, its ability to evoke the warlike rage of Theseus, comes precisely from this lack of a transition. Yet on another level of narrative development something is missing, and this something is provided by a very lengthy gloss appended to the first line of octave 14. The gloss adds a transition from the Theseus scene to the Mars scene—based on causation rather than formal resemblance—by explaining that Mars's association with the forest arises from the devotion shown him there by Tideus, who fought off a band of fifty knights sent to attack him, and that it was the news of Tideus's victory over fifty men that finally motivated Theseus to fight a band of mere women. Had this causal explanation, a kind of psychological motivation linking Mars through Tideus to Theseus, been inserted into the text, it would not only have destroyed the drama of the juxtaposition of Theseus and Mars but would also have constituted a kind of narrative digression. Instead, the gloss permits Boccaccio to change the reader's apprehension of the text without revising the text itself. To establish successful transitions in this way among temporally disparate levels or episodes of a text is to accomplish a first step in creating the illusion that the text is in some way freed from ordinary notions of time and history. The movement out of the linear temporality of the narrative of Theseus and the Amazons to the completely different temporal sequence of Tideus and Mars and then back again creates a sense that the text belongs to a time that is plural rather than singular.

Still other glosses contribute to the illusion of multiplication of the narrative's temporal sequence by making explicit a subtheme that is only implicit in the text. For example, they may introduce as a subsidiary adjunct to a relatively early point in the narrative some element that will later reappear in connection with an important event. These glosses are examples of what is today called "foreshadowing," an essential device for the distortion and denial of time. By far the most important subtheme so introduced is from the story of the house of Thebes—specifically, the rivalry between Etiocles and Polynices. Various episodes from and comments upon the struggle in which this pair of Theban brothers engaged to win a kingdom fill the glosses to the early books of the *Teseida* and constitute in themselves an important, distinct, and continuing (though entirely "marginal") story that foreshadows the main plot: the contest of Etiocles and Polynices over the kingdom parallels and precedes the struggle in which the Theban cousins, Arcites and Palaemon, engage to win Emilia.

Another major subtheme in the glosses relates Palaemon and Arcites, respectively, to light and to extinguished light or darkness; Emilia, correspondingly, is linked to both the sun and the moon. First introduced in the gloss to Book IV, octave 14, the significance of this recurrent subtheme is stated explicitly only in Book VII, with the glosses to octaves 91 through 94—in which Boccaccio, as he usually does in the glosses, refers to himself in the third person, as the *auctore*: "Qui dimostra l'auctore in questi due fuochi quale dovesse essere il fine de' due amanti, cioè di Palemone e d'Arcita" (Here the author shows in these two fires what is to be the end of the two lovers, that is, of Palaemon and Arcites). The two fires, one of them extinguished and then rekindled and the other extinguished permanently, are thus "shown" to foreshadow the poem's end. From Book X onward, what would without this foreshadowing seem to be gratuitous allusions to night, to the sun, and to the constellation Gemini (the twins: that is, Arcites and Palaemon) assume great significance in the glosses. Additional subthemes (disguises, menacing weapons of warfare) also serve to prepare later turns in the plot and thus modify what would otherwise be a linear temporality.

Still other glosses subtly modify the linear temporality of the text by emphasizing more than they elaborate or explain, thus "unveiling" patterns in the text. Allusions to night and day once again provide an excellent example. Throughout all of Books X and XI the same gloss recurs again and again: "cioè la notte" (that is, night). While it appears to offer simply a definition and thus to be exclusively exegetical, this recurrent gloss is in fact appended to a variety of phrases whose meaning is already perfectly clear and requires no explanation: for example, "del tempo perso" (of the dark time)—"cioè della notte" (that is, of night; X.7.8); two stanzas later, "el tempo tenebroso" (the shadowy time)—"cioè la notte" (x.9.4); and yet again, "nel tempo che tutto nasconde" (in the time that hides all)—"cioè la notte" (x.89.6). To be sure, "perso" is a literary form, but it has already been glossed repeatedly; "tenebroso" is certainly more learned than *ombroso*, but it is hardly obscure; and "tempo che tutto nasconde" is a quite simple example of *circumlocutio* based on a verb that is definitely less learned than its synonym *celare*.

The many, many repetitions of the gloss "that is, night" are thus largely superfluous as exegesis. They are unusual in that Boccaccio (who here indeed might appear to be "pulling our collective leg") does not give a literal rendering of all the other phrases that are as simple as the ones cited. The effect of the repetition as one reads the poem and glosses together is significant in an entirely different way: through the gloss, metaphors expressive of night that are not quite close enough to constitute a mnemonic pattern are regularized to form a refrain. In other words, while a reader would not necessarily remember all these phrases and perceive their semantic equivalence, the insistently repeated gloss brings them together. These are the two books in which the twin associated with night, Arcites, slowly dies and in which his funeral rites are celebrated. The repetition of the gloss thus erases verbal differences to give the impression of unveiling a hidden pattern, which implies that the verbal differences are mere matters of surface and that the text indeed hides a "kernel" of significance, though it is not immediately visible. In the terms employed by both Dante in the *Vita nuova* and Boccaccio in the *Genealogy*, such unveiling constitutes a defense of poetry. It also constitutes the fabrication of an illusion that the text is made up not "just" of words but of surface and core. This implies that its significance is not limited merely to one temporal framework.

Boccaccio's glosses, then, serve several important functions in addition to those served by such a gloss as Lactantius Placidus's. The general effect of many of them seems to be to show the reader how to read a poem as a structure that has a power beyond its own plot and a temporality beyond the temporal framework of that plot. That the reader for whom these glosses were created may have been Boccaccio himself suggests that he may have needed to convince even himself that this was so. The idea that a secular, vernacular text could have such importance was new. It entailed a new status for the author and responded to a new concept of the reader. But Boccaccio's concern was above all the text itself; indeed, he was one of the principal inventors of the notion of the autonomous text and of the concomitant notion that a text assumed to be timebound, because of its secular origin, could nevertheless lead the reader into the timeless realm opened up by sacred texts.

A literary theorist of Boccaccio's sophistication could not turn away from the hermeneutic problems created by the notion of the autonomous text and the timeless text. Fifteenth- and early sixteenth-century humanism inherited in some part from Boccaccio an acute awareness of these problems. The ardent wish to recover or create words whose value would not pass away or even change continued as an ideal throughout the Renaissance (and, *a fortiori*, the Reformation). But this wish was accompanied by an equally acute, often painful consciousness of the instability of textual meaning. Christine de Pizan would laboriously develop structures meant to give their full due both to what she regarded as unstable and to what seemed timeless in the texts she studied. Cristoforo Landino,however, entirely abandoned the allegorical interpretation of Vergil espoused in his *Disputationes camaldulenses* (ca. 1475) for detailed exegetical study in his edition of Vergil (1487); he was unable to conceive of any hermeneutic model that would do justice to the historical changes in the text's meaning and at the same time preserve a vision of the text as changelessly true.[21] His hermeneutic despair, and his retreat to a philology that wears hermeneutic blinders, represents a more general retreat that continues to give philology an undeservedly bad name among many literary theorists today.

Indeed, the period known as the Renaissance has no exclusive claim on the tension between the wish for an exegetical ideal and despair over textual mutability. One might well argue that "Renaissance" (a term now being abandoned by many scholars for the more neutral "Early Modern") should be used not so much to designate a historical period as to evoke a hermeneutic conflict that arises again and again in many "periods." "Renaissance" indicates the two bases of the conflict: the awareness that something is dead, gone, missing; and the hope or belief that the lack can be remedied, the dead resurrected.

In writing of the (purportedly) romantic author, Gérard de Nerval, Sarah Kofman describes this ever-repeated "Renaissance."[22] Her characterization rings true in everything except, perhaps, in attributing

21. I am grateful to William J. Kennedy for drawing this illustration to my attention.
22. Her account clearly draws its structure from psychoanalytic theory; see Sarah Kofman, *Nerval, Le charme de la répétition: Lecture de Sylvie,* (Lausanne: L'Age d'Homme, 1979), p. 63): "The renaissance ritual (which perhaps helps one better understand Nerval's taste for the Renaissance period . . .) is an attempt to fix in the subject,

exegetical optimism solely to narcissism. The censoriousness of such an explanation tends to limit its applicability if it is taken to suggest that "the renaissance ritual" is performed only by such motherless madmen as Nerval or, perhaps, by deluded humanists performing countless philological exercises in an attempt to reach a goal that is aways beyond reach. In fact, if this is a ritual that Narcissus performs, then every book is his pool, and every reader is at times a Narcissus.

Philip Sidney was not immune to the ambiguities that reading entails, and his writing shows that he felt the attraction of both polar extremes, exegesis and interpretation.[23] As a late-arriving performer of "the renaissance ritual," however, he may be taken to represent a movement still further from the attitude toward the reader which Dante achieved. As this chapter's epigraph, quoting his famous defense of poetry, indicates, the concept of poetry that Boccaccio began to articulate made poetry, once again, first an enticer and only then a teacher. The roles are subtly different from those envisioned by Dante, the intention of whose work is didactic first and foremost.[24] Sidney's hostility to "interpretations" that "blur the margent," although di-

---

through phantasm and image, a good, perfect object: the Actress (read: Antiquity) is seen as an all-powerful character, suited to fulfill all the subject's whims . . . possessing all perfection. But these perfections are only the correlates of the spectator's narcissism, the projection of his desire to be all-powerful." Kofman adds (p. 64) that the need for "the renaissance ritual" arises from a sense of lack of an origin (in Nerval's case, lack of a mother), which must be "mastered" through performance of the ritual. For other instances of this "ritual," see the discussions of Newman in the "Introduction" and of Baudelaire in Chapter 6.

23. For an account of the genre to which Sidney's *Defense* belongs and its concern with the text's "body," see Margaret Ferguson, *Trials of Desire: Renaissance Defenses of Poetry* (New Haven, Conn: Yale University Press, 1983).

24. The evolution of roles may be seen as part of the change in the assignment of poetry from ethics (human behavior on earth), in the Middle Ages, to theology, where the Boccaccio of the *Genealogy* wants to place it. The shift is traced by Judson Boyce Allen, *The Ethical Poetic of the Later Middle Ages* (Toronto: University of Toronto Press, 1982). Dennis Costa, *Irenic Apocalypse* (Saratoga, Calif.: Anma Libri, 1981), chap. 3, "Learning to Read Irenically," shows how Dante's presentation of the character of his poetry is intimately bound to theological concepts of textuality. For the sixteenth-century development of a poetic strategy which, instead of elevating secular verse to the level of scripture, reduces scripture to the status of ordinary language, see David Quint's analysis of Ariosto in *Origin and Originality in Renaissance Literature* (New Haven, Conn.: Yale University Press, 1983), esp. p. 90: "As the source of all intelligibility, the presence of the Word prevents any text from closing off its system of meaning: further allegorization will always be possible. But it is precisely to effect such a closure that Ariosto dismisses the Logos with a joke, wittily reducing the status of the scriptural Word to the level of the words of his poem."

rected at commentaries on nonpoetical works, may nonetheless stand as an emblem of the beginnings, in the Renaissance, of a certain authorial diffidence about readings and readers. Boccaccio plays an important role in the articulation of a view of the reader as someone whose readings threaten to displace the author's, a projected being with whom the author must struggle for control of the text.

An interesting and by no means coincidental aspect of Boccaccio's initial contribution to the developing view of the author-reader relationship as one of struggle rather than cooperation is his depiction of female reader figures. While Dante from his youth explicitly regarded gentlewomen as an essential part of the audience for which he wrote in the vernacular, he cast the female reader in a negative light at least once—in his Eve figure, Francesca. Boccaccio, however, took the depiction of the female reader *in malo* a bit further, creating not only the stupid, maundering old crone of the *Genealogy* and the narcissistic and stupid Donna Lisetta (see above, p. 66) but also the more famous "oziose donne" of the *Decameron* prologue: ladies with time on their hands and mischief in their hearts, very unlike the extremely hardworking writer who made them up.

While it is no doubt true that Boccaccio's late treatments of women were likely shaped by his growing misogyny, notoriously explicit in the *Corbaccio*, the instances in which he depicts women *readers* as moral or intellectual inferiors suggest not merely a general contempt for women but, more interestingly, a realization that authors and readers are no longer necessarily cut from the same cloth. There is no better way to dramatize for oneself that one's words will be read by someone different from oneself than by seeing the projected reader as a member of the *other* sex.

Thus, the inevitable split between the time of writing and the time of reading, often rendered as a spatial split (like that between "autonomous" text and "marginal" gloss), may also be rendered as sexual difference. The effort to erase the split will then become an episode in the "war of the sexes." The sexual figuration of the temporal split between the time of writing and that of reading looks different, to be sure, when drawn by a woman author. Such is the case in the work of a well-known participant in the *querelle des femmes*, Christine de Pizan. Though she wrote nearly two generations after Boccaccio, her work displays not a further increase in diffidence about the reader but a greater concern for "him," a concern figured as maternal rather than fraternal. Christine's attitude toward her public may correctly be seen as more conservative than Boccaccio's, harking back to Dante's and even earlier, to that of biblical commentators with quasi-pastoral concerns. When seen within the context of her perspective on the temporality of reading, however, her view of the relation of author to reader seems distinctly unorthodox: less a throwback to medieval models than an anticipation of the modernist urge to deconstruct language's illusory atemporality.

Chapter 4

From Boccaccio to Christine de Pizan: Reading the Corpus

Affin que ceulz qui ne sont mie clercs poètes puissent entendre
CHRISTINE DE PIZAN, *L'Epistre Othéa*

I have suggested that certain of Boccaccio's negatively cast allusions to female readers express a diffidence on his part about readers in general, a movement away from the fraternal concerns of author for reader which I identified with Dante. I am *not* suggesting that such Boccaccian allusions are a reaction to a growth in numbers of women readers in Boccaccio's era or indeed the result of any great interest in women on Boccaccio's part at all. The generalized "woman" who reads on the surface only or who distorts the author's intention is a rhetorical commonplace found frequently in both classical and patristic literature, which Boccaccio simply took up on several occasions as a rhetorical tool to help him explore what seems to have been his increasingly profound concern with the relation of books and time.[1]

In other words, just as the relation of marginal gloss to text may be a figure for that of later readers to earlier text, so the relation of readers of one sex to a text written by a member of the other may figure the radical but nonsexual difference between later readers and earlier text. Why should this recasting as sexual difference of a split which is in fact temporal hold a certain appeal for Boccaccio, and for many male writ-

---

1. I have discussed this commonplace in "On the Superficiality of Women" in *The Comparative Perspective on Literature,* ed. Clayton Koelb and Susan Noakes (Ithaca: Cornell University Press, 1988), pp. 339–55.

ers? An answer may be found through examination of explicit bodily imagery that Boccaccio uses to evoke the temporal relation of later readers to earlier texts, imagery found above all in the proem of *Genealogie deorum gentilium libri*.

To study this proem is to encounter (for the first time in this book) a Boccaccio who thinks of himself primarily not as editor (of the *Vita nuova*), or self-glossator (of the *Teseida*), or compiler (of the then completed thirteen books of the *Genealogy*)—all of these being semi-authorial roles—but rather as reader. The *Genealogy*'s proem is not, like its fourteenth and fifteenth books, the product of Boccaccio's mature thought: its modern editor dates it early (1350–59), indicating that the last two books (and the interpolated allusion to them in the proem) were the product of a later revision of the beloved work on which Boccaccio labored until his death in 1375. Although the *Teseida* glosses have yet to be securely dated and indeed were written at various times, it is reasonable to think they are very roughly contemporary with the first draft of the *Genealogy*, for which, it has been asserted, they serve as a kind of preparatory stage.

At this period, then, when Boccaccio composes—in the proem and perhaps also parts of the *Teseida* gloss—texts in which he seems to be identifying himself above all as a reader, his attitude toward reading is extremely complex, profoundly ambivalent. In certain passages from the proem he seems to see himself as just one member of a plundering mob, hacking the body of the text to pieces. In others he backs away from the imagery of violence by means of a certain levity in response to a despair typical of this period of humanism: he throws up his hands and shrugs his shoulders at the plight of both ancient and "modern" readers, who must face each other across an unbridgeable abyss. A glimpse of hope appears when Boccaccio mentions the possibility that occasionally a prudent reader (not himself) may happen along, but this is not a hope on which he dwells. In a passage very near the conclusion of the proem, he describes himself as a reader who is a physician, possessed of powers that challenge the divine in their ability to heal the dreadful bodily damage wrought by time and the readers who have been time's henchmen. The proem ends with Boccaccio's return to the sense of himself as author more than reader as well as a return to the tone of violence; he vehemently curses those future readers who may attack the work: "detractantibus . . . delusio, ignominia, dedecus, et eterna damnatio!" (to all detractors . . . confusion, ignominy, disgrace, and eternal damnation; Romano 10, Osgood 13).

Time and the Text as Body: Boccaccio's
Ambivalence

In the previous chapter, I quoted a passage from the fifteenth
book of the *Genealogy*, in which Boccaccio represented poetry without
glosses as "non solum . . . neglecta, atque deiecta, sed etiam . . .
lacerata." This image of poetry as sadistically "lacerated," appearing in
the final book of Boccaccio's lengthy mythological compendium, derives from a much longer and more complex passage in the proem.
Extended attention to the language of this earlier prefatory passage is
necessary to an understanding of how Boccaccio's concern about the
effects of time, and the readers time brings, comes to be figured as
concern for the integrity of the body.

In the *Genealogy* proem Boccaccio depicts himself as engaged in
dialogue with Donino of Parma, a royal emissary sent to ask him to
compose a work tracing the genealogy of the pagan gods and the
heroes descended from them, and setting forth the meaning that the
learned have found in such mythological stories. "Boccaccio," of
course, must object at some length that the task is too difficult. One of
his reasons for demurring is that many necessary books have been
destroyed by the enemies of poetry. Among these enemies the avaricious make up the largest class, including nearly everyone.

It is in describing the attitude of this class toward poetry that Boccaccio uses a triple series of adjectives later echoed in his final book:
"Ex quo consecutum ut aurum non afferentia, non solum neglecta, sed
despecta atque deiecta sint" (the avaricious man . . . not only neglects
anything that gets no money but despises and rejects it; Romano 6,
Osgood 9). *Despecta* is used where the later passage reads *lacerata*—but
Boccaccio goes on to describe an enemy of books even more insidious
and ineluctable than avarice, one that lacerates prey much sturdier than
books: "Ceterum si cetera pepercissent, non eis, restauratore caren-
tibus, pepercissent labile tempus, cui et taciti et adamantini sunt dentes,
nedum libros, sed saxa conterentes durissima et ferrum ipsum, domans
cetera" (But if all these enemies [the avaricious, etc.] had relented, they
[books] would never have escaped the silent and adamantine tooth of
fleeting time, which slowly eats away not books alone, but hardest
rocks, and even steel; Romano 6, Osgood 9).

While it will be well to keep in mind Boccaccio's description of time
as "labile" (perhaps "fickle" conveys its negative connotation better
than Osgood's poetic "fleeting"), what is important in relation to Boccaccio's physical imagery of the text is the attribution of teeth to time,

making it a kind of beast from whose silent and powerful jaws fragments of pages can be seen to dangle. (The image anticipates certain of those used by Baudelaire to describe time, but it could hardly be further from Newman's optimism, which sees time as bringing enhanced meaning to books.) One might think Boccaccio is referring only to natural forces that damage books over a period of time: light and moisture, for example, may be said today to "eat" away at paper. It becomes clear, from alimentary terms appearing later in the passage, however, that Boccaccio is also alluding to the traditional and especially patristic image of reading as eating (attested in English by such phrases as "digesting an author's works," "ruminating on a poem"). He is not only concerned with the fact that time eats away at the book's physical nature; he is painfully aware that time eats away at its hermeneutic nature as well.

Indeed, what may from a modern viewpoint seem two entirely distinct forms of decay over time—physical and hermeneutic—are, from the viewpoint of the manuscript era, intimately connected. Especially if one does not work with old manuscripts, it is easy to think that Boccaccio is concerned with books that simply crumble with the passage of time, the fault being not that of readers but of the materials from which the books are made. Nothing, however, could be further from the truth. Although everyone who owns many books today is likely to have the unpleasant experience of seeing bindings come unglued and paper disintegrate, this is in no way comparable to the kind of experience Boccaccio would have had with books, and to interpret what he says here with so modern an image in mind would be seriously misleading.

During the centuries before printing, the physical decay of books was primarily the *result* of hermeneutic decay, not of defects in materials or manufacturing. When Boccaccio elsewhere laments the state of manuscripts partly consumed by mold, he is no doubt aware that the mold is caused not by some defect in the parchment but rather by the neglect of readers who did not grasp the manuscripts' importance and therefore did not store them properly. Parchment is much, much stronger and more enduring than paper, especially the paper on which most modern books are printed. And if writing on parchment fades, it is misguided to blame this decay on light; medieval manuscripts were stored in chests, not on shelves, and would be exposed to the light for long periods only if some reader took them to contain unimportant material and thus neglected to replace them in the *armadium*.

Even more often, readers caused the physical decay of books not through mere neglect but through active mutilation. If a book's contents were regarded as no longer important (and classical texts were frequently so regarded in the Middle Ages, because their authors were pagan), it might have several nuggets "torn out" from it by recopying in some *florilegium* and then be "rubbed out," to become a palimpsest. Sections of it might be used to form the interior of a binding for a newer and more interesting book. Its parts might be forever sundered by a reader who chose to save one fascicle and not others. Or, in the most frequent form of "decay," its text might become seriously distorted when it was copied by a scribal reader too ignorant or careless to recognize properly its letter forms, spelling, or syntax. All such acts of violence against books merely express physically a more fundamental hermeneutic decay: books were neglected, dismembered, and erased only when they were no longer read as being in any important way meaningful. With all these forms of destruction in mind, "Boccaccio" is forced nonetheless to admit to Donino that, despite the harm done by the various enemies of books, the number of those *not* chewed to bits is considerable: "negari tamen non potest, quin multa supersint" (and yet . . . I cannot deny that much is left; Romano 6, Osgood 9).

Yet, he again objects, since references to the topic in question are so scattered (in this sense, the problem being one of too *many* books), a researcher would be put to a lot of trouble to carry out Donino's request. "Boccaccio" uses three verbs to describe such labors:"Que quis, queso, pro minime seu saltem parum fructuoso labore velit exquirere et tot volumina *volvere, legere*, et hinc unde *excerpere* perpauca?" (But pray who is there that would wish, for no useful result, or at least very little, to hunt them all up, read, and finally gather a few notes?; Romano 6, Osgood 9; emphasis added). These three words form a dispassionate image of research; they might literally be translated as "turn [the pages]," "read," and "excerpt." But the clever and persuasive Donino transforms the three-part series to add a note of passionate energy: "*volve* et *revolve* et *exentera* libros . . . tuum nomen in longissimum deduc evam!" (turn the books over, nay, inside out . . . make your name reverberate to remotest time; Romano 7, Osgood 10). Again, Osgood's translation is a bit too poetic for present purposes. The repetition in "volve et revolve" builds to the imperative "exentera," meaning "disembowel [an animal]," "torment [a person]," "empty" or "exhaust [a thing]."

The books, one begins to suspect, may in some sense fare no better hermeneutically at the hands of the scholar Donino is seeking than physically in the jaws of time. In Donino's speech, however, time gives up its role as archdestroyer to reappear as a long path into the future down which the fortunate scholar may send his name; that is, time here wears its *other* guise, as preserver rather than destroyer, each of these being a role that time may assume, depending upon whether one reads at a given moment under the primary influence of the interpretive or the exegetical pole.

"Boccaccio" is at last persuaded to become the scholar Donino describes in such quasi-heroic terms:

> unique . . . non aliter quam si per vastum litis ingentis naufragii fragmenta colligerem sparsas, per infinita fere volumina deorum gentilium reliquias colligam, quas comperiam, et collectas evo *diminutas* atque an *semesas* et fere *attritas* in unum genealogie corpus, quo potero ordine, ut tuo fruaris voto, redigam.
>
> (Everywhere . . . I will find and gather, like fragments of a mighty wreck strewn on some vast shore, the relics, scattered through almost infinite volumes, shrunk with age, half-consumed, well-nigh a blank, I will bring into such single genealogical order as I can.) [Romano 7, Osgood 10–11; emphasis added]

Once again, three past participles evoke the pitiful condition of the text fragments to be sought; they are (in terms more literal then Osgood's) "by time reduced in size," "half-eaten," and "nearly rubbed away."

"Boccaccio's" proposal is to make these badly damaged bits into one "body" ("corpus") so far as he can. He proceeds to expand upon this corporeal image:

> Non expecta . . . corpus huiusmodi habere perfectum; mutilum quippe, et utinam non membrorum plurium et fortasse distortum seu contractum gibbosumque habendum est iam rationibus premonstratis. Porro, princeps ecimie, uti componendo membra deveniam, sic sensus absconditos sub duro cortice enucleando procedam, non tamen ad unguem iuxta intentionem fingentium fecisse promittam.
>
> (I would warn you now not to expect . . . that a work of this sort will have a body of perfect proportion. It will, alas, be maimed—not, I hope, in too many members—and for reasons aforesaid distorted, shrunken, and warped. Furthermore, O excellent Prince, to arrange the members in any order, I must proceed to tear the hidden significations from their tough sheathing, and I promise to do so, though not to the last detail of the authors' original intentions.) [Romano 8, Osgood 11]

It is important to note that in this passage Boccaccio chooses to describe the text in terms that strongly connote bodily deformity or disproportion and yet are traditionally used in literary discussion. The characteristic triad of adjectives is in this case preceded by "mutilum," which indicates a body that has been violently treated but also commonly describes a manuscript that lacks some essential part—primarily because a reader has, for the reasons mentioned above, mutilated it. The series "distortum . . . contractum gibbosumque"—again softened slightly in translation—literally means "twisted, shrunk, and hunch-backed," powerfully evoking the incongruities of a body made by sewing together chewed-up members scattered here and there on a beach. Yet each of these words has a literary sense as well: one thinks readily of textual distortion and contraction and of crooked speech.

The double corporeal/textual meaning of another word, "enucleando," is still more important to the coherence of the proem as a whole. Osgood translates *enucleare* in this instance as "to tear," whereas on the very next page he will render "enucleationibus" as "interpretations." In this he is quite faithful both to the semantic tradition and to Boccaccio's text. The central revelation of this text is indeed that reading is a kind of tearing. This is a hermeneutic point of first importance, not to be lightly passed over. It expresses Boccaccio's profound ambivalence about reading. In the context of all he has already said about the destruction of books, there can be no doubt that he sees reading, including his own, as a kind of violence. But it is a violence necessary ("I must") to the accomplishment of his end, which is the ordering and partial healing of what has always been already mutilated.

In this first instance of the use of *enucleare*, Boccaccio stresses the literal sense of the word by placing it after "sub duro cortice," but the remainder of the sentence clearly moves from the literal to the literary level. His alter ego may seem almost modern in the candor with which he confesses that he will not be able completely to repossess the authors' intentions, but in fact, such a realistic assessment of the limits of exegesis is extremely common among humanists;[2] it had to be reintroduced to hermeneutics by Friedrich Schleiermacher after the Enlightenment had obscured it.

"Boccaccio's" explanation of why he will not be able to extract the author's complete intention merits particular scrutiny: "Quis enim

---

2. This has been demonstrated by Thomas M. Greene, *The Light in Troy* (New Haven, Conn.: Yale University Press, 1982).

tempestate nostra antiquorum queat terebrare pectora et mentes excutere, in vitam altam iam diu a mortali segregatas, et, quas habuere,
sensus elicere?"(Who in our day can penetrate the hearts of the Ancients? Who can bring to light and life again minds long since removed
in death? Who can elicit their memory?; Romano 8, Osgood 11). Here
Osgood's translation renders wholly literary several verbs that are in
Latin quite physical. "Terebrare" comes from *terebra*, an auger or gim-
let or, especially in this case, a surgical instrument (trephine) for cut-
ting out circular sections of, for example, bone or cornea. "Excutere"
means "to shake out." "Boccaccio" is thus describing (and asserting the
impossibility of) the search for the original intentions of ancient authors in terms suggestive of autopsy: a surgical drilling into the breast
("pectora") to make possible a shaking-out of what is inside. Once
again, as in his first use of *enucleare*, he represents reading as a form of
violence carried out in the service of a good end.

The task is all the more impossible because the corpses of the authors
are set apart, isolated ("segregatas") from the living by death. "Boccaccio" thus sees time as having interposed, through death, an abyss or
barrier between these authors and the would-be interpreter. To perform such an autopsy and bridge such a gap is, he asserts, a job for
gods, not mortals: "Esset edepol divinum potius quam humanum!" (A
divine task that—not human!; Romano 8, Osgood 11). The relation
between the ancient authors and the latter-day interpreter is after all,
then, not to take the form of an autopsy. The argument turns from a
notion of reading as violence to one of reading as creation: "Boccaccio"
asserts that the reader's function is a kind of multiplication of possible
meanings, among which even the weak ones will be useful in stimulat-
ing the proposal of sounder ones. He then suggests that such multiplication is the only kind of exegesis available to mortals, and his
description of this notion of reading is extremely rich rhetorically,
drawing together what is most difficult—even paradoxical—in
hermeneutics:

> Veteres quippe, relictis licteris suis niminibus insignitis, in viam uni-
> verse carnis abiere, sensusque ex eis iuxta iudicium post se liquere
> nascentium, quorum quot sunt capita, fere tot inveniuntur iudicia. Nec
> mirabile; videmus enim divini volumnis verba ab ipsa lucida, certa, ac
> immobili veritate prolata, etiam si aliquando tecta sint tenui figura-
> tionis velo, in tot interpretationes distrahi, quot ad illa devenire lec-
> tores. Et ob id in hoc minus pavescens accedam, nam, et si minus bene
> dixero, saltem ad melius dicendum prudentiorum alterum excitabo.

(The Ancients departed in the way of all flesh, leaving behind them their literature and their famous names for posterity to interpret according to their own judgment. But as many minds, so many opinions. What wonder? There are the words of Holy Writ, clear, definite, charged with unalterable truth, though often thinly veiled in figurative language. Yet they are frequently distorted into as many meanings as there are readers. This makes me approach my own task with less misgiving. Where I do not perform it well, at least I shall arouse a wiser man to do it better.) [Romano 8, Osgood 11].

It is important to notice that Boccaccio adopts the pose of one untroubled by this multiplication of interpreters and interpretations. A kind of natural balance is suggested by the semantic balance between the ancients who die and depart and those who are being born ("Veteres . . . nascentium"). Moreover, the tone is light when "Boccaccio" asserts that as many judgments will be found about the meanings of the words the Ancients left as there are heads among those "coming to birth." One has the impression that the writer has attained a kind of hermeneutic peace of mind, as Dante had in the *Paradiso*—though, of course, Dante's grounds were religious, while Boccaccio's are secular and historical.

To demonstrate that such variety in interpretation should cause neither trouble nor surprise, Boccacio cites the limit case of an ideal form of language. This ideal form is described with yet another triad of modifiers; in this instance, however, they are for the first time positive in connotation. The words of scripture not only are "clear" and "certain" but also "set forth with unchanging truth." The word "immobili" stands in implicit contrast to the earlier "labile [tempus]."

When he presents even these ideal scriptural words as being dragged off ("distrahi") into as many interpretations as there are readers, "interpretation" would seem to have taken on a negative connotation. Paradoxically, however, "Boccaccio" asserts that the notion of such infinite multiplicity in interpretation makes him tremble less, not more, at the task he faces. To be sure, if he were an author, his feelings might be different; but as someone charged only to read and compile, he takes comfort in knowing that his will be just one in an unending series of readings. (Again, the attitude parallels that of Dante in the *Paradiso*.)

He therefore sets forth his plan of action, which comprises two forms of "reading":

Et hoc faciens, primo, que ab antiquis hausisse potero, scribam, inde, ubi defecerint seu minus iudicio meo plane dixerint, meam apponam

sententiam; et hoc libentissimo faciam animo, ut quibusdam ignaris
atque fastidiose detestantibus poetas, a se minime intellectos, appareat,
eos, etsi non catholicos, tanti fuisse predentia preditos, ut nil ar-
tificiosius humani ingenii fictione velatum sit, nec verborum cultu
pulchrius exornatum.

(It is, therefore, my plan of interpretation first to write what I learn
from the Ancients, and when they fail me, or I find them inexplicit, to
set down my own opinion. This I shall do with perfect freedom of
mind, so that men who are ignorant and fastidiously despise the poets
whom they do not understand, may see that the poets, though not
Catholics, were so gifted with intelligence that no product of human
genius was ever more skillfully enveloped in fiction, nor more beau-
tifully adorned with exquisite language, than theirs.) [Romano 8, Osgood 11]

In the terms employed earlier in this study, "Boccaccio" plans first to
perform exegesis on the ancient texts, but a human form of exegesis
which is a plucking out from them, in their ancient context, of as much
as he can ("hausisse potero"); he will not attempt the kind of absolute
exegesis previously mentioned, which must be left to God alone. He
will then pass on from exegesis to interpretation, which he will undertake when the ancient text is in some way lacking or when his judgment (one among many) tells him the text is hiding something in its
depths.

In either case he will inevitably add to the text ("apponam") his own
opinion. Moreover, such additions will be made in the service not of
the authors' intentions but of appearance: "Boccaccio" will substitute
his intelligence for that of the Ancients in order to produce and maintain among the public a high opinion of ancient letters, a belief that
faith in the meaningfulness of texts is warranted.

This statement of motive for the additions he will make seems to
impel Boccaccio away from himself as a reader and back toward a view
of himself as an author. He moves toward the proem's conclusion by
citing the terms of the original royal request. He asserts that from his
interpretations ("ex . . . enucleationibus"; literally, "from these tear-
ings out of kernels") the reader will not only find that the request has
been fulfilled but also have cause to marvel at the way natural truths
have been poetically hidden. He then proceeds to the thoroughly authorial (and indeed scholastic) task of explaining the divisions and
outline of the work to come and disposing of certain objections that
may be made against it.

The image of the ancient texts as dismembered bodies returns, however:

> Satis advertere possum, quid michi faciendum sit, qui inter confragosa vetustatis aspreta et aculeos odiorum membratim discerptum, attritum, et in cineres fere redactum ingens olim corpus deorum procerumque gentilium nunc huc illuc collecturus et, quasi Exculapius alter, ad instar Ypoliti consolidaturus sum.

> (I can quite realize this labor to which I am committed—[can well imagine what I have to do, who am about to gather] this vast system of gentile gods and their progeny, torn limb from limb and scattered among the rough and desert places of antiquity and the thorns of hate, wasted away, shrunk almost to ashes; and here am I setting forth to collect these fragments, hither and yon, and fit them together, like another Aesculapius restoring Hippolytus.) [Romano 9, Osgood 13]

Such reading becomes a daring and miraculous act, challenging the power of a god (as, in Zeus's view apparently, Aesculapius did). It is therapeutic reading, a response to and countermodel of the violent reading evoked earlier in the proem. Reading as re-membering—that is, putting the members back together—and reading as dismembering stand side by side in Boccaccio's exposition as two necessary aspects of the same process.

It is important to recognize that if Boccaccio does in the conclusion of his proem see reading in a positive rather than negative light, it is to some degree because he is talking about what he sees as an exceptional case—his own. Like many rhetoricians of his day, he praises himself as a reader of extraordinary powers, who is presenting the fruit of his reading to the public. But Boccaccio's overall picture of reading in the proem—the one passed on, by and large, to the Italian humanists who came after him—is ambivalent, and passionately so. There is hermeneutic despair over the changeability of the historical meanings of texts. At the same time there is hermeneutic zeal to refine philological method in the service of interpretation.

Italian humanism, however, was unable to transmit this legacy of hermeneutic ambivalence intact to the present day. So much has the pessimistic view of reading as inevitably violent faded away that its reassertion in recent years, notably by Paul de Man and Jacques Derrida, has been met in some quarters with accusations of a new philistinism. It has even been implied that to argue that the power of human exegesis has necessary limits is antihumanist—an ironic label for a viewpoint that parallels a major current in humanist thought.[3]

It is not possible, in a book devoted to tracing the persistence of hermeneutic ambivalence, to trace also the general fading of awareness of this negative view of reading, under the shadow cast by an ardently cultivated belief in the power of reading and readers. But it is possible to point out and explore the single fundamental structure that motivated the ardent, and nearly successful, repression of the humanist understanding of reading as dismemberment. For centuries, Western culture with few exceptions turned away from the recognition of the temporal nature of reading because of a need to maintain a notion of changeless truth. This notion is defended with all the vigor invested, in another context, in the defense of bodily integrity. Boccaccio's choice of language in the *Genealogy* proem is not casual. He saw the text as a body constantly and inevitably menaced by successive generations of readers. Concomitantly, he envisioned these readers as radically different from the text (and its author).

It is this view of reading as an attack on the body of the text's truth which gives the image of the destructive reader as female its special appeal, notably for authors who are male. This image, to be sure, is nothing more—or less—than image. It is an allegory rather than a reality; rhetorical commonplace, not historical fact. It would not be unreasonable to expect a female author to use different images of the readers she expects time to bring and of the reading process in which they would engage the text. The reader, to be "other," might well be imagined as male, for one thing. And other differences in the representation of the reading process might ensue. Traditionally, concern with bodily integrity belongs to the male more than the female province. Because a female writer's experience of her body has included its multiple changes over time (the appearance of breasts at puberty, the recurrence of the monthly cycle, perhaps the very great changes of pregnancy, childbirth, and the postpartum state), her imaginative repertory for thinking about the text as body will necessarily be quite different from that of a male writer.

The present study is written by a woman, which will no doubt detract from its persuasiveness in some quarters but may also offer

3. Cf. Clayton Koelb, "The Authority of the Text: Paul de Man and the Humanistic Tradition," in *Humanism and the Humanities in Historical Perspective*, a special issue of *Storia della Storiografia*, no. 9 (1986), 91–103.

some rhetorical resources that would be unavailable to the hermeneutic tradition if this tradition were an exclusively male one. When a woman writes in a field that has long cast women in the role of misreader (no pun intended), she must seek ways to invert that role, to create another allegory to replace the allegory of woman as misreader. Clearly, its central positive figure must be a female reader.

For this purpose, I have chosen Christine de Pizan and have placed her at the literal and metaphorical center of this book. Christine is not introduced to complete a three-part series of medieval writers, to be followed by three nineteenth-century authors, with a woman completing that triad, too. The symmetry I wish to create is an entirely different one, devoid of tokenism. My discussion of Christine is preceded and followed by studies of, in each case, two male authors who occupy positions in the currently accepted European canon much more central than hers because their work is regarded as of more importance to a movement (Nerval in French romanticism), a genre (Boccaccio in narrative and Baudelaire in lyric), or even to the Western literary tradition as a whole (Dante). Christine's centrality is constructed by my argument; it is presented as allegory rather than something found in the "neutral" landscape of European literary history. It is not a "legend" in quite the same sense that I used this word when I made Saint Louis the key figure in Chapter 1, but it is as close to my treatment of the boy reader, on the one hand, as it is to my discussions of Newman, Dante, and Boccaccio, on the other.

The reasons for my assignment of Christine to this allegorical position are several. First, there is the vast discrepancy between the reception in its own century and in the present one of the text I discuss here. *L'Epistre d'Othéa la Deese, que elle envoya a Hector de Troye quant il estoit en l'aage de quinze ans* (*The Letter of the Goddess Othéa, Which She Sent to Hector of Troy When He Was Fifteen Years Old*) was recopied many times, appeared in several fifteenth- and sixteenth-century printed editions, and was three times translated into English (the third printed as late as 1540). This publication history reflects an enormous interest in it among late medieval and early Renaissance readers[4]—yet today,

---

4. Susan Schibanoff, "Taking the Gold out of Egypt: The Art of Reading as a Woman," in Flynn and Schweickart, *Gender and Reading*, pp. 83–106, comments: "The *Othéa* was extraordinarily successful; more contemporary manuscripts (forty-three) of this work can be verified than of any of Christine's other numerous writings. Within a hundred years, it had been translated into English at least three times, and early publishers, such as Caxton, frequently printed and reprinted the *Othéa*" (p. 92). I cannot

there exists no critical edition of it. I take this sharp decline in popularity to reflect not a lack of quality but rather a hermeneutic problem. What made this text readable and interesting in its own time but not similarly readable now? What role do exegesis and interpretation play in this change?

Second, Christine wrote during a period that has in a sense been lost to French literary history. The fifteenth century is seen as neither fully medieval nor yet fully Renaissance. Its best-known representation is as Johan Huizinga's "waning" Middle Ages. I take this literary-historical fact also as symptom of a hermeneutic problem rather than evidence of a lack in the quality of fifteenth-century literature. A literary-historical period designation is above all a strategy for reading. It permits the reader to ask how a work reflects the features of its period and then to confirm the quality of the work (and of the reading, and reader) through appropriate responses. When a period concept is largely unavailable, as it is for the fifteenth century in France (only François Villon being still "readable"), a special and interesting problem for the relation between exegesis and interpretation is posed.

Third, the text in question is notable for its hermeneutic candor and sophistication. It lays out in the open the problematic a reader faces in trying, in the light of present situations, to read words written long ago. It also attempts to make the nature of these problems comprehensible to readers with no specialized theoretical background (and for this reason is open to patronizing criticism). In both these respects it differs markedly from the other texts I treat. It seems to recapture an awareness of hermeneutic complexity and a power to make that complexity accessible which have been largely lost.

Finally, it uses a hermeneutic language much different from that of mainstream hermeneutics. This discrepant language, which concerns, for example, the mother-child relationship and games, makes it difficult to take the text seriously as a contribution to the Western hermeneutic tradition; at the same time it makes awareness of certain

---

agree with Schibanoff's presentation of the *Othéa* as a text in which Christine reads only as a male exegete would, a zero-point against which her later and (in Schibanoff's account) more purely feminist works develop. A reliable introduction to the *Othéa* is provided by Charity Cannon Willard, *Christine de Pizan: Her Life and Works* (New York: Persea, 1984), 91–99. Willard notes (p. 91) that Christine "may. . .have become acquainted with Boccaccio's ideas on poetry expressed in his treatise *De Genealogia Deorum.*" See especially Willard's discussion of Christine's "new concept of poetry" (p. 93). Also, see below n. 18.

hermeneutic problems more compelling to those prepared to listen to it.

It should not be supposed that my placement of Christine in a central position is meant to suggest that she has a better understanding of the reader's role or is herself a better reader because she is female. I would contend, however, that she has at her disposal different rhetorical resources because she is a woman. One might adapt Judith Fetterley's concept of the "resisting reader" to designate Christine's hermeneutic rhetoric a "resisting rhetoric."[5] Indeed, some aspects of hermeneutic tradition are called into question by the very fact that a woman treats them at all. Her hermeneutic arguments would necessarily be *read* as meaning something different from the "same" arguments written by a man, given especially that hermeneutic theory must endlessly address the problem of authority and that concepts of authority are fundamentally shaped by concepts of gender.

The relative inaccessibility of the text constitutes an unfortunate inconvenience for the reader but represents something more: that the text is unedited and must be transcribed from a manuscript constitutes, to be sure, a reminder of the necessity of exegesis even for a reading striving toward interpretation.[6] The particular character of the recuperative effort undertaken in this study is emblematic of a number of problems posed by the relation of exegesis and interpretation and thus serves a function that outweighs in importance the inconvenience it inevitably entails.

Christine de Pizan is placed in the center of my argument, then, not so much because her sense of the reader differs from that of others as a result of her sex or her age (although on both accounts I think it does) but rather because of the ways, both exegetical and interpretive, in which her words can be read. Her language in describing texts and readers in fact differs markedly from Boccaccio's. In what she considers her first serious work, composed in France very roughly three decades after Boccaccio's death, she compares reading not to dismemberment but to a game—not an easy or frivolous but a subtle game,

<hr>

5. Judith Fetterley, *The Resisting Reader: A Feminist Approach to American Fiction* (Bloomington: Indiana University Press, 1978).

6. The very name "Pizan" requires that a hermeneutic operation be performed before it can be written. From one viewpoint it must be spelled with a "z" because it derives from the town of Pizzano, where her family originated; from another, it is written as "Pisan" because she wrote in French, and French tradition associated the family with the better-known city of Pisa. The first reading of her name is primarily exegetical; the second is interpretive in that it looks not to origins but to later impact.

which she compares with chess.[7] Its goal is to strengthen the reader's soul, as jousting (she thinks of her reader here as male) strengthens the body. She makes no mention of any Aesculapian need to restore the text to its original form or condition.

In fact, however, the *Epistre Othéa* might well be read as having been composed by means of a complete and wanton dismembering of a much older "text," the story of Troy, and a most incongruous rearrangement of its parts by comparison with the original narrative sequence of the Trojan cycle. To paraphrase Boccaccio, Christine's *Epistre* is a "twisted, shrunken, and hump-backed" *Iliad*. One might use Boccaccio's image of the student of ancient literature who awkwardly reassembles severed limbs washed up on a beach: Christine has taken arms and put them where the ears should be, then put one ear behind the knee and the other where the big toe should go. Moreover, she has then had the audacity to introduce the distorted whole by saying in effect: "The shape of the old narrative doesn't matter. This is how it makes sense to look at the Trojan story now." Her commitment to interpretive reading is indeed extreme, but her dismemberment of an ancient text is by no means the product of ignorance—female, medieval, or otherwise. She knows where the members *used* to go but chooses to put them elsewhere. In an important sense, then, she represents the kind of reader Boccaccio most deplored, even when he felt himself to be one of "them."

Christine, however, does not describe what she is doing as dismembering. She shows no ambivalence about reading and, even more unlike Boccaccio, no diffidence with respect to her readers. Like Dante, she gives evidence of keeping in mind her actual readers and their needs while she cuts away at the story of Troy to make it suit them. She puts the concerns of her readers above the interests of textual integrity. Rosemund Tuve suggested that it was Christine's ability to teach her readers how to read the *Othéa*'s allegory which kept demand for the work strong during the fifteenth and first half of the sixteenth century.[8] Contemporary readers, as noted above, responded well to

7. I thank SunHee Kim Gertz for drawing my attention to a parallel passage in Augustine, *De doctrina christiana* xxx.

8. Rosemond Tuve, *Allegorical Imagery: Some Medieval Books and Their Posterity* (Princeton, N.J.: Princeton University Press, 1966), p. 33, describes Christine's work as passing on to Renaissance secular readers certain medieval clerical "distinctions." To my description of the *Othéa* as a dismemberment of an ancient text, compare Tuve, p. 285: Christine "will escape the dreadful flaw, of shattering into fragments the unified work being allegorized, because she had no great work to shatter."

Christine's debut as a serious writer. They liked her work, had it copied over and over again, and then printed repeatedly. Only after several generations did the *Epistre Othéa* fade from popularity, and by then it had presumably accomplished its ends. Readers had changed, as its author had hoped they might and had assumed, with equanimity, that they would.

The Embracing of Temporal Ambiguity and the Qualitative Development of Literacy

While the disappearance from the literary canon of the once-popular *Epistre Othéa* thus makes Christine's book a suitable emblem of the text that welcomes rather than rejects interpretive reading, this same decline in interest creates difficulties for the kind of exegetical reading that must be attempted here. Late-arriving (in this case, post-Renaissance) readers without special interest in the fifteenth century are unlikely to know anything about the *Epistre*, so that all the elements contributing to exegesis must be explicitly provided. Moreover, because there has been no critical edition—that ultimate product of exegetical reading—there is no one accepted text.

One version of the *Epistre*, the British Library's Harley MS. 4431, recommends itself for examination particularly because it has recently been discovered to be in the author's own hand; moreover, it was extensively illustrated, apparently under Christine's direction.[9] One possible obstacle to the choice of this version as an object for exegetical reading, however, is precisely its relative lateness: while scholars continue to reassess arguments about the precise dating (within the first decades of the fifteenth century) of the first version of the text and of the one represented in the Harley copy, all agree that the latter is the result of revision of an earlier text.[10] In this case, revision seems to

9. Cf. Gilbert Ouy and Christine Reno, "Identification des autographes de Christine de Pizan," *Scriptorium* 34 (1980), 221–38.

10. See Gianni Mombello, *La tradizione manoscritta dell' 'Epître Othea' di Christine de Pizan. Prolegomeni all' edizione del testo* in *Memorie dell' Accademia delle Scienze di Torino.* Classe di Scienze Morali, Storiche e Filologiche, series 4a, no. 15 (Turin, 1967). Charity Cannon Willard, "A Fifteenth-Century View of Women's Role in Medieval Society: Christine de Pizan's *Livres des Trois Vertus*," in *The Role of Woman in the Middle Ages*, ed. R. T. Morewedge (Albany: SUNY Press, 1975) p. 94, suggests that the date ca. 1402 connected with the text may be that of its first copying rather than its composition; she dates the Harley MS ca. 1410 or 1411 (p. 113). See also Sandra Hindman, "The Composition of the Manuscript of Christine de Pizan's Collected Works in the British Library: A Reassessment," *British Library Journal* 9 (1983), 93–123.

have meant that Christine rethought her earlier text with a new and quite specific group of readers more forcefully present to her mind than they had been on a previous occasion.

Since the basic form of the work is that of a letter from the goddess of wisdom, Othéa, to Hector at the age of fifteen, it has been plausibly suggested that the first reader Christine envisioned was her own son.[11] He is thought to have been about this age and entering into training for his life's work (courtly service) at the time of the *Epistre*'s composition, and frequent maternal imagery in the work tends to support this inference. Still, since various copies are dedicated to several of the most influential aristocrats of the day—no doubt chiefly in an effort to gain their patronage—it is not legitimate to think of the work as in any sense private, intended for a narrowly restricted audience. Moreover, the inclusion of the Harley copy in the edition of her collected works that Christine made for Isabeau of Bavaria, queen of France and wife of the infamous mad king Charles VI, would seem to suggest that the author hoped the *Epistre* would interest not only squires and knights but also high-born ladies in need of edification.

Perhaps Christine's only explicit description of the readers she envisioned appears in the notation she placed before the opening of the *Epistre*'s first chapter in the Harley copy. It is written in purple ink, seemingly to make sure the reader would not miss it; it stands apart visually from both the text and the other headings in the usual red:

> Affin que ceulz qui ne sont mie clercs poètes puissent entendre en brief la significacion des histoires de ce livre, est à savoir que par tout ou les ymages sont en nues c'est à entendre que ce sont les figures des dieux ou deesses de quoy la letre en suivant ou livre parle selon la manière de parler des ancians poetes. Et pour ce que deyte est chose espirituelle et eslevée de terre sont les ymages figurez en nués et ceste première est la dèesse de Sapience.

> (So that those who are hardly learned writers may understand succinctly the meaning of the stories of this book, one must know that wherever the images are in clouds it is to be understood that they are the figures of the gods or goddesses of which the following letters or book speaks, in the manner of speaking of the old poets. And because deity is a spiritual thing and high above earth, the images are figured in clouds, and this first one is the goddess of Wisdom.)[12]

11. Edith Yenal, *Christine de Pisan: A Bibliography of Writings by Her and about Her* (Metuchen, N.J.: Scarecrow Press, 1982), p. 42.

12. All citations are from the British Library's Harley MS 4431. Transcriptions are

Christine's characterization of her readers in the first line of this purple rubric requires some explication: what does it mean that the intended readers of this copy, presented at court, are not "clercs poètes"? To a modern reader, the phrase may sound condescending, as if Christine is designating those who will read the queen's copy as less knowledgeable than herself; she would thus be, however gently, looking down at her readers as inferior to her from an educational viewpoint. Her attested success as a court writer suggests that she was hardly so maladroit. In fact, the characterization does indicate an author-reader hierarchy but not the one modern readers are accustomed to seeing: it indicates first of all that the readers of Isabeau's copy are rulers rather than servants—as clerks, scribes, and even chancellors were.

It also means, however, that these highborn readers lie outside the class that most often read this kind of material. This class was by the beginning of the fifteenth century certainly not limited to priests, so "cleric" would not be a proper translation of "clerc." Christine uses the term to describe both her father and her maternal grandfather, for example, men who earned the designation by their learning. A reader who is "scarcely a clerk poet" is one who can command the services of a clerk—to translate, copy, read aloud, or expound a text. Christine offers precisely such services when she explains the nature of the "ymages" (miniatures)—that is, that they give "en brief" the meaning of the following "letre"—and when she identifies the figures depicted in the clouds and explains why they are so depicted.

The latter explanation suggests that Christine expected from her patrons neither minimal iconographic knowledge nor the ability to understand a visual metaphor such as the relation between spiritual and spatial elevation. The modern, university-educated reader may well be

---

diplomatic to emphasize the exegetical character of this chapter, but I have expanded common abbreviations, added essential modern punctuation and accents, written "i" as "j" where modern orthography requires it, and occasionally added letters in brackets to bring spelling closer to modern usage. All translations are mine. I indicate the location of passages by chapter number to assist the reader who, lacking access to the Harley MS or a microfilm of it, is using another MS or one of the early English translations, for example: *The Epistle of Othéa*, trans. Stephen Scrope, ed. Curt F. Bühler (Early English Text Society, o.s. 264) (London: Oxford University Press, 1970). Bühler, p. xii nn. 2, 5, mentions three early sixteenth-century French editions titled *Cent histoires de Troye*, as well as a translation by the English printer Robert Wyer with a colophon designating it as "The C Hystories of Troye" (ca. 1540).

led thus to wonder whether Christine was not expending her efforts in a hopeless task when she wrote in the manner of "ancians poètes" for patrons so little attuned to even common visual convention; today, even a child exposed to no more than comic books is likely to know how to interpret a figure leaning out of a cloud. If Christine's royal patrons could not be assumed to know how to "read" this basic visual convention, in what sense could she have expected them to know how to "read" her text?

This question concerns not the (more often studied) quantitative growth of non-clerkly literacy but rather its qualitative development: what kinds of things did a reader who had mastered the ABC's and knew how to construe a sentence have to learn in order to go on to material beyond the elementary level? Fourteenth- and fifteenth-century writers addressing a non-clerkly public show awareness that lay readers needed to acquire many skills in order to achieve qualitatively advanced literacy. They needed, for example, to recognize forms different from those of their own dialects and to grasp plays on words. Like Prince Louis, they needed to learn to spot organizational clues to a text's structure, beginning with the most basic organizational literacy skill: remembering the details of a plot. They had to develop stylistic sophistication so that they could, for example, notice ironies and changes in tone. They needed to acquire a kind of "intertextual" facility, enabling them to recognize and interpret citations from or allusions to other works. Because of the importance of illustrated books in the late Middle Ages, one must include, as an aspect of such "intertextual" facility, the ability to read pictures and words as mutual commentary and to grasp pictorial allusions, puns, and so on. Most difficult of all, the lay reader needed to acquire a certain hermeneutic sophistication, to learn some rules for relating books to life—an activity fraught with peril, as the case of Paolo and Francesca illustrates.

During the fourteenth and early fifteenth centuries three factors above all laid the foundation for the development of qualitatively advanced literacy among nonscholarly readers. First, the laity increasingly gained access to those books most important to European commerce, politics, and culture and was therefore no longer wholly dependent on clerks for information from or interpretations of them; even lay biblical scholars, university trained in textual study, appeared in the fourteenth century. Second, lay persons in high places, in court circles and in the middle classes, supported lay literacy by enriching the corpus of vernacular literature, writing new works and translating older ones. The author of the *De vulgari eloquentia* was only the foremost among the numerous fourteenth-century writers who stimulated the growth of literature in the language of the laity. In the early fourteenth century the university professor Giovanni del Virgilio, in an epitaph for Dante, found it worthy of comment that a learned man like Dante should write the *Commedia* in a lay "mode" consciously shaped to lay understanding; as the century wore on, however, works of a learned character written for the laity became less remarkable. Third, institutions and traditions developed which ensured literacy a place in upper- and middle-class lay life. Most obviously important was the establishment of an increasing, though not large, number of secular schools. In addition, the second half of the fourteenth century saw the emergence of an international court culture, which gave vernacular literary works a quasi-diplomatic value as fruits of a court's accomplishments that could be exchanged and admired abroad. Moreover, such works were important to individual courtiers across Europe because they provided a standard for the measurement of taste and learning. Members of the middle class, too, incorporated books more firmly into their activities. In Tuscany, reading became a fixed feature of domestic life in successful fourteenth-century merchant families to such a degree that members were admonished to take some time from commerce each day to study the classics.

The *Epistre Othéa*'s Temporal Structure

The single feature of the *Epistre Othéa* that contributed most effectively to the qualitative development of literacy was that very structure which I have described, using Boccaccio's term, as the result of a "dismemberment" of the story of Troy. It is evident at a glance that this structure is so highly complex that modern readers may consider it cumbersome; Huizinga, for example, calls it "awkward,"[13] and Sidney would no doubt have regarded it with distaste because it is so "blurred" with Christine's interpretive glosses. The immense contemporary success of the work, however, and Christine's continuing pride in it throughout her career urge an effort to understand how the very complexity that has repelled some later readers formed one of the *Epistre*'s attractions in the fifteenth century.

13. Johan Huizinga, *The Waning of the Middle Ages* (1949; rpt., Garden City, N.Y.: Doubleday, 1954), p. 318.

The structure is dictated not by narrative concerns but by hermeneutic ones. Each of the *Epistre*'s hundred chapters is divided into three parts. The first, labeled *texte*, is always in verse and usually short: in most cases, only four lines. The second and third parts, in prose, are labeled *glose* and *allegorie*. An examination of one chapter will clarify the distinction between the two.

Like one of the passages from Boccaccio's *Teseida* discussed earlier, Chapter 11 of Christine's *Epistre Othéa* concerns Mars. Its *texte* reads as follows:

> Mars ton père, je n'en doubt pas,
> Tu ensuivras bien en tout pas,
> Car ta noble condicion
> Y trait ton inclinacion.
>
> (Mars, your father, I have no doubt
> You will surely follow at every step,
> For your noble state
> Draws in that direction your inclination.)

The *glose* explicates the *texte* exegetically by relating its words to secular learning and to the story of Troy. It comments on the name *Mars*, treating its relation to the day, "mardi" (Tuesday); to the metal, iron; and to the planet "qui donne influence de guerres et batailles" (that governs wars and battles). It then explains for readers unaccustomed to such metaphorical usage why the fictive addressee of the *texte*, "Hector de Troye quant il estoit en laage de quinze ans" (Hector of Troy when he was fifteen years old), is referred to as the son of Mars "non obstant fust il filz au Roy Priant" (even though he was the son of King Priam): any "chevalier" (knight) devoted to and renowned for military valor "peut estre appellé filz de Mars" (may be called son of Mars). Thus, the *glose* explains that "Mars ton père" (your father Mars) is an analogy and provides the reader with a means of understanding that analogy and its relation to the literal level of the Troy narrative (Hector's identity as Priam's son). The very form of this account of the relation between Hector as adolescent fictive addressee of the work and Hector as a more general figure of the knight makes clear that there is a corresponding difference between the narrator of the *texte*—Othéa, the *texte*'s *je*—and the voice of the *glose*, which refers to Othéa in the third person: "pour ce Othéa nomma ainsi Hector" (for Othéa called Hector by this name). Next, this voice, which might be termed the "glossatrix," justifies Othéa's assertion that Hector will follow his meta-phorical "father," by asserting in turn that this is what "tout bon chevalier doit faire" (every good knight should do). The *glose* ends with the citation of "un sage" (a wise man): "Par les oeuvres de l'omme peut on cognoistre ses inclinacions" (By a man's works one can know his inclinations). This proverb brings to the text's last word, "inclina-cions," the new idea of its effect in "oeuvres," thus extending the *texte* beyond its literal sense by introducing the idea of another person, the "sage," and by moving from the reasoning of the *texte* to its corollary.

The *allegorie* then reads the *texte* interpretively, extending the moral still further and introducing an entirely new frame of reference: "Mars" is interpreted to mean "the Son of God." This major change, from an ancient to a Christian perspective, is legitimized by the seemingly minor addition of an adverb to a verb phrase. In the *glose* it was said that any knight devoted to military valor "*peut* estre appelle filz de Mars" (*may* be called son of Mars). In the *allegorie* the optative auxiliary *pouvoir* is strengthened by the addition of "bien" (indeed). Thus the transition from Mars as the sire of military inclination to Mars as Christ is marked by a formula that stresses, in seeming proleptic defense of itself against an anticipated question, that this "reading" has been chosen for good reason, though it is not the only reading possible: "Mars le dieu de bataille *peut* bien *estre appelle* le filz de dieu" (Mars, the god of battle, *may indeed* be called the Son of God; emphasis added). Similar phrases frequently mark the beginning of the *allegorie* sections; for example, in the next two chapters, the phrases "*pouvons* prendre que" (we may take it that) and "nous *pouvons* entendre" (we may understand) introduce the connection between pagan myth and Chris-tian faith which forms the premise of the *allegorie* exposition. The use of the first person plural emphasizes that it is the group comprising Christine and her readers (as opposed to the Ancients) which draws forth from the *texte* the particular interpretive reading in question.

After the Christian premise of the *allegorie* is thus set forth, the focus shifts from Mars as Christ to Hector as "le bon esperit" (the good soul), a term that replaces "Hector" in each *allegorie*. As Hector will follow the military inclination of his father Mars, so "le bon esperit" will follow the example of Christ in doing battle against vice. Next comes a quotation, identified as the words of Saint Ambrose, employ-ing the vocabulary of warfare in a way that simply reiterates what has just been said about the Christian soul. The reader is then reminded that it is vain to give battle to the city's external enemies on the field outside a city when there are traitors within the city itself, and this observation becomes the ground for the argument that concludes the *allegorie* and, with it, the chapter: it is impossible to conquer the vices that surround one without first conquering the sins within one's soul. After a final remark in the vernacular—"Et est la plus glorieuse victoire qui soit que vaincre soy mesmes" (And the most glorious victory one can have is conquering oneself)—the chapter ends with a citation in Latin, from the last chapter of Paul's epistle to the Ephesians, also comparing the Christian's spiritual battle to the earthly soldier's battle "adversus carnem et sanguinem" (against flesh and blood).

In what does the movement from *glose* to *allegorie* consist, then? Why does Christine make this "division"? One useful analogue for the relation of these two units is provided by the widespread medieval practice of three- or four-part allegorical interpretation, best known in the form in which it was used in the *Letter to Can Grande*.[14] Christine's *glose* provides what the letter calls "literal" and "moral" interpretation, much like the commentary employed by grammar masters in ancient as well as medieval schools: the verse text is rendered into a prose paraphrase: the proper name it mentions is futher identified and some figurative language explained; and a parallel passage from an *auctor* serves as the basis for a secular moral interpretation. Christine's *allegorie* goes on to provide what the Can Grande letter terms "allegorical" and "anagogic" interpretation. Such non-clerkly readers as Can Grande and Isabeau needed to learn the difficult clerkly art of relating nonscriptural texts to salvation history, especially the concepts asssociated with the Last Judgment.

Late medieval allegorical interpretation, however, is not entirely adequate to explain Christine's distinction between two types of glosses. Her early fifteenth-century *Epistre* differs from the early fourteenth-century Can Grande letter in being addressed to readers who, though lay people, have a somewhat different consciousness of history. That they see a contrast between two temporally distinguishable ways of understanding a text is suggested by a contrast in verb forms. A simple assertion of exegetical necessity is implied by the unmodified and impersonal verbs most often used in the *glose*: "De Mars *est* le jour

14. This classic of medieval literary theory, long attributed to Dante, may be consulted in *Le Opere di Dante*, 2d ed., ed. Michele Barbi et al. (Florence: Società Dantesca Italiana, 1960); Allan H. Gilbert, *Literary Criticism: Plato to Dryden*, pp. 202–6, translates excerpts from it.

de mardi nommé" (The day Tuesday *is* named for Mars). The assertion in the *allegorie* is qualified by a form of *pouvoir*: "*peut* estre appellé filz de Mars" (*may* be called son of Mars). The content of the *glose*, secular even in its morality, relates the terms of the text to each other and to information and concepts associated with them in antiquity. The reader is unlikely to be in a position to question or add to this information. The frequently emphasized use of *pouvoir* to qualify the connection between *texte* and *allegorie*, however, alerts the reader that an interpretation of Mars as Christ, for example, is not compelled by the ancient text itself. Rather, it represents a choice made by the commentator on the basis of an understanding different from that of the ancient authors. In my terms, it is interpretive, and so announces itself.

The difference between the two modes of reading represented as *glose* and *allegorie*, then, is only apparently a difference between literal/moral interpretation and allegorical/anagogic interpretation, or between secular and sacred subject matter. At its foundation it is, rather, a difference between two modes of knowing that are distinguished temporally. While the *glose* relates the *texte* to what is believed to have been known in the period in which its sources originated, the *allegorie* relates the text to the belief system of the period of the *Epistre Othéa* itself. In a paragraph interpolated in the Harley manuscript before the beginning of the first *allegorie*, Christine explains the theory behind her allegorical practice by rendering into the "lay mode" the principle of anagogic interpretation long practiced by "clerks"; that is, she makes anagogic interpretation comprehensible in somewhat secularized terms. An *allegorie*, Christine says, is produced when one has "en continuelle mémoire le temps futur qui est sans fin" (continually in memory future time, which is without end). She thus alludes to the Apocalypse but omits to mention explicitly so technical a term which might be an obstacle to her lay readers.

Christine's *allegories* are the result of considering a moral problem in the present or a story from the past in relation to the future. This kind of consideration (even leaving aside for the moment its Christian setting and its relation to the humanist emphasis on prudence) inevitably makes reading a process whose results are not absolute but relative. An apocalyptically oriented viewpoint, as Dante has Saint Thomas explain in the *Paradiso*, sees all human interpretation as provisional; Christine, with her optative "pouvons entendre," offers up this provisionality in somewhat secularized terms. Her *gloses* involve learning to understand a story or opinion from the past—which may in itself seem outrageous or nonsensical—by respecting what was valuable in the past, understanding the reasons for differences between past and present states of knowledge, and mastering the means of transforming material from the past into something useful for the present.

While each of these forms of reading, *glose* and *allegorie*, is founded on a different form of temporal apprehension of the *texte*, they are not dichotomous but interdependent. Between them lies no gap but, rather, a continuous space to be constantly traversed by the reader in first one direction and then the other. The reader envisioned by the *glose* reads exegetically—that is, by looking to the past for information to make possible the reading of a text from the past—but the goal is nonetheless always an interpretive one, that of bringing the past text to make sense in the present. The reader envisioned by the *allegorie* reads interpretively: that is, by looking first at the present as a time in movement, a time of change, and only then, as a consequence of the future, back at the past to see how it too was in movement toward the same distant future. The intertwining of these two temporal perspectives is best evoked by Christine's own description of her method of allegorical interpretation, whose terms, read literally, are paradoxical. To keep "in perpetual *memory* the *future* time which is without end" is to look toward a perennial future known only through, as if from, what has been known in the past.

The *Epistre*'s Hermeneutic Themes

The structure of the *Epistre Othéa*, then, is hermeneutically rather than narratively motivated: it frankly presents a series of readings of each text which move from exegesis to interpretation, and it teaches the reader to consider the relationship among these readings. While this structure makes the *Epistre* seem a failure to some modern readers, it appears to have held great appeal for contemporary lay readers who needed to learn the most elementary of hermeneutic operations. Many of the *Epistre*'s themes, as well as its structure, derive from hermeneutic concerns. The most telling is presented in chapter 83. Its *texte* and *glose* concern the invention by Ulysses of games for the amusement of the Greek knights during periods of truce in the long siege of Troy, games with which "Hector" may also amuse himself at suitable moments. The *glose* mentions that chess may have been among them. Only in the *allegorie* does the focus shift from what seems, for the *Epistre*, a rather light subject to a serious one: "Les gieux Ulixes

peu[v]ent estre entendue que quant l'esperit chevalereux s'est lassé
d'aourer et d'estre en contemplacion, il pourra bien soy esbatre à lire les
saintes escriptures" (Ulysses's games may be understood [to mean]
that, when the knightly soul has tired of praying and contemplating, it
may well amuse itself by reading Holy Scripture).

The notion that one might amuse oneself, as with a game, by reading Holy Scripture seems at first sight rather astonishing. It is eluci-
dated in the quotàion that follows, attributed to St. Jerome: describing
scripture as a mirror held up before the eyes of the heart, it recommends the study of scripture as a means of self-examination. Interpretation of sacred texts thus appears in this *allegorie* as a demanding
"game" of great importance because it enables the soul to strengthen
itself even in moments of repose from the battle against vice. Lay
people, then, may improve themselves by engaging in interpretation—
if they know the rules of the game.

In a number of chapters of the *Epistre*, the glossatrix illustrates such a
"game" by pointing out that a particular figure in one of the *textes* is
susceptible of several interpretations. She goes on to use this multiplicity of possible interpretations as a basis for providing guidance to
the reader who knows little about the "game" and may find this situation, in which a great number of possible "moves" present themselves,
hopelessly confusing. In this way, Christine gives concrete form to
what is suggested by such formulae as "pouvons entendre."

In the *glose* on the story of Pygmalion (chapter 22), for example, she
asserts that stories susceptible of multiple interpretations are so made in
order to sharpen the wits of their readers—they are set up, presumably, like a good game of chess: "A ceste fable peu[v]ent estre mises
plusieurs exposicions et semblablement aux autres tels fables. Et pour
ce les firent les poètes que les entendements des hommes . . . soubtillas-
sent à y trouver diverses exposicions" (To this fable there may be
provided several expositions, and similarly to other such fables. And
poets made them for this [reason], that the understanding of men . . .
might grow subtle by finding various expositions for them).

The *glose* on Perseus's slaying of the Gorgon (chapter 55) states that
"mainte exposicion peut estre faite sus ceste fable" (a number of expositions may be made of this fable); after explaining two of them—
involving interpretation of the Gorgon as a wealthy city and as a
beautiful woman—the *glose* comments that "autres plusieurs entendements y peu[v]ent estre mis" (several other meanings may be applied
to this [text]). While there is no implication that any one of these

"expositions" or interpretations is superior to another, there may be, in the account of Perseus's shield, the suggestion of a way for the reader to protect him- or herself from attractive but dangerous interpretations: the shield that can mediate one's gaze at the seductive Gorgon is to be found in "l'estat de perfeccion" (the state of perfection), which is exemplified in the lives of and written about by wise men. To look into Perseus's shield is to study books; perhaps the way to avoid seductive but destructive interpretations is to study more and better books and study them more deeply.

The *glose* on the story of Hermaphroditus (chapter 82) again emphasizes the need to penetrate the interior of a text:

> Ceste fable peut estre entendue en assez de manières. Et comme les clercs soubtilz philosophes ayent muciez leur grans secres soubz couverture de fable y peut estre entendue sentence appartenant à la science d'astronomie et autressi d'arquemie. Si comme disent les maistres. Et pour ce que la matière d'amours est plus délitable à ouyr que d'autre firent communement leurs fictions sus amours pour estre plus délitables mesmement aux vides qui n'y prennent fors l'escorce et plus agréable aux soubtilz qui en sucent la liqueur.

> (This fable may be understood in quite a number of ways. And, like clerks, subtle philosophers have hidden their great secrets under cover of fable; there may be understood in it a meaning belonging to the science of astronomy and also of alchemy. So the masters say. And because the matter of love is more delightful to hear than any other, they usually made their fictions about love, to be more delightful even to the empty ones who take nothing from it but the shell and more pleasing to the subtle who suck its juice.)

Christine's reader thus learns that among various possible readings of a fable, some will answer the needs of some readers (for example, astronomers) while other readings will answer the needs of others (for example, alchemists). The explanation makes clear, moreover, that there exists a hierarchy of readers: at the bottom are those who seek only the delight of the surface; higher up are those who seek the liquor hidden within.

A theme that parallels the interpretation of books is the interpretation of dreams. Christine uses her treatments of dreams to place before her reader other basic notions about the nature of interpretation; indeed, she is not treating dreams so much as she is treating the interpretation. Chapter 68, about Paris's dreams, admonishes the reader against accepting his own interpretation of a dream, describing solitary interpretation as dangerously arrogant. Since Christine has elsewhere stressed the necessity of learning how to interpret other kinds of "material" for oneself, perhaps the general hermeneutic principle her reader is to infer here is that one should both develop one's own reading and consult with others before committing oneself to a final interpretation. Chapter 78, on the god Morpheus, cautions that "pour ce que songe est chose moult trouble et obscure, aucune fois riens ne signiffie et aucune fois le rebours peut signiffier de ce que l'on a songié" (because [a] dream is a very difficult and obscure thing, sometimes it means nothing and sometimes it may mean the opposite of what one has dreamed). Since dreams can mean nothing or the opposite of what they appear to mean, one must be reticent about interpreting them and avoid unwarranted anxiety about their meaning. In the following chapter, exposition of the story of Ceyx and Alcyon includes admonition to seek good counsel for the interpretation of dreams. Alcyon, who interpreted her dream correctly but whose interpretation was ignored by her doomed husband, is compared to the Church and to Joseph, interpreter of the Pharoah's dreams.

The Nature of the Reader's Presence in the *Epistre*

All these chapters treat the interpretation of myths, of scripture, and of dreams in such a way as to center attention not so much on the *product* of any particular act of interpretation as on the interpretive *process* itself. Christine presents interpretation as a serious and demanding game undertaken to sharpen the wits, to refine, revitalize, and nourish the intelligence, a game that requires both study and consultation if it is to be played well. Just as the tripartite structure of each of the *Epistre*'s chapters provides the reader with examples of exegetical and interpretive procedure, the stories recounted give the reader a series of hermeneutically instructive models and countermodels.

Still more instructive than either the stories or the structure of individual chapters, however, is the *Epistre*'s overall narrative organization. Its foundation is an epistolary fiction, established in the work's first chapter, whereby Othéa, the goddess of wisdom, is the letter-writer and Hector, "quant il estoit en l'aage de quinze ans" (at the age of fifteen years), is the letter's recipient. Othéa is the figure telling each story, and Hector is the figure to whom it is told. The numerous

allusions to "wise women" throughout the *Epistre* seem to tease especially the unsophisticated reader to "read" Othéa as representing
Christine herself. But who is the fictive reader Hector "en l'aage de
quinze ans"?

In other words, how is the *Epistre's* recipient represented, and what
does his representation say about his analogue, the reader, as envisioned by Christine de Pizan? Virtually nothing is said of Hector's life
and deeds between the first chapter, which establishes his epistolary
relation with Othéa, and the eleventh; the intervening chapters introduce, instead, the four cardinal virtues and the seven planets. The first
bit of information about the fictive addressee and princely protagonist
is revealed in chapter 11, when Othéa refers to Mars as Hector's father
and the glossatrix explains that Hector is nonetheless the son of Priam.
Chapter 12, on the god Mercury, has nothing more to say about
Hector's life. Chapter 13 closely parallels chapter 11: the glossatrix says
of Hector that Othéa called him the son of Minerva even though he
was the son of Queen Hecuba of Troy. Chapter 14 brings no further
details.

Chapter 15, however, is devoted to an event of capital importance in
Hector's life: his death. The choice of this particular chapter for a
treatment of his death is no doubt connected to the initial identification
of Hector-as-addressee as a youth of fifteen years. Othéa admonishes
him: "Ayes chiere Panthassellée / De ta mort sera adoulée" (Hold
Penthesilea dear; she will be saddened by your death). This is not a
mere general prophecy that Hector will die, spoken by a Sibylline
goddess of prudence with the habit of ambiguity. Much more than an
instance of the *momento mori* motif, it is a specific description of something (Penthesilea's mourning) that will follow Hector's death; with
eighty-five *textes* still to come, the fifteen-year-old Hector is told of the
aftermath of his own death. His deeds and life are passed over for
another twenty-five chapters, until the *glose* of chapter 40 mentions
that Achilles was responsible for his death—or, rather, *will* be responsible for it: with the announcement of Hector's death the temporal
framework of the *Epistre* has been necessarily rendered double. From
chapter 15 onward the fictive temporality of the epistolary fiction
("Once upon a time there was a goddess named Othéa who wanted the
boy Hector to learn something of wisdom") is explicitly admitted not
to be the only temporality of the *Epistre*; it exists both in a temporal
framework that precedes Hector's death and one that follows it.

Obviously, Christine is not attempting to narrate the story of Hector in a chronological fashion. The narrative of Hector, hero of the Trojan cycle, is not what interests her. She is extracting from it fragments that help her elaborate the narrative that does interest her: the writing of Othéa's epistle to Hector, described as a young prince. To do this, she links the discrete moments represented by the *textes*, fragments of an earlier narrative, into a new continuity, a new reading time.[15]

Killing her fictive addressee, so to speak, is a necessity for the kind of text Christine is writing. By constructing Hector and then taking him apart, she opens to question everything in the work. She removes it from the mimetic realm and makes it all a game, albeit a very serious one: a hermeneutic game for high stakes, like interpreting scripture. When Hector's death is "recalled" to him in his youth, any possibility that the *Epistre* can be read as mimetic, as narrative, ceases. Young Hector, the aftermath of whose death is treated while he is an adolescent at the threshold of knighthood and has yet to perform a single heroic deed, never becomes a protagonist. Moreover, the *Epistre*, which looks as if it is going to tell the stories of Troy (and was indeed misleadingly titled "The C. Historyes of Troye" in its first English edition), never becomes a historical narrative. Christine rejects narrative temporality and its powerful seduction of the reader in favor of a kind of hyperallegory that keeps readers emotionally distant from the text while simultaneously urging them to seize and play with the text in unaccustomed ways.

To persuade the reader of a narrative to go along with the transitions from one chapter to another and from one level of a chapter to another (as Boccaccio wished to do with the *Teseida* glosses) is to accomplish a rhetorical act that must be seen both *in malo* and *in bono* (as Dante showed in the Geryon episode). A kind of seduction into the fictive world of the narrative must be accomplished, and the means are, presumably, justified by the end. The *Epistre*, especially after chapter 15, attempts no such seduction.

Hector, the fictive addressee, remains a cipher to whom stories are

---

15. That she chooses to create this sort of narrative rather than another is not surprising, given the French literary history of her time. Among the features singled out by Paul Zumthor, *Essai de poétique médiévale* (Paris: Seuil, 1972), chaps. 8 and 9, as typical of later medieval French literature which are present in the *Epistre*, none is more important than the impulse to give to a collection of narratives of different periods a unity with its own meaning in its own time.

recounted. Some have taken place during "his" lifetime; others, after it. The question "when" is, fundamentally, never raised. Hector's life is not presented in any way even remotely resembling a chronological account, and he is not to be thought of historically at all. He is set up as existing at a particular historical moment ("quant il estoit en l'aage de quinze ans"), only to have his historicality erased (in a chapter with the same number as his age) by the choice of a moment following his death as the very first event from his "life" to be recounted.

Hector thus belongs to no single time but rather to two temporal frameworks: that of the Trojan narrative and that of the epistolary framework. This dual temporality is a successful antimimetic strategy, making it clear that the reader should not read the *Epistre* to find in it a mirror of history. Hector's separation from mimetic temporality is made strikingly evident by his insertion into a matrix that recalls strongly the chronological movement of the Trojan cycle—its character as a series of events—and by the *Epistre*'s insistence on his dual position, both inside and outside that chronology. The story of Troy, as a continuous series of events occurring one after the other, is divided into discrete, episodic units that are then reordered in a meaningful, but not chronological structure. In Boccaccio's terms, it is "dismembered," and by means of this dismemberment Christine creates an achronological work. Her motive in doing so is nurturant and didactic, the same motive that led her to divide the commentary on her *textes* into *glose* and *allegorie*. The *Epistre* implicitly suggests that texts may be reinterpreted at any future time and stresses the need for readers to learn how to perform such future interpretation. Whereas Boccaccio, in the proem to the *Genealogy*, treated multiplicity in interpretation with distaste, Christine welcomes it and invites her readers to reap the benefits of entering into what she calls the "game" of interpretation.

She did not, it would seem, share Boccaccio's passionate concern for the integrity of the textual "body," if chronological structure is regarded as essential to that integrity. Whereas he worked first to bring into the vernacular the chronological structure of a classical epic and then, especially in his glosses, sought to add to this chronologically ordered recounting of events some multiplicity of meaning, she focused her attention less on maintaining and enhancing the text and more on training the reader. She sought to bring her readers to a more qualitatively advanced form of literacy, a concern demonstrated, at a simple level, in her efforts to teach them very basic notions about understanding pictures and metaphors and, at a more sophisticated level, in her efforts to make them aware of the complex temporality of reading.

Why should such a difference between these two writers be discoverable? One answer, to be sure, is provided by gender. Classical epic predominantly portrays the martial struggles of men and generally relegates women to marginal roles unlikely to hold much appeal for a woman of Christine's resourcefulness and abilities: disruptive temptress (Helen), prize in a contest (Emilia), helpless victim (Andromache), self-mutilating or mad eccentric (Hyppolita, Cassandra). Such epic did not provide a mirror of the life of her sex which Christine was likely to have a great stake in maintaining. Her identity as a woman, however, did provide her with the rhetorical resources to remake the story of Troy into something that addressed her concerns.

But a second answer is required to account for the nature of Christine's concerns and their subtle difference from Boccaccio's. Both writers seem acutely aware that reading is a complex process, that a poor reading impoverishes even a very rich text and vice versa. But Boccaccio's hermeneutic awareness expresses itself in a much less explicit and evangelical form than Christine's. In the *Genealogy* he writes in Latin and rails against professional critics and the "avaricious" who devote no time to reading. In the *Teseida* glosses he is exploring some interpretive problems, it seems, primarily for himself, not for a wide and explicitly acknowledged public. Even if one regards the *Decameron* as a work with a hermeneutic doctrine to convey, such a doctrine is notably inexplicit compared with that of the *Epistre*.

It seems likely that the different forms in which these two writers express their hermeneutic awareness reflect differences in their perceptions of their readers. Moreover, there is reason to think that these differences in perception had some basis in the actual character of Boccaccio's and Christine's readers. Boccaccio may, like Dante, have envisioned in the abstract the possibility of a hermeneutically sophisticated lay reader, but there is no evidence that he directly encountered any. One might argue that his lectures on the *Inferno* were meant to educate the lay reader, but their substance is above all anecdotal. And in his many reference works, including the *Genealogy*, he provides a wealth of information to enlighten the ignorant but does not provide the guidance that would enable those of his contemporaries who were not "clerks" to learn to make something of difficult works on their own. His orientation is toward content rather than process—and perhaps anecdote and information were all that his readers were prepared to receive. Vittore Branca has traced manuscript evidence of the alterations the earliest readers of the *Decameron* made to its text; above all, these merchant-readers seem to have delighted in substituting the names of their own friends and enemies for the names of characters in the stories.[16] The physical evidence of the character of their reading resembles graffiti more than it does a series of glosses with, say, moral concerns.

Christine, by contrast, had a very specific audience not merely present in her mind but often before her very eyes. For her, the lay reader was no longer an ideal vision but a concretely attainable possibility. Within the circle of her court patrons she sought to create a readership for vernacular literature written more to edify than to entertain. The extraordinary popularity of the *Epistre* in the fifteenth century strongly suggests that it met important demands on the part of contemporary readers. One of those demands no doubt arose from the vogue for the antique in fifteenth-century France, but this must have been accompanied by a demand to learn how to read antique stories; otherwise, the early printers could have simply brought out editions of the antique romances of the French Middle Ages and saved themselves the considerable trouble and expense of setting in type the *Epistre*'s complex page layout. But that would not have suited readers who, for whatever reason, wished to learn how to read better. The lay reader of French medieval romance and the lay reader of Rabelais and Montaigne are, I submit, two very different figures. One can explain the evolution of the former to the latter only by recourse to the mediating figure of the fifteenth-century reader as one bent over a group of now unpopular texts, learning to interpret complex literary structures without clerical guidance.

Alongside the studied and apparently successful nurturance of the fifteenth-century readers who were not "clercs poètes" stands another aspect of Christine's endeavor: not merely the "dismembering" of the narrative but also a kind of fictive "murder" of the character evoked as fictive reader. The need for early acknowledgment of the narratively distant death of the fifteen-year-old "Hector" is emblematic of a need always present in what I have been calling "timely reading," reading conscious of its own temporal character. Christine wishes to demon-

16. Vittore Branca, *Boccaccio medievale,* 4th ed. (Florence: G. C. Sansoni, 1975), p. 3n. 1, pp. 4–5, p. 6n.2.

strate and teach interpretive reading, which can be practiced only by those who regard their own readings as provisional. Such an attitude can be achieved, however, only by those who maintain awareness, while reading, of their own mortality, those who know already at an early age that the text will have a life, and will find readers after their own deaths. Certainly, the *momento mori* motif is basic to both devotional literature and the literature of the Hundred Years' War, and insofar as the *Epistre* is assigned to both those categories, it must be expected to recall its reader's death. Yet this motif's pertinence is not topical only: it is fundamental to Western hermeneutics, at any time, for readers of either sex or any religious persuasion.

But the thought that a text will have a life and readers after one's own death is a thought very hard to keep in mind while one is reading. "Intimations of mortality" threaten, in more ways than one, to interrupt the reading process. Christine sets up a very rigid structure to contain not only the dismembered story of Troy but also the corollaries of her reader's (approaching) death. The *Epistre* goes perhaps as far as one can in distinguishing the two poles of the temporality of reading: one looking backward to the moment of textual origin, the other looking at the present as movement into a future in which the reader will vanish. Indeed, the very awkwardness Huizinga pointed out in the structure of Christine's *Epistre* suggests how cumbersome it is to try to read both exegetically and interpretively, while knowing what one is doing.

In this chapter, I have presented some of the results of my reading the *Epistre Othéa both* exegetically and interpretively. The two impulses have, in the case of this text, made similarly taxing demands upon my skills as a reader, but as I mentioned earlier, investing such a double effort in the *Epistre* has been essential because, unlike many other texts more easily legible (and more often read), this long-forgotten work provides me with at least a partial allegory of the task I am attempting in this book. I have argued that Christine's text has a double structure: one ordered according to the familiar principle of chronology, the other not chronological but temporal in a different sense, a hermeneutic one. One structure relates the occurrences of discrete moments one to another in sequential fashion. The other relates occurrences of discrete moments one to another, and to ideas, in a fashion that produces not a sequence but a meaning. When sixteenth-century printers (see n. 12) called the *Epistre* "One Hundred Stories of Troy," they were promising Christine's readers much less than she was prepared to offer. She had, in the *Epistre*, deliberately rejected the seductive power she could have given her text with a chronological narrative structure and provided instead a hermeneutic structure that could not be successfully masked as a narrative one.

At this point in my own text I feel a strong impulse to indulge in creating a narrative about the history of lay reading, and the metamorphoses of exegesis and interpretion, in the Reformation. To tell "what comes next," after Christine de Pizan, is the natural course to take.

But the more compelling such an impulse may be, the more energetically it must be rejected. Now that my argument has established a chronological thread, from Saint Louis to Christine de Pizan, the time has come to re-emphasize that my goal is not to recount a history of reading, or even one small segment of that history. I am less interested in the historical narrative that could be read as the product of my reading of Dante, Boccaccio, and Christine than I am in the process of reading itself and what it has to show about the complex interdependence of exegesis and interpretation. I conceive of myself as writing at a particular moment in the history of reading, addressing readers characteristic of that moment. They, you, are "clerks": that is, professional readers of texts, historians, interpreters, and critics in several disciplines, some a good bit younger than I, others with much more power in the influential realm of texts and readings than I am ever likely to have. And lately, you have most often been divided into two camps, which I see as fundamentally exegetical and interpretive, respectively.

To address such readers, I must make a deliberate break with the apparent chronological structure of this book. It is a history of reading only to the extent that the *Epistre Othéa* is "One Hundred Stories of Troy." Had I thought it appropriate to compose a history of reading, I would now go on to some figure in the Reformation, then discuss European education in the late sixteenth and early seventeenth centuries, and follow this with a chapter on Diderot. All this material is "missing," because this book is not a history.

The chapter which follows this one should not be read as about a *later* period in the history of reading.[17] Instead, it moves more insis-

---

17. However, on the privileging of the Middle Ages as a period that engenders many questions for modern thinkers and thus has special hermeneutic value, see Paul Zumthor, *Speaking of the Middle Ages*, trans. Sarah White (Lincoln: University of Nebraska Press, 1986), esp. pp. 8–9.

tently than what has gone before into a theoretical framework. Its argument will, I hope, help make clear that what I have been presenting is less a history of reading than a series of figures of the complex temporality of reading. The next one may even be given a name drawn from the study of figures, for it is essentially a special temporal form of irony. But just as other figures of the temporality of reading have been misread (Dante's divisions as puerile errors, Christine's allegory as awkwardness), so this temporal irony is misread—as madness.[18]

18. On political allegory in the *Epistre Othéa,* especially as it may be understood through analysis of the accompanying miniatures, see Sandra L. Hindman, *Christine de Pizan's "Epistre Othéa": Painting and Politics at the Court of Charles VI,* Studies and Texts 77 (Toronto: Pontifical Institute of Mediaeval Studies, 1986).

Chapter 5

Nerval: Reading between the Lines

> . . . comme si l'intelligence n'avait pas la permission de les voir
> (as if the understanding were not permitted to see them).
>
> MARCEL PROUST

Through the narrator of her first serious prose work, Christine de Pizan embraced two roles with great explicitness: that of reader of an ancient textual tradition and that of writer of a fictional epistle. Yet this explicit duality created no ambiguity. Just as she gave no indication of seeing herself as dismembering an ancient text (as Boccaccio had), she associated no sense of loss, pain, or tension with either her authorial or her readerly role. In part, the coherence of her text results from her view of her readings as authoritative (in every sense of the word) and helpful to a clearly envisioned audience. When read as an allegory applicable to the problem raised in the present study, her *Epistre Othéa* provides a figural pattern of exegesis and interpretation successfully brought into dialogue with each other, a pattern in sharp contrast to the pattern I earlier associated with Boccaccio.[1]

To be sure, no one, not even an allegorist, can quite read a text from two such different viewpoints at the same time, but Christine's structure permits her to give the illusion that she can. By forging links between questions about values and behavior as they were formulated

---

1. A more recent analogue is M. M. Bakhtin's concept of productive dialogism. "Every utterance participates in the 'unitary language' . . . and at the same time partakes of social and historical heteroglossia": *The Dialogic Imagination*, ed. Michael Holquist, trans. Caryl Emerson and Michael Holquist (Austin: University of Texas Press, 1981), p. 272. What I have been calling exegesis strives to see a text as what Bakhtin terms "unitary language"; interpretation, as I have used the word, belongs to the domain of heteroglossia.

in ancient times and similar questions formulated in a fifteenth-century framework, Christine makes what could loosely be called a metaphor, as medieval allegorists had done before her and as many humanists would do in her century and the century to come. Her goal is rhetorical: like the other humanists at the court of Charles V, her most direct models, she adds to the persuasiveness of her recommendations about the present by making them appear to be based on doctrines enunciated in the distant past. She thus creates a fictive "depth" to underlie what she writes. Her views about what her readers should do to deal with the problems of the present take on a power that is in fact purely fictive and rhetorical but appears to be historical.

Yet even more than it is humanistic or allegorical, Christine's strategy must be seen as fundamentally literary. The delineation of two parallel temporal structures, ancient and contemporary, is a representation of the writer's relationship to her language. When one writes, and especially when one writes an epistle, a future moment when the words written will be read is envisioned. One hopes the words will have a life in the future. This gives them, fictively, a double temporal framework, present and future, which writers often represent instead as a link between present and past.

Similar representations of the fictive duality of written language, translated from a present/future to a present/past structure, may be found in many mimetic texts. One of the most telling appears in the major prose work of the late French romantic writer Gérard de Nerval, a work that was to be his last. In several ways it presents a figural pattern of the temporal character of reading which is precisely the converse of the pattern identified in the *Epistre*. In the long short story *Aurélia*, Nerval functions as a *writer* of the greatest originality (his narrative techniques being later explicitly adopted by Proust), yet he projects himself, through the character of a first-person narrator, as a *reader*. This reader, moreover, is not "authoritative," like Christine's glossatrix, but one who fails over and over again to read successfully and is driven to despair by his continuing readerly failure.

The hallucinatory framework encountered in numerous romantic texts serves in *Aurélia* merely as a pretext for the presentation of a literary defeat. The narrator's repeatedly described malaise, deriving from his inability to distinguish dream from life, assumes the general form of an inability to distinguish past from present; it gives rise to a conflation of moments that the narrator strives unsuccessfully to distinguish, above all in the reading of books. Again and again he tries to read exegetically in order to learn what such writers as Swedenborg, Apuleius, Dante, and Petrarch "intended to tell him," but he continues to find in his readings only what he himself, as an interpretive reader, puts into them.

Although critical tradition has tended to merge *Aurélia*'s reader-narrator with its writer, the latter by no means shares the former's confused state; Nerval creates a structure just as clearly defined as Christine's in the *Epistre* and much more complex. Whereas, for example, Christine on only one occasion (chapter 85) uses changes in verb tense to signal her break with traditional narrative structure, Nerval makes of departures from standard verb usage an entirely new kind of ironic narrative structure. The critical approach taken by Nerval's very first editors may suggest that such departures should be seen as indicators that the text is unfinished (the manuscript having been found in Nerval's pocket at the time of his suicide; see below n. 14): this would imply that the murdering of the reader-narrator's sanity, so bitterly complained of in the text, should be blamed for a kind of dismemberment of the traditional temporal framework. A less condescending view, however, would see the author as successful, as having escaped his reader-narrator's failure. Nerval, that is, succeeds in doing as a writer what his narrator wishes vainly to do as a reader: having it temporally both ways, engaging at once in the discourse of both past and present.

The Failed Dialectic of Exegesis and Interpretation

Aurélia begins with a catalogue of the narrator's mental library and his statement that his readings have driven him mad: "[Cette folie] est la faute de mes lectures" (My readings bear the blame for [this madness]).[2] It is important to distinguish this statement from Francesca's, for Nerval's narrator sees his madness as the fault not of

2. This passage is cited from Gérard de Nerval, *Oeuvres*, ed. Albert Béguin and Jean Richer (Paris: Editions Gallimard, Bibliothèque de La Pléiade, 1966), 1:360. To facilitate reference by those using other editions of *Aurélia*, further citations are made by part and chapter number (the chapters being very short). All translations are mine. Portions of this chapter appeared in my "Self-reading and Temporal Irony in *Aurélia*," *Studies in Romanticism* 16 (Winter 1977), 101–19. Shoshana Felman, *La Folie et la chose littéraire* (Paris: Seuil, 1978), pp. 67–69, analyzes the doubling of the pronoun *je* as the key feature of *Aurélia*, rather than the doubled tense structure.

his books but of his readings of those books, of the mistaken way he has interpreted them. Again, near the end of the story a voice from the beyond reproaches the narrator for his failure as a reader: "Tout cela était fait pour t'enseigner le secret de la vie, et tu n'as pas compris. Les religions et les fables, les saints et les poètes s'accordaient à expliquer l'énigme fatale, et tu as mal interprété. . . . Maintenant il est trop tard!" (All that was done to teach you the secret of life, and you have not understood. Religions and myths, the saints and the poets agree in explaining the enigma of fate, and you have misinterpreted. . . . Now it is too late; II.3). The narrator's last important human contact in the story is with one final interpreter of the "fatal enigma," "un interprète sublime . . . prédestiné à entendre ces secrets de l'âme que la parole n'oserait transmettre ou ne réussirait pas à rendre. C'était l'oreille de Dieu" (a sublime interpreter. . . predestined to understand these secrets of the soul which language would not dare to convey or would not succeed in rendering. It was the ear of God; II.6). But the ear not being an organ of speech, the sublime interpreter does not pass on the messages received, so that at the end of the story the narrator is, by his own qualitative standards, still illiterate.

If this reference to God as the ultimate interpreter calls to mind the theological framework in which Dante presents reading, the association is certainly no accident: of the four authors listed at the beginning of *Aurélia*, Dante is the one whom Nerval mentions most frequently throughout his writings.[3] Perhaps his key allusion to Dante appeared

3. The *Commedia* is the only work Nerval's narrator cites as a model both in the preface to *Les Filles du Feu* and in the opening paragraphs of *Aurélia*. In the preface (Nerval, *Oeuvres*, 1:151), he claims that had he succeeded in focusing his memories into a single masterwork, he would have written something like "le Songe de Scipion, la Vision du Tasse ou *la Divine Comédie* de Dante." Instead, the first chapter of his *livre infaisable* "semble faire suite au *Roman comique* de Scarron" (looks like a sequel to Scarron's "Comic Novel"). In the first paragraph of *Aurélia*, the narrator retains Dante, classing the *Commedia* with *The Golden Ass* as a model study of the soul and citing Emmanuel Swedenborg's *Memorabilia*, too, as an example of the dream-vision. He continues to allude to Dante throughout the introductory section: his struggle to balance reason and imagination he calls a *vita nuova* (1:259); because he has taken poetic fictions too seriously, he has, he confesses, made of an ordinary person of "our" century a Laura or a Beatrice (1:360). In *Sylvie*, Beatrice appears again as a key image for the beloved. Adrienne "ressemblait à la Béatrice de Dante qui sourit au poète errant sur la lisière des saintes demeures" (resembled Dante's Beatrice, who smiles at the poet wandering along the edge of the realm of the holy; 1:246). François Constans, "*Aurélia* ou l'itinéraire de la délivrance," in *Gérard de Nerval devant le destin* (Paris: A.-G. Nizet, 1979), pp. 263–94, emphasizes that the final version of *Aurélia* seems to have been

three years before the publication of *Aurélia*, in *Les Nuits d'octobre* (*October nights*). The narrator, about to be introduced to the Parisian market by a friend, recalls Rousseau's invective against the "moeurs des villes" (city ways; Nerval, *Oeuvres*, 1:94) and remarks, in a tongue-in-cheek reference to the opening of the *Inferno*: "Si je n'étais sûr d'accomplir une des missions douleureuses de l'écrivain, je m'arrêterais ici" (If I were not sure of carrying out one of the writer's painful tasks, I would stop here). Since the tense of the main clause is the present (not the past) conditional, it is clearly the narrator as writer, as well as the nocturnal *flâneur*, the urban vagabond, who "would stop"; the doubling parallels that of Dante the poet and Dante the character. The Dantesque allusion then becomes explicit as the friend quotes *Inferno* XVII (the Geryon episode):

> . . .mais mon ami me dit comme Virgile à Dante: "Or sie forte e ardito;— omai si scende per sì fatte scale . . ."
> A quoi je répondis sur un air de Mozart: "Andiam'! andiam'! andiamo bene."
> —Tu te trompes! reprit-il, ce n'est pas là l'enfer; c'est tout au plus le purgatoire. Allons plus loin.

> (But my friend said to me, as Vergil did to Dante: "Now be strong and daring;—henceforth one goes down on stairs made like this . . ." To which I answered, with a snatch from Mozart: "Let's go! Let's go! Indeed, let's go." "You're mistaken!" he said, "that's not Hell; at most, it's Purgatory. Let's go farther on.")

The narrator's response in misremembered words from an erotic seduction scene in Mozart's *Don Giovanni* are as lightheartedly inappropriate as his friend's Dantesque quotation. Indeed, misreading ("Tu te trompes!") is the point of this comic passage, in which Nerval pokes fun at the impulse to emulate Dante which frequently emerges in his work, inevitably to be frustrated.

Dante's theologically grounded view of "reading" represented for Nerval a totally unattainable ideal. Dante's pilgrim can "hear" Beatrice as an indicator pointing to Mary, who in turn indicates the Divine

---

undertaken with an apostolic zeal akin to that more commonly attributed to Dante; according to Constans, Nerval at this time wished to shape "the spiritual destiny . . . of those among his brothers who were troubled by visions" (p. 266). Constans also notes (pp. 285–86) that the influence of the *Commedia* becomes more recognizable in Part II.

Word (*Paradiso* XXIII.70–75; cf. *Paradiso* IV;1–12), without either finding himself lost in a series of signifiers without end (ceaseless interpretation) or conflating the signifiers and the historical moments of their
appearance so as to lose the essential human sense of their difference
(deadening exegesis). Dante's model, in other words, can remain fully
open to continuous *change* in meaning without resulting in an ultimate
lack of meaning; indeed, constant change in meaning and ultimate
meaningfulness are, in this fully dialectical model, inextricably interdependent.

But the narrator of *Aurélia* cannot find ultimate meaning in what he
reads. Like the pilgrim in Paradise, he sees people as signs that point to
something else, but for him this something else is always another
word, or a person seen as a word—something to be further interpreted, not final. The narrator's failure in reading is like that of the
young Dante: "I have deified my love and I have worshipped [her]."
One woman dissolves into another, and still another:

> La déesse m'apparaissait, me disant: "Je suis la même que Marie, la
> même que ta mère, la même aussi que sous toutes les formes tu as
> toujours aimée. A chacune de tes épreuves, j'ai quitté l'un des masques
> dont je voile mes traits, et bientôt tu me verras telle que je suis."

> (The goddess appeared to me, saying to me: "I am the same as Mary,
> the same as your mother, the same one also under all the forms whom
> you have always loved. At each of your trials, I have dropped one of
> the masks with which I always veil my face, and soon you will see me
> as I am.") [II.5]

When Beatrice pointed to Mary, it was as the incarnatrix of the eternal
Word; Nerval's goddess is a metaphor for metaphor, for things that
stand for other things that lead back in an endless series.

Near the end of the fifth chapter in the first part, one of the narrator's
friends asks tearfully: "N'est-ce pas que c'est vrai qu'il y a un Dieu?"
(Isn't it true that there is a God?). In effect, he wants to be reassured
that all the words the narrator has said, all the symbols he has seen as
pointing each to the next, must point to something final. "'Oui!' lui
dis-je avec enthousiasme" ('Yes!' I said to him with enthusiasm). The
narrator goes on: "Quel bonheur je trouvai d'abord dans cette conviction!" (What happiness I found at first in this conviction!). Later, however, his certainty vanishes.

Temporal Irony

Because the Dantesque model of reading does not work for him, Nerval must devise a narrative structure wholly different from Dante's. The *Commedia*, on the other hand, is the product of the tension between two narrative perspectives, that of narrator and that of pilgrim.[4] These two figures stand at different points along a "then/ now" axis. In *Aurélia*, on the other hand, Nerval uses two voices not separated by a fixed moment of conversion to "new life," distinguishing "then" from "now." These voices are so equal in narrative power that the reader would be unable to decide which voice is the "original" and which the "double" did not the voice that speaks the first words of the story also end it. And yet, because the two voices have functioned in such perfect polyphony throughout the tale, it is the voice of the double, which does not speak at the end, that gives *Aurélia* its unwritten afterword. The story's ending appears unsatisfactory if judged by the criteria of traditional narrative structure, for although at an explicit level it asserts itself as a conclusion, at another level the story's problem continues after the story's end. It is the voice of the double that gives the ending this continuing quality and makes it, rather than a narrative failure, a narrative tour de force.

The conceptual basis for the temporal double in *Aurélia* is the physical double often encountered in romantic narrative.[5] It first appears shortly after the narrator falls into a hallucinatory fit in the night streets of Paris (1.3). Taken to a police station, he senses the presence of his double behind him as he lies stretched on a cot and later believes he sees his friends taking the double out of the station, mistaking it for the narrator. When his friends finally retrieve him, denying that they came to the station earlier in the evening, the narrator continues to be troubled by the knowledge of the existence of his double. He later realizes that his beloved Aurélia, already lost once, to Death, will be taken in by the same fraud that deceived his friends (1.9). Then, dreaming that he is in a room where a group has gathered to await the arrival of a bridegroom, he remarks, "J'imaginai que celui qu'on attendait était

4. Gianfranco Contini, "Dante come personaggio-poeta della *Commedia*" in *Un'idea di Dante* (Turin: Einaudi, 1976).
5. Claire Gilbert discusses psychoanalytic aspects in *Nerval's Double: A Structural Study*, Romance Monographs 34 (University, Miss.: Romance Monographs, Inc., 1979).

mon *double*, qui devait épouser Aurélia, et je fis un scandale qui sembla consterner l'assemblée" (I imagined the person they were awaiting was my *double*, who was to marry Aurélia, and I made a scene that seemed to upset everyone; I. 10). Threatened with physical violence, the narrator prepares to fight back, and his upraised arm is stopped only by a woman's mournful cry. He awakens, knowing that the cry was real, not a dream, and that the voice was the dead Aurélia's.

Two details in the depiction of the traditional physical double suggest the willed blindness toward the threat of death which forms the conceptual basis for Nerval's temporal double: first, the narrator decides not to look at the double; second, he recalls that seeing one's double indicates death's approach. Since the narrator's death would bring the narration to an end, his refusal to advance from intuiting the double's presence to seeing it makes possible the continuation of the story. He merely glimpses someone of his size retreating from the room. His later violence directs itself toward those who are awaiting the double's appearance, not toward the double itself, and no second appearance of the physical double is represented in *Aurélia*.

Rather than growing out of a struggle between the narrator and his physical double, the story develops from the tension between the narrator and his temporal double. The narrator, in other words, maintains his existence as narrator by ignoring the commentaries of the temporal double, which tend to undermine his own story. Like the physical one, the temporal double must be glimpsed only in passing. The relation between the two voices is not at all that between two characters (narrator-then/narrator-now) but rather that between two texts. Each text reads the other and comments upon it; each finds in the other a gloss that modifies its own value and meaning. But the relation between text and commentary is not regular and continuous, with the two laid out in a predictable pattern as they are in the *Vita nuova* or the *Epistre Othéa*. Instead, single discourse often splits in two at the most unexpected junctures, just when the narrator's voice has imposed itself as univocal.

An especially disorienting eruption of the voice of the temporal double occurs as early as the story's second paragraph. Up to that point, the temporal structure is simple. The narrator states that he has, in a time prior to the time in which he is writing, gone through "une longue maladie" (a long illness), which he associates with "rêve" (dream), the "monde invisible" (the invisible world), "limbes" (limbo), and "le monde des Esprits" (the Spirit world). By the time he begins his story, he has come back from the other world to the world of "ce que les hommes appellent la raison" (what men call reason). It is a straightforward then/now structure: "then," the narrator was sick, asleep, and imagining; "now," he is healthy, awake, and reasoning.

But this clear structure is rendered ambiguous by the verbs of the last sentence of the second paragraph. In the penultimate sentence the narrator refers to the ecstasies that his imagination brought him during his period of sickness, now past. His voice, firmly grounded in the time frame in which he is writing, describes his past self as past. "Parfois, je croyais ma force et mon activité doublées; il me semblait tout savoir, tout comprendre; l'imagination m'apportait des délices infinies" (Sometimes, I thought my strength and activity were doubled; it seemed to me that I knew everything, understood everything; imagination brought me infinite ecstasies). But the verbs of the last sentence of the paragraph move the narrator backward for an instant into the realm of those lost ecstasies. Instead of being the person he was in the preceding sentence, someone who was once blessed with "imagination" and "ecstasies" but is so blessed no longer, he becomes someone who still possesses these gifts but, balanced on a threshold, anticipates the approaching moment when he will have to give them up: "En recouvrant ce que les hommes appellent la raison, faudra-t-il regretter de les avoir perdues?" (Recovering what men call reason, will it be necessary to regret having lost them?)

The first element to be noted in this important sentence is the tense of the verb *falloir*. The clarity of the then/now structure would have been better maintained if *falloir* had been placed in the present tense: *faut-il*. It would then be clear that the narrator continued to speak from the healthy, awake, reasoning viewpoint of "now," asking whether "now" he should regret having lost the "délices" "then": "faut-il regretter de les avoir perdues?" The structure would have been clarified even further if the participial phrase that opens the sentence had been based on a past rather than a present participle. But Nerval's use of the future tense, "faudra-t-il," makes the question quite a different one, blurring what had been a clear demarcation between past and present. The lack of temporal specificity of the phrase "en recouvrant" permits modulation away from the tense norms already established, though not in itself implying any deviation. The narrator, with "faudra-t-il," asks whether he will have to regret the loss of the "délices" in the future when he experiences it; the loss has yet to occur. The voice that says "faudra" cannot have returned from the "monde invisible"; that

voice speaks from a moment prior to the time in which the two preceding sentences are written.

What is important about the form "faudra" is not merely that it is in
the future tense but rather that its tense deviates slightly from the
pattern established by the immediate context. It does not initiate a
flashback or a reverie of any substantial duration; its power lasts no
longer than the ellipsis which follows the question mark: "faudra-t-il
regretter de les avoir perdues? . . ." Not a change in the color or line of
the whole canvas of *Aurélia*, it is only one very light brushstroke, but a
brushstroke that nonetheless changes the appearance of everything
around it. The two paragraphs that precede this sentence establish a
norm for the use of tenses and the description of temporality from
which *faudra* deviates just enough to call the norm into question. They
have together formed a prologue to the account that begins with the
third paragraph: "Cette *Vita nuova* a eu pour moi deux phases. Voici les
notes qui se rapportent à la première" (This *New Life* has had two
phases for me. Here are the notes relating to the first).

As the prologue closes, what it explicitly announces about the account to come is thus cast into a new light, if only for an instant. The
assertion of the first two paragraphs that the narrator has returned
from the state labeled "maladie" is, with the syntactic structure, called
into question. The reader must look back and reevaluate what has gone
before. This instant of questioning passes but leaves the question behind, even as the narrative returns to the clear temporal order set up by
the main body of the prologue. In a move crucial to the rhetorical
structure of the work, Nerval has rendered visible the discrepancy
between the two narrative voices that will tell the story.[6] If his next
sentence, the first of the text proper, hides the discrepancy once again,
that does not mean that the reader is to forget what has been glimpsed:
the crucial sentence embodies the moment of transition between two
states of being and two moments of knowing, which—according to
the first paragraph—it is the purpose of *Aurélia* to describe. "Les pre-
miers instants du sommeil sont l'image de la mort; un engourdisse-
ment nébuleux saisit notre pensée, et nous ne pouvons déterminer

6. W. M. Bronzwaer observes that "the use of tenses is governed by the author's
decision to make certain contrasts visible at certain moments": *Tense in the Novel: An
Investigation of Some Potentialities of Linguistic Criticism* (Groningen: Walters-Noordhoff,
1970), p. 62. Relevant here is Sarah Kofman's description of *Aurélia* as a text that tries to
create a rhetoric of lucidity; the reader must be made to think the narrator capable of
distinguishing past from present (*Nerval*, p. 15).

l'instant précis où le moi, sous une autre forme, continue l'oeuvre de l'existence" (The first instants of sleep are the image of death; a vague numbness takes hold of our thought, and we cannot fix the precise instant in which the I, in another form, continues the work of existence). The final sentence of the prologue, then, not only treats but also exemplifies the breaking through of past into present. It is particularly important to *Aurélia* because it shows for the first time how the story's themes will be worked out in its structures.[7]

Reading between (the Lines of) Past and Present

The opening paragraphs of *Aurélia* thus announce, in detail as well as in general terms, both the structure and the themes of the work as a whole. In his prologue Nerval writes *about* and also *in* two periods of time. The two might be called "remembered time," time past, the time of sickness; and "text time," the present time of narration, the time of recovered health. The prologue might then be described as written *in* the time of recovered health *about* the time of sickness— except for "faudra," a word spoken in the time of sickness about the time of recovered health, to which it looks forward with some ambivalence. Thus, to label the period of sickness as "remembered time" or "past time," implying that it is definitely over when *Aurélia* begins, is to falsify the story's temporal structure and to simplify Nerval's conception of memory. Similarly, to label the period of recovered health as "text time" or "present time," implying that the entire text is written in that time frame, is to fail to perceive *Aurélia*'s complexity. Even the opening paragraphs, which establish the traditional setting of the traveler returned and about to tell the story of his journey, are not written entirely from the point of view of the "returned" time frame.

The only satisfactory labels for the time frames the story is written about and in are those suggested by the subtitle, "le rêve et la vie"

---

7. Some general features of this first temporal disruption recur at other points in *Aurélia*. First, a preparatory element implies transition from one stage or state to another and permits modulation away from the normal tense pattern; in this case, the preparatory element is the initial participial phrase *en recouvrant*. Second, the syntactic context establishes a specific temporal and tense norm, laid down with definiteness so that deviation from it can be noted. Third, the semantic context emphasizes the importance of this temporal norm to a proper understanding of the story. Fourth, the deviation, made visible by the regularity of its syntactical context, in turn reflects its own ambiguity onto that context, calling it into question.

(dream and life), or "dream time" and "life time." Dream time is to be associated with the double, life time with the one who is doubled. In the first sentence of *Aurélia*, the realm of dream is given a secondary status with respect to the realm of life: "Le Rêve est une seconde vie." The implication is that a dream is a duplicating of life, a mode of being and knowing modeled on life. But considering *Aurélia* as a whole, it is by no means clear that the "second life" is inferior merely because it is second.

The entire story presents itself as an inquiry into one question: is the dream state, as compared with the waking state, a time of diminished or of heightened awareness?[8] But by asking which voice has access to the truth, that of the Double or that of the one who is doubled, Nerval poses two more general problems deriving from the relation between time and knowing. The first has to do with time conceived as normative, predictably continuous, the stable background against which events are measured and through which events are described. The second has to do with time conceived as moving.

The first problem is posed directly by the tenses, which ordinarily function according to conventions. The conventions pertaining to the relation of one tense to another effectively restrict what is seen or, more particularly, what is spoken or written about what is seen. They keep the individual speaker in conformity with those notions accepted a priori by a linguistic community as to what is "then" and what is "now," for example; they thus privilege some moments as present and relegate others to nonpresent status. In order to question these notions, *Aurélia* must break the syntactic conventions on which they depend.

The second, more complex problem is how to conceive time as moving, a vehicle of transition. Nerval's extended speculation about the way change occurs from one form of understanding to another depends upon explorations of this problem. His concern with this process is suggested by the line from the story's first paragraph already cited: "We cannot fix the precise instant in which the I, in another form, continues the work of existence." The moment of transition is indeed itself the unknown which is to be explored ("nous ne pouvons déterminer") and not merely a passage toward the unknown. To understand the moment of transition is to understand a process that

8. Paul de Man, "The Rhetoric of Temporality," in *Interpretation: Theory and Practice*, ed. Charles S. Singleton (Baltimore, Md.: Johns Hopkins University Press, 1969), pp. 173–209, has shown the importance of "'slumber' [as] a condition of non-awareness" to the temporal structure of one of Wordsworth's Lucy poems.

changes the known into the unknown, perhaps the most powerful kind of alchemy.

Death must form a part of this inquiry, even if only at one remove, as figured in sleep; for it is death that places a limit on both human time and human knowledge, and the limit position is always the one that promises the explorer the greatest rewards. The twilight consciousness, whether a transition to the darkness of death or to the darkness of sleep, is a state in which the self knows it is passing from one mode of being to another but is unable to determine at exactly what moment that passing occurs. It knows it is experiencing something that it does not understand, that seems just beyond its grasp. The twilight state is, then, the point of intersection between the known and the unknown; in it the self does not know whether to say: "I am awake; I will sleep" or "I was awake; I do sleep." When it does not know what time it is, it recognizes the extent of its own ignorance.

It was in this focus on the difficult moment of transition between two modes of being and two time frames that Marcel Proust found the strength of Nerval's narrative technique. Commenting on Nerval's *Sylvie*, Proust noted that "One is obliged at every moment to turn the preceding pages to see where one is, whether it is present or recollection of the past." He describes his own desire to fix the "pictures" seen in the moments of transition between one state of consciousness and another: "Sometimes, at the moment of falling asleep, one perceives them, one wishes to fix and define their charm, and then one awakens and sees them no more, one lets oneself go and before one has been able to fix them one is asleep, as if the understanding were not permitted to see them." Proust found that Nerval had not only succeeded in seizing such moments as isolated instances but had also been able to see in these moments general patterns: "these mysterious laws of thought which I have often wished to express and which I find expressed in *Sylvie*." What is great and "inexpressible" in *Sylvie* "is not in the words [but] all mixed in between the words."[9]

This is even more the case in *Aurélia*, where the movement from one time frame to another and back again is more rapid still than in *Sylvie*. It is to be glimpsed in the relations between words, specifically between verbs, rather than in individual words themselves.[10] The way

9. These quotations (as well as the chapter's epigraph) are taken from Marcel Proust's essay "Gérard Nerval," printed in the Pléiade volume *Contre Sainte-Beuve: Précédé de pastiches et mélanges* (Paris: Gallimard, 1973), pp. 238, 235, 239, 242.

10. On the significance of the difference between words, see the discussion of the interpretant in the Conclusion.

the verbs refer to each other and thus give rise to the effect Proust notes may be seen in a paragraph in which the narrator asks himself whether the figure glimpsed in the police station was "the *Double* of the legends" (1.9). What is at issue throughout this paragraph is, once again, the relation between time and knowing, between the way the narrator knows the earthly world, "vie," and the way he knows the supernatural world, "rêve." Nerval's use of tenses in this paragraph to mark off different periods of time and the attitudes toward "vie" and "rêve" in each period is careful and regular, once again establishing a definite norm with respect to which deviation can be noted. The first sentence begins: "Je ne sais comment expliquer . . ." (I don't know how to explain . . .). The time frame is the present: the moment of writing is life time rather than dream time. "Mais quel était donc cet esprit . . ." (But who, then, was this spirit . . .): this standard use of the imperfect tense makes clear that the spirit's existence has some undefined duration, but its context by no means suggests that this duration extends into the moment of *Aurélia*'s writing. "N'avais-je pas été frappé de l'histoire de ce chevalier qui combattit toute une nuit dans une forêt contre un inconnu qui était lui-même?" (Had I not been struck by the story of that knight who fought all night in a forest against an unknown who was himself?). The past imperfect tense beginning this sentence emphasizes that the narrator, in the present, knows not only that the Double's appearance in the police station took place in the past but also that something occurred ("N'avais-je pas été frappé . . .") in an even more distant past. That is, the paragraph shows a clear sense of the distinctions among discrete periods of time.

But the paragraph ends in temporal as well as epistemological ambiguity: "Quoi qu'il en soit, je crois que l'imagination humaine n'a rien inventé qui ne soit vrai, dans ce monde ou dans les autres, et je ne pouvais douter de ce que j'avais *vu* si distinctement" (Whatever the case may be, I believe the human imagination has invented nothing that is not true, in this world or in the other, and I could not doubt what I had so distinctly *seen*; original emphasis).[11] This sentence moves from a present-tense affirmation of belief in the truth of the imagined to an imperfect-tense assertion of inability to doubt that truth.

Although, with respect to verbal convention, there is nothing even slightly aberrant in Nerval's use of tenses here, the relation between the

---

11. The italicization of *vu* is dropped in the alternate versions presented below, so that the variant forms of *pouvoir* may be emphasized instead.

two principal verbs creates precisely the effect of uncertainty that Proust describes. Each of the two coordinate independent clauses carries the same message—belief in imagination in the first clause, and non-doubt of vision in the second—yet each of them is constructed around a different tense. The impact of the imperfect tense in this context is clearer when one considers how the two clauses would function together if the present tense, the near past tense, or the past definite tense were substituted for the imperfect (necessitating tense changes elsewhere in the sentence as well):

je crois que l'imagination humaine n'a rien inventé qui ne soit vrai . . . et je ne *puis* douter de ce que j'ai vu . . .

je crois que l'imagination humaine n'ait rien inventé qui ne soit vrai . . . et je n'*ai pu* douter de ce que j'ai vu . . .

je crus que l'imagination humaine n'avait rien inventé que ne fut vrai . . . et je ne *pus* douter de ce que j'avais vu . . . .

What is significant is the effect of the juxtaposition of the imperfect with other tenses, for it indicates that whether the narrator's belief in his vision of the Double continues into the moment of narrating the story is an unsettled question. It would have been answered affirmatively by the first two of the foregoing models, negatively by the third. It is instead left open, because to provide an answer to this question would be to eliminate the problem that is the story's motive force. A grammarian has described the imperfect tense (from *imperfectus*, not completely finished or carried out) in the following terms: "There are [implicit in the imperfect tense] limits . . . but one does not see them (*or does not want to see them*)."[12]

That the inability to doubt the imagination is expressed in the imperfect tense indicates that the narrator does not see the beginning or the end of his inability to doubt. Indeed, it is crucial to *Aurélia* that the narrator see neither a moment when he begins to believe nor a moment when he ceases to believe his imagination. There must be no discoverable dividing line between belief and unbelief, for the narrator must know that his visions are simultaneously false and true. *Aurélia* is

12. Holger Sten, *Les Temps du verbe fini (indicatif) en français moderne*, Det Koniglige Danske Videnskabernes Selskab, Historisk-filologiske Meddelelser, 33, no. 3 (Copenhagen, 1952), p. 127. Emphasis added in my translation.

subtitled "le rêve *et* la vie," not "le rêve *ou* la vie." Dream and life are concurrent.

The ambiguous relation between two selves, two time frames, and two ways of knowing is, in *Aurélia*, most typically expressed in this way, through the juxtaposition of a verb in the imperfect tense with a verb in some other tense. To paraphrase Proust, it is in the space "mixed between" imperfect tense verbs and verbs in other tenses that the narrator's double makes its presence, or its present-ness, felt. The narrator generally relegates to a clearly demarcated past time, cut off from the present, those attitudes characteristic of dream. He speaks in tenses indicating that the past is over and that he is, at the moment of writing the description, cured of the delusions he describes. Often, however, there is a sudden movement from those tenses that represent cut-off past time to an imperfect tense implying that the dream attitudes have not been banished and that dream continues in wakefulness. A traditional description of the French imperfect tense is "a present in the past." Nerval's use of the imperfect, however, often inverts this formula by bringing the past into the present.

Sometimes in *Aurélia*, other tenses in various combinations also serve to create rapid shifts in temporal perspective.[13] As Proust says of the earlier *Sylvie*, one must constantly look back to see whether one is reading about a state of vision or a return from vision. Each verb, in fact, must be questioned in a deliberate attempt to slow the fluctuations in temporal perspective: that is, to understand them rather than simply to feel their effect.[14] The initial theme of *Aurélia* is made manifest in its structure; the reader must try to measure just how distant dream time is from life time at particular moments in the narrative, thus imitating the narrator's inquiry.

Authorial Mastery, Readerly Madness

But the oscillation between temporal perspectives which struck Proust as innovative is, however remarkable, new in only a quite specific sense. Rapid changes in the narrator's viewpoint occur in any

---

13. Among the most revealing examples of temporal ambiguity are the brusque movements between imperfect and past definite in a passage that imitates memory while being about memory (II.2) and from past definite to near past in a passage on the sun (I.10), that which marks time and later comes to represent the disruption of time through imagination (II.4; see also I.6).

14. Certainly, one must first have questioned whether Nerval's irregularities in tense usage are not simply errors, especially in the light of the critical tradition—initiated by

number of well-known texts and are designated by the traditional rhetorical term "irony." What is unusual about Nerval's changes in perspective is that they are temporal; they are, nonetheless, not different in structure from other types of irony, all of which are based on doubling. In *Aurélia* it is the time frame fixed at the very start of the story which is made to appear double in structure. The temporal irony consists in oscillation between this time frame and another, between one that is continuous and one discontinuous with the moment of the opening of the narrative. The moment of beginning to write signifies a time frame in which the narrator records: "Je vais essayer . . . de transcrire les impressions" (I am going to try . . . to transcribe the

---

Aurélia's first editors, Théophile Gautier and Arsène Houssaye—that regards the text, found in proof at the time of Nerval's suicide, as unfinished because of lacunae in both manuscripts and proofs. Béguin and Richer, however, specifically reject the notion that *Aurélia* is incomplete, and in introducing his facsimile edition of the manuscript fragments, Richer comments: "[The reader] will note that almost nothing, in Nerval's literary manuscripts, reveals the threat of insanity": *Les Manuscrits d' "Aurélia" de Gérard de Nerval* (Paris: Société d'Edition "Les Belles Lettres," 1972), p. 2. Henri Lemaitre, in an edition of Nerval's *Oeuvres* (Paris: Garnier, 1966), p. 750, argues that the lacunae in the second part do not suggest an unfinished work, for the two parts show careful symmetries. My examination of the fragments of the "Première *Aurélia*" formerly in the collection of Dr. Lucien-Graux, now at the Bibliothèque Nationale, leads me to agree with Richer. It therefore seems legitimate to follow Proust in seeing the irregularities as representing a major innovation in narrative technique, especially since they are by no means random but present features that follow a pattern. Proust was himself criticized for using the verbs as Nerval did; parts of *A la recherche du temps perdu* have been taken to be unfinished or weak because of their irregularities in tense. According to Robert Vigneron, in one passage, for example, "the imperfects and past definites follow each other with no apparent reason, as if the author, unable definitively to adopt one viewpoint rather than another, had left its temporal transpositions unfinished": "Structure de *Swann*: Prétentions et Défaillances," *Modern Philology* 44 (1946–47), 127, translation mine. Gérard Genette, in *Figures III* (Paris: Seuil, 1972), translated by Jane E. Lewin as *Narrative Discourse* (Ithaca, NY: Cornell University Press, 1980), disagrees with Vigneron and seems almost ready to call Proust's syntactic aberrations deliberate: "This ambiguity does not thereby justify the explanatory hypothesis of an 'incomplete temporal transposition.' I believe that I even glimpse a presumption, at least, to the contrary" (*Figures*, p. 172; *Discourse*, p. 147). "Even if we must make (considerable) allowances for external circumstances, there undoubtedly remains in Proust, at work in such pages just as we have already met it elsewhere, a sort of undertow of will— perhaps scarcely conscious—to liberate the forms of narrative temporality from their dramatic function, to let them play for their own sake" (*Figures*, p. 178; *Discourse*, pp. 154–55). The uneasiness of Proust's critics in the face of his syntactic innovation emphasizes the very novelty of his attempt. According to a pattern not unfamiliar in the rhetoric of criticism, attention was first focused on a crucial aspect of Proust's work only through a misreading of it; in short, the copy suffered much the same critical fate as the model.

impressions). Transcription is his characteristic activity in this—rather than in the imagining—time frame, and it is the concept of transcription that is undercut by the temporal irony.

The time frame of transcription is to be associated at first with "vie" more than with "rêve." In the time of "vie," the narrator claims, an effort is made to transcribe—that is, to double or repeat graphically—the experiences of the time of "rêve." In fact, though, the time in which the imaginative experiences to be transcribed occur and the time in which the actual transcription takes place are one and the same; that is, the writing time is not and cannot be double in structure. As it is made to appear doubled, however, there occurs a redistribution of connotation between the paired terms of the subtitle, coloring all the concepts associated with each. The relative positions of "rêve" and "vie" are nearly inverted as the notion that the fiction is a transcription of past feelings remembered rather than a present creation of them in writing becomes more convincing. "Vie," clearly associated with transcribing time at the outset, becomes more and more associated with the fictive remembered time as the second life takes on increasingly privileged status, becoming a more deeply real form of life than the "first."

The fictive doubling of the writing time, with the consequent redistribution of value from "rêve" to "vie," is brought about by the same device that is used to achieve doubling within the story: repetition. Characters, events, images, and ideas that are presented as occurring in one time and therefore as temporally discrete are shown to be similar to those occurring in another time and are no longer temporally discrete but part of a repetitive temporal structure. In the second part of *Aurélia* (II.5) there is an especially striking example of such a metamorphosis of something that is single, first, into something that is related by similarity to something else and, then, into something that is part of a repetitive series extending across time.

Pendant mon sommeil, j'eus une vision merveilleuse. Il me semblait que la déesse m'apparaissait, me disant: 'Je suis la même que Marie, la même que ta mère, la même aussi que sous toutes les formes tu as toujours aimée. A chacune de tes épreuves, j'ai quitté l'un des masques dont je voile mes traits, et bientôt tu me verras telle que je suis.'

(During my sleep, I had a marvelous vision. It seemed to me that the goddess appeared to me, saying: "I am the same as Mary, the same as your mother, as well as the same woman whom you have always loved in all the different forms. At each of your trials, I have dropped one of the masks with which I always veil my face, and soon you will see me as I am.")

Such extensions of what are essentially metaphors into the temporal realm unify—or, rather, constitute—the narrative. Because two images are similar, the two time periods in which they occur seem to reflect each other. One moment, so mirrored in another, will therefore appear to have been extended, and the resemblance between what occurs within the two moments will be taken as duration, just as reflections in a sequence of mirrors will be taken as depth.

In the same way, one moment of writing is made to seem doubled through the creation of apparent repetition. The writing, it is claimed, is not discrete, something unto itself, but rather a copy of something else, for example, an insight or inner experience. The relationship of similarity between insight or experience, on the one hand, and a copy, on the other, creates the double structure of the writing. Once this double structure is established, it is metamorphosed from a doubling derived from similarity to a doubling extended over time. Metaphor becomes history. The insight or inner experience is said to be a memory, an inner copy of an event that occurred in the past. In the writing, then, by means of the same two-step process used in the story, what is written in the present is cast onto the screen of the past. The present thus appears to acquire duration, a quality that it cannot, in fact, possess.

One of the important consequences of such literary metamorphosis is a fundamental change in the status of the writer, a change that may be the writer's primary motivation in bringing about the metamorphosis. A synchrony that recalls human limitation becomes instead a synchrony that implies omniscience. The synchronic reality, an image written in a single passing moment, is fictionalized into a diachronic narrative structured through repetition, and this repetition in turn suggests a synchrony visible from a point of view larger than that of mortal beings.

Nerval described the desire to perceive such a superhuman synchrony in the preface to his translation of *Faust*; the preface, published in 1840, anticipates the concerns of *Aurélia*, interpreting Goethe's work in terms of the relation between time and knowledge:

Cet infini toujours béant, qui confond la plus fort raison humaine, n'effraye point le poète de *Faust*; il s'attache à en donner une définition et une formule. . . . Bien plus, non content d'analyser le vide et l'inexplicable de l'infini présent, il s'attaque de même à celui du passé. Pour lui, comme pour Dieu sans doute, rien ne finit, ou du moins rien ne se transforme que la matière. . . . Il serait consolant de penser, en effet, que rien ne meurt de ce qui a frappé l'intelligence, et que l'éternité conserve dans son sein une sorte d'histoire universelle, visible par les yeux de l'âme, synchronisme divin, qui nous ferait participer un jour à la science de Celui qui voit d'un seul coup d'oeil tout l'avenir et tout le passé.

(This always gaping infinite, which confounds the strongest human intelligence, does not at all frighten the poet of *Faust*; he is intent on giving a definition of and a formula for it. . . . What's more, not satisfied with analyzing the abyss and the unexplainable of the present infinite, he takes on as well that of the past. For him, as for God no doubt, nothing ends, or at least nothing is transformed but matter. . . . It would be comforting to think, in fact, that nothing of what has struck the understanding dies, and that eternity preserves in its breast a kind of divine synchronism, which would one day make us participate in the knowledge of the One who sees in a single glance all the future and all the past.)[15]

In the following chapter I discuss a passage from Baudelaire that also asserts the immortality of everything that has ever been thought. Did such immortality exist, both exegesis and interpretation would be fully possible. But, even though this "synchronisme divin" is not available to mortals, at least something quite like it can be constructed, through writing. The one who constructs it—that is, the one who convincingly presents him- or herself as seeing from a point of view beyond that actually available to a finite being—is elevated to a superior position. The writer's position is especially privileged when a conviction is awakened, in the writer as well as others, that she or he actually has seen a "synchronisme divin" and not merely constructed it. The reader will follow the same impulse toward immortality when pursuing exegetical reading with too much passion.

Nerval, perhaps unfortunately for his personal equanimity, recognized the falsity of any sense of authorial mastery over time and the reading process. Traces of irony in his description of Goethe's undertaking indicate mockery of the writer who pretends to an understanding which is, for temporal reasons, unavailable to him: "Bien plus, non content d'*analyser le vide* et l'inexplicable de l'*infini présent*. . . . Pour lui,

15. Gérard de Nerval, *Oeuvres complémentaires, La Vie des lettres*, ed. Jean Richer (Paris: Minard, 1959), 1:13–14, translation mine.

comme pour Dieu *sans doute* . . ." Nerval's awareness of the futility of undertaking a project that demands a knowledge exceeding human temporal limits had made him describe ironically his *Les Filles du feu* (The Daughters of Fire) in which he had believed he was capturing the series of all his past lives (Nerval, *Oeuvres*, 1:15), as a "livre infaisable" (unwriteable book). The slightly later *Aurélia* is in this sense even more "unwriteable."

If only fleetingly, *Aurélia* makes visible what exists in invisible form in other works. Temporal doubling has the same form as the writer's relationship to his or her language, insofar as writing is a creation of duration for a lived moment that vanishes: the moment of writing.[16] The temporally doubled structure is, however, a simplification. Writing meant to be read, so far as its writer knows (and hopes), potentially exists in an infinity of future moments, which the writer envisions by reference to a series of past moments that he or she purports to be "transcribing." The moments associated with writing are thus multiple rather than merely double.

When schematically reduced to two, however, these moments may be described as the relative present and the relative past. I introduced these concepts in Chapter 2, when I described the structure of Francesca's speech. In relation to the author, the present is the time *of* writing, and the past is a remembered experience *about which* he or she writes in an effort to make the moment of that remembered experience recur in some future moment when the text is read. In relation to the reader, the present is the time of reading (which was the writer's future), and the past is the time of writing (which was the writer's present) as well as, in some cases, the time about which the writer seems to write. The writer has no real access to the future (the reader's present), just as the reader has no access to the writer's present (the reader's past). Yet each struggles to have what cannot be had, to see what cannot be seen.

16. Juliet Flower MacCannell has shown how a similar notion of the relationship between writing and temporality functions in Rousseau: "Repetition is the mechanism for extending the life of a present which is in fact impossible to extend. Just as the fiction of the idyll of the cherries—its being written—was the source of that 'duration' Rousseau ascribed to a past moment, so, too, in the *Dialogues* Rousseau settles on a fiction as that which gives 'constancy' to 'Jean-Jacques'' manner of being": "History and Self-Portrait in Rousseau's Autobiography," *Studies in Romanticism* 13 (1974), 297. This notion, at work in the *Essai sur l'origine des langues*, is described by Paul de Man, "The Rhetoric of Blindness," in *Blindness and Insight*, pp. 102–41.

To simplify the model further, one might say that the past always belongs to the author as the present belongs to the reader, and that each wants to possess not only his or her own time frame but also the other's. Each has one but is driven to seek another. At times, a dialectical exchange between moments may seem to occur in passing, as it does in the fictive structure Nerval constructed by means of temporal irony. More often, however, the attempt at exchange will be felt to end in failure—as it does for the narrator, whose madness is, he says, caused by his readings.

It is never quite possible to read both in the past and in the present. One inevitably reads in only one moment while nonetheless desiring to read in two: that is, to make one's mind live in a moment other than one's own, to know something as it was known (or, from the writer's viewpoint, will be known) at another time. The "other" moment in which one wishes to have one's mind exist, however, is always the province of someone else: for the reader, the author; for the author, the reader. For this reason, author and reader are often seen as inevitably locked in struggle; and the author (like Boccaccio) imagines the reader's victory as bringing dismemberment, while the reader imagines the author's victory as bringing madness. In fact, however, they struggle not against each other but against the common enemy: time.

Chapter 6

Baudelaire:
Battling the Reader

> . . . to disclose the structure of timely utterance. . . .
> GEOFFREY HARTMAN,
> *Deconstruction and Criticism*

The temporal structure of Nerval's *Aurélia* intermittently makes visible a process of substitution that Western literature regularly hides: the substitution of an apparent battle between author and reader over control of the text's meaning for what is instead really a struggle against time. The transformation of the desire to use written language as a device to conquer time into a struggle between reader and author for control of the text serves to mask the true character of this desire, which must be admitted to be utopian, futile, ultimately even mad. One might well construe the comment of the Nervalian narrator, "This madness is the fault of my reading," to indicate a madness caused not by certain books themselves but by a particular hermeneutic stance taken with respect to them. To conceive the relation between reader and author as one of bitter rivalry rather than fraternal assistance is to set up a screen on which a kind of hierarchical struggle is endlessly projected and which thus hides the temporal element that is the crux of all hermeneutic activity.

As I pointed out early in the first chapter, the conception of reader and author as enemies plays a recurrent role in the writings of Charles Baudelaire. Its best-known appearance is in "Au Lecteur," a poem discussed in the present chapter, along with other writings by Baudelaire which treat the hostile relations between author and reader in contexts that nonetheless inevitably betray their hidden temporal concerns. First, however, it is essential to inquire into the setting in which Baudelaire's works initially met their readers. What features of the history of reading in France in Baudelaire's time helped him mask the character of the author's and reader's common struggle against time as a struggle, instead, between author and reader? I argue that the change in attitude from Dante's fraternal concern for the reader to the contempt shown by Baudelaire reflects historical change in the character of reading and, especially, a major change in the readers these authors addressed.

"Dans le bon temps du romantisme"

The phrase used to head this section appears in the first, highly ironic, sentence of one of Baudelaire's earlier works, *La Fanfarlo* (published in 1847).[1] It indicates a particular attitude toward the romantic movement, which had dominated Parisian literary life in Baudelaire's formative years: a kind of nostalgia voiced with tongue in cheek. An English equivalent might be "in the good old days of romanticism," suggesting (1) the loss of something, (2) the high value assigned by some individual or group to what is lost, and (3) skepticism about that assignment of high value, created by the ironic tone of the phrase as a whole. It raises the question, should one (in 1847) lament the passing of romanticism?

The year 1830 is often taken to represent the heyday of French romanticism: in that year Hugo's *Hernani* had its first, clamorous public performance, and the July Revolution brought France its first constitutional monarch. Albert George points out one reason why Baudelaire, almost twenty years after the triumph of Hugo and Louis-Philippe, may have had to look back at the good old days of romanticism with a very skeptical eye:

> Successful romanticism was to receive a great shock when, after *Hernani*, it discovered itself facing a public quite unlike any ever known, one that lived under conditions undreamed of by literary rebels. When the patrons disappeared in the rubble of the old regime, writers sud-

---

1. All citations of Baudelaire's works refer to *Oeuvres complètes*, ed. Claude Pichois, 2 vols. (Paris: Pléiade, 1975–76), © Editions Gallimard Bibliothèque de la Pléiade. Translations are my own except where indicated. My treatment of the new relation between poet and reader in mid-nineteenth-century France may be understood by reference to Hayden White's discussion of the ambivalence toward rhetoric evinced by historians during the period; see his *Metahistory: The Historical Imagination in Nineteenth-Century Europe* (Baltimore, Md.: Johns Hopkins University Press, 1973).

denly discovered that they must woo the buying public in order to make a living. But the purchaser of books had changed character since as recently as the Restoration [of the Bourbons in 1814]. To make a decent living, a writer found himself forced to cater to the whims of large numbers of the newly educated who were scarcely literate enough to appreciate the old poetic values. The men who had struggled so hard for verse came to realize that the 19th century had become the age of the masses and that two new factors now had to be considered: the reading tastes of the multitude and the effects of the Industrial Revolution. . . . On the eve of the July Revolution, the romanticists found that they had won a Pyrrhic triumph.[2]

The "good old days of romanticism" marked the advent of an entirely new kind of relationship between author and reader. Thereafter, a successful romantic author had to master a new species of authorial hustle. The need to find an audience and, in some sense, to sell one's works to that audience in order to live was hardly new. Joachim Du Bellay, for example, had satirized "Le Poète courtisan" (The courtier poet),[3] criticizing with great bitterness those conditions in mid-sixteenth-century France that forced talented young men of his class to choose between financial insecurity and life as courtly flatterers. But DuBellay could jab at the courtly poet only because it was in his day becoming possible to write for a new class of readers, the cultured urban professionals.

Baudelaire and Nerval no longer had the luxury of the choice available to their sixteenth-century predecessors. The reader whom their education had trained them to address had, for all practical purposes, vanished.[4] The Parisian salons of the seventeenth and eighteenth centuries, where a thinker or writer could find an audience capable of providing both moral and monetary support, had largely disappeared.

2. Albert Joseph George, *The Development of French Romanticism: The Impact of the Industrial Revolution on Literature* (Syracuse, N.Y.: Syracuse University Press, 1955), p. 37. Also pertinent to this discussion are Walter Benjamin's extended meditations on Baudelaire's relation to his historical and his rhetorical reader, "On Some Motifs in Baudelaire," and, in a more general sense, the classic essay "The Work of Art in the Age of Mechanical Reproduction," both translated by Harry Zohn in Benjamin's *Illuminations*, ed. Hannah Arendt (New York: Schocken Books, 1969), pp. 155–200 and 217–51. Compare also Chapter 1, n. 29, on Jauss's analysis of the problem.

3. The poem appears in Bernard Weinberg's anthology *French Poetry of the Renaissance* (Carbondale: Southern Illinois University Press, 1954), pp. 65–69.

4. Paul de Man, *The Rhetoric of Romanticism* (New York: Columbia University Press, 1984), p. 253, alludes to the reputation of both Baudelaire and Nerval as neoclassicists, though denying the utility of such a label.

According to George, "the middle class . . . had replaced the nobility as the arbiter of a writer's fate."[5] George goes on to describe the new nineteenth-century readers in France as lacking "the habit of literature." They were, he suggests, interested only in content, and content related to their own experiences; they were quite blind to "subtleties of form" (p. 38).

In this regard, it is significant that neither Nerval nor Baudelaire succeeded in earning a living by publishing the kinds of writing for which they are best remembered today: poetry, prose poems, poetic narrative. Their work in these genres unquestionably requires a reader well trained to interrogate "subtleties of form," but neither writer was able in his own day to find such readers in large enough numbers. Both Nerval and Baudelaire relied for support during much of their adult lives on what was then a relatively new field of endeavor—journalism.

For Nerval, this meant, above all, travel literature: *Voyage en Orient, Loréley: Souvenirs d'Allemagne, Un Tour dans le nord, Lettres d'Allemagne, Lettre des Flandres*, and so on; he was extremely productive in a genre whose roots Roland Barthes has traced to the rise of the nineteenth-century bourgeoisie.[6] He also succeeded in placing a certain amount of drama criticism with periodicals, allowing him to derive some income

---

5. "Nobility" here must be understood to mean not just the blood nobility but also the *noblesse de robe*, the legal and administrative class that played a prominent role in supporting French literature of the seventeenth and eighteenth centuries.

6. In his essay "The *Blue Guide*," which he published in *Mythologies*—cited here from the English translation by Annette Lavers (New York: Hill and Wang, 1973)— Roland Barthes discusses the "myth" of the picturesqueness of the Alps as dating from the nineteenth century, recalls Gide's association of it with "Helvetico-Protestant morality," and asserts that "the mythology of the *Blue Guide* [a well-known series of French travel books] dates back to the last century, to that phase in history when the bourgeoisie was enjoying a kind of new-born euphoria in *buying* effort" (p. 74). Barthes suggests that eighteenth-century travel was "based on human realities" and adds that "this myth of travel [as search for the picturesque] is becoming quite anachronistic, even among the bourgeoisie" (p. 76), thus closely tying the vogue for the kind of travel literature Nerval wrote, focused on "riches" and the marvelous, to the nineteenth-century middle-class audience. They would "buy" what Nerval wrote about fabulous lands even if they could not yet buy enough freedom from their commercial activities to travel themselves. For an earlier dating of the advent of the "picturesque mountain," however, see Marjorie H. Nicolson, *Mountain Gloom and Mountain Glory: The Development of the Aesthetics of the Infinite* (Ithaca: Cornell University Press, 1959). Cf. also Denis Diderot's discussion of the relation between landscape and sentiment in "Entretiens sur 'Le Fils naturel,'" III, in his *Oeuvres esthétiques*, ed. Paul Vernière (Paris: Garnier Frères, 1968), pp. 135, 158, 160, 170.

from the extraordinary level of interest in the theater of Paris during the reign of Louis-Philippe.[7] Pierre Gascar's analysis of Parisian box-office receipts in relation to population for the 1830–31 season indicates a rate of theater attendance never since equaled; he offers two plausible explanations, both of which suggest useful perspectives on the changing relations between author and reader during the period in which Nerval and Baudelaire struggled unsuccessfully to support themselves as writers:

> To be sure, the bourgeoisie, a larger group than formerly, feels the need in the evening to leave the sales counters behind in order to show itself in public in its very best finery, and it has more money than ever before with which to do it. But the resurgence or development of the drama also derives from the quest on the part of writers for a more vigorous means of expression than that provided by the book. It is a matter not only of desire for better communication with the public but also of the desire to convey passion with all its accents, which will always resonate better on a stage than on printed pages.[8]

Gascar's clear preference for drama over all other genres, including fiction and poetry, cannot entirely disguise the nature of the situation he is describing. The continuing high esteem in which *Madame Bovary* and *Les Fleurs du mal* are held suggests that mid-nineteenth-century French fiction and poetry might be taken "to convey passion with all its accents" at least as successfully as the numerous plays of the period that have been forgotten.

What is really at stake in the situation Gascar describes is the mid-nineteenth-century public's minimal interest in "printed pages" and the sense, ascribed to writers of the time, that to write books is not to express oneself "vigorously." I take this to mean that writing books to be read rather than plays to be performed brought the writer less sense of himself as a powerful actor in the cultural arena. The public was much less a reading public desirous of displaying its refined sensibility in salon conversation about novels and poems than a theatrical public desirous of displaying its refined taste in and ability to purchase attire. The style was being set (no pun intended) for a time when the names of

7. Numerous examples appear in Gérard de Nerval, *Oeuvres complètes*, ed. Jean Guillaume, Claude Pichois, et al. (Paris: Pléiade, 1984), pp. 1165–1261.
8. Pierre Gascar, *Gérard de Nerval et son temps* (Paris: Gallimard, 1981), p. 47.

fashion designers would be better known to the Parisian "public" than those of novelists.[9]

If Nerval made the barest of livings as a travel writer and drama critic,[10] Baudelaire found an intermittent market for his art criticism; well-known examples include the monographic *Salons* of 1845 and 1846. The latter opens with an introductory section addressed "To the bourgeois," indicating that he expects his critical monograph to be purchased by the bourgeoisie, with its growing interest in the acquisition and display of art objects and in the display of its own finery and aesthetic perspicacity while visiting exhibitions and galleries. Baudelaire makes no attempt to disguise the cynicism of his appeal to these readers:

> You are the majority,—[in] number and intelligence;—thus you are the force,—which is justice.
>
> Some [are] knowledgeable, others [are] property owners;—a glorious day will come when the knowledgeable will be property owners, and the property owners will be knowledgeable. Then your power will be complete, and no one will protest against it.
>
> While awaiting this ultimate harmony, it is proper that those who are only property owners should aspire to become knowledgeable; for knowledge is a pleasure no less great then property. . . .
>
> It is thus to you, bourgeois, that this book, by nature, is dedicated; for any book which does not address itself to the majority,—[in] number and intelligence,—is a foolish book. [2.415–17][11]

Baudelaire makes clear in this dedicatory passage that he sees the bourgeoisie ("property owners") as lacking knowledge of the arts. The

9. I use "public" in this paragraph with Erich Auerbach's analyses of changes in the meaning of that term in mind. See esp. his "La Cour et la ville," in *Scenes from the Drama of European Literature* (New York: Meriden Books, 1959), pp. 133–79.

10. Kofman, *Nerval*, pp. 19–20, cites a pathetic letter that Nerval wrote to his father some six months before his suicide: "My works are a form of capital which I will increase, if it please God, and which, even if it is after my death, would suffice to settle my account with mankind." François Constans ("Aurélia," p. 266) notes that proofs for the second part of *Aurélia* were sent to Nerval at a small hotel, which sent them back a few days after his suicide with the indication that his name was unknown there. This suggests that Nerval, rather recently released from a doctor's care, had found no fixed address at the time of his death. See also *Oeuvres* 1:1488–89 for the public debate just after Nerval's suicide as to whether it was attributable to extreme poverty or to sickness alone.

11. The translation is mine; since the language of the text is not analyzed here, I have not provided the French, nor do I do so in quoting other passages from Baudelaire's prose where precise nuances are not at issue.

two pages that I have indicated by ellipsis urge the bourgeois, tired out from "public affairs and commerce," to feel no obligation to acquire such knowledge and to substitute feeling: "It is through feeling alone that you are to understand art" (2: 416). That such advice is given with a sneer must be clear from the tone of the dedicatory section; one need not have recourse to Baudelaire's own artistic practice, which constantly calls "feeling alone" into question.

To remember Christine de Pizan's dedicatory references to "those who are hardly learned poets [*clercs poètes*]" is to realize how vast is the gulf separating the author in early fifteenth-century Paris—when a poet was still basically a kind of servant or clerk and the intended reader a royal or noble—from the author writing in the same city four and a half centuries later. In both periods, rule is understood to be in the hands of those without learning, but there is a sense in the works of Baudelaire, a poet unquestionably nostalgic for the *ancien régime*,[12] that this is not a desirable state of affairs. While Christine can without any bitterness whatever see herself as both more learned than and a servant to her patrons, Baudelaire finds such a situation deeply offensive.

Possessed of a sterner will and greater shrewdness than Nerval, he discovered in the essay form still another journalistic genre through which he could buy the support he needed to write poetry. But the preoccupation with his own continuing flirtation with poverty and the need to pay court to a public for which he has contempt certainly did not vanish. In an essay first published anonymously in 1845, whose title translates as "how a person of genius pays his debts," Baudelaire presents a sneering and no doubt jealous picture of Balzac. Now Balzac had created in *Illusions perdues* (*Lost Illusions*) and its sequel a wholly chilling portrait of the early nineteenth-century French writer as a young man forced by poverty into a life of prostitution and chicanery. Lucien de Rubempré's lessons on how to manipulate the world of journalism are merely the starting point on a long downward path that ultimately leads him to suicide in a prison cell. The Balzac envisioned in Baudelaire's essay, however, profited from those lessons in a way Lucien could only have dreamed of. Crushed one evening by the need to pay the next day a note for 1,200 francs, he successfully persuades the editor of two journals to buy from him two articles, to be signed with his own illustrious name, for the sum of 1,500 francs. He then

12. The best-known suggestion of such nostalgia is Baudelaire's poem "Le Cygne" (1:85–87), the second part of which begins with the exclamation "Paris change!"

engages two less well-known writers to write the articles for 150 francs each, and everyone involved winds up satisfied.

This essay is remarkable in two senses. First, it identifies itself, with some legitimacy, as providing a realistic representation of the contemporary Parisian literary world, for it uses real people as characters: not only Balzac but Théophile Gautier, Nerval, and several others are recognizable from prominent clues, and the whole episode has been tied by Baudelaire's editors to two actual articles published in September 1839. Second, the essay shows how strong was Baudelaire's desire to metamorphose writerly poverty from real-life suffering into rhetorical dazzle. The Balzac one encounters in biography was hardly so sublimely clever as the figure Baudelaire's resentment creates; he was plagued by debt, not just occasionally but constantly, because of speculative investment that was anything but clever. But Baudelaire mythologizes this titan of financial anxiety into a kind of monetary Houdini and concludes that he has "wished to show that the great poet knew how to unknot a banknote as easily as the most mysterious and complex novel" (2.8). Baudelaire thus equates financial dealings with plot construction. He takes the very real predicament of not only Balzac but also the lesser lights who will ghostwrite on very short notice for little pay and turns this predicament into evidence of literary skill. He is deluding himself, but no doubt the illusion is a necessary one to the Baudelaire of 1845.

Nearly twenty years later, in 1863 (1:XLVIII), Baudelaire himself sold to a publication the rights for *Les Fleurs du mal* and *Le Spleen de Paris*, knowing that he had already sold these rights to another publisher in 1861. When this "genius"-like attempt to pay his debts was unsuccessful, Baudelaire actually left Paris for Brussels in 1864, both to avoid his creditors and to earn honoraria that had (misleadingly) been promised to him for a projected series of lectures. It was in this state of financial exile that he became ever more gravely ill and was brought back to Paris when he was no longer able to function, only to live out his final year in a hospital. Even as early as 1845, Baudelaire saw what the life of a writer in mid-nineteenth-century France was likely to be; he observed Balzac, Gautier, and Nerval. But he transformed this repellent reality into an aspect of the myth of the gallant romantic artist, creating the fantasy of a fiscal Don Juan who manipulates his world with dazzling success, just as he manipulates words on the page.

The very extent of Baudelaire's activity as a writer of essays is an index of the urgency of his need to support himself through journalism, criticism, and translations; his poems did not find readers numerous enough or wealthy enough to relieve him of financial pressure. Like Nerval, Baudelaire was essentially homeless throughout his adult life, forced to move frequently from one temporary lodging to another. This homelessness was quite different from Dante's. Dante was forced to learn "how bitter it is to eat another man's salt" because of a politically motivated exile. It was his relation to his readers that brought him the possibility of shelter with his several patrons. Baudelaire's painful situation was *caused* by his readers, specifically by their failure to respond to his work in a way adequate to his needs. His "Advice to Young Writers," first published in an 1846 essay, established an essential relation between reader and writer which could hardly be more different from Dante's evocation of a fraternal relation (or Christine's of a maternal one): "Today, one must produce a lot;— one must thus make haste slowly; it is therefore necessary that every shot strike its mark, and that no stroke be wasted" (2:17). Here is the language of military crisis applied to the act of writing. Indeed, the language of armed stuggle pervades the entire essay.

In the passage just cited the young Baudelaire assesses the situation of contemporary writers, who could ill afford to spend a lifetime (as Baudelaire himself was to do) refining one volume of verse and a related volume of prose poems. Albert George emphasizes one reason for this pressure to "produce a lot": to make a living after the patrons disappeared, "a writer found himself forced to cater to the whims of large numbers" (p. 37). To be sure, technological innovation contributed as much to this change as did the elimination of the patron class in the Revolution. As George also shows (chapters 6–7), the introduction of much faster presses in France in the 1830s brought the writer a new market to replace the one the Revolution had destroyed; with the advent of the *roman-feuilleton* to keep readers purchasing regularly, attention turned definitively away from poetry and toward prose.

Baudelaire's evocation of conflict between reader and author, then, does reflect the economic reality of his life as a writer. But this reflection does not remain an end in itself in Baudelaire's work. Between the reality of the anxious poet cranking out journalistic pieces to survive and the picture of the gallant bohemian writing a preface addressed to the bourgeois who (he hopes) will buy his book there is a further distorting element that makes the picture rather more heroic than the reality. This element is Baudelaire's powerful desire to use his writing to overcome time.

Baudelaire's struggle is not so much against the bourgeois reader as it is against time, in all its guises. "One must therefore move *quickly*": it is the passage of time that is the writer's most powerful enemy. The passage of time does violence to the writer not only because he "must produce a lot" but also because he is robbed by history, deprived of the elite audience that would have appreciated his talents. Most fundamentally, it means that the writer can never be sure his words will be understood by his readers. The new insensitive public is a historical reality, which is *also* a figure for the old, ever-insensitive public.

Playing to the Gallery: The Poet as Spectacle, the Reader as Voyeur

To struggle to locate a thousand bourgeois "patrons," in the form of bookbuyers, to replace the wealthy patron one might have had in an earlier day was to fight a battle with no hope of success—unless one changed one's weapons. This Baudelaire was willing to do to only a very limited extent. He would write journalistic criticism, but no novel. His poems, both verse and prose, nonetheless project a kind of phantom novel, the protagonist of which is the poet.

Albert George's study of the impact of the Industrial Revolution on French romanticism emphasizes, along with the advent of a new literary audience and the changed economics of publication, two additional results: the triumph of prose—especially the novel—over verse, and the elaboration of a new literary mythology. Both developments figure prominently in Baudelaire's career or, rather, in his representation of his career and specifically of his relation to the readers upon whom that career depended. According to George, "the Revolution smashed the old mythology ruthlessly. . . . The suppression of the universities and the famous schools almost obliterated classical learning" (pp. 173–74). An important hero in the new mythology that replaced it, George asserts, was "the Poet" (p. 184).

Baudelaire does everything possible in his writing to invent himself as a peculiar kind of mythic hero-poet. He thus creates a fascinating persona likely to hold his reader's interest as firmly as that of the most scandalous roman-feuilleton. He further continues the romantic transformation of the role of the poet, from a person of intellect and taste into a titillating spectacle of passion and depravity.

Such a transformation had necessarily to be accompanied by a corresponding transformation in the fictive representation of the reader. How thorough this was may be judged by returning to landmarks in the vernacular literary tradition to recall the vernacular readers as they had been represented earlier. Dante and Christine are able to condescend to their readers, even depicting them as children, without sacrificing the sense that both poet and readers belong to the same community, a community uniting all Christian souls. Somewhat later writers are able to include both themselves and their readers in other imagined communities—of *honnêtes hommes*, say, or men of reason. The condescension of the late medieval vernacular writer in particular is qualified by an awareness, on the part of both writer and reader, that the vernacular writer is a servant and thus inferior to the most immediately intended circle of readers, the royal or noble patrons.

Baudelaire's condescension to his reader assumes an entirely different tone. It is above all angry: the condescension of a performer who puts on a spectacle (of "evil") that he knows will titillate his audience and therefore divest it of its money, even while he himself sometimes condemns what he does and those who urge him on to do it. The reader become a voyeur, and reading parallels pornography.

Thus develops the Baudelairean myth of reader and author as complicitous enemies, linked in a coupling that they hate and that augments their hatred of themselves: "hypocrite reader, my image, my brother." The material from which the myth is constructed is, as I have indicated, economic and historical reality. But this superstructure rests upon and covers a foundation laid by neither the French Revolution nor the Industrial Revolution but rather by the character of Western hermeneutic activity and its fundamental ambivalence about time.

To mythologize reading as a voyeuristic encounter with a titillating spectacle is to fabricate a fiction that will screen the desire to triumph over time, which forms the basis of Western hermeneutics. The hermeneutic myth that Baudelaire develops is like those that have gone before it (some of which have been traced in earlier chapters of this book) in that its elements are derived from contemporary history. Yet the organization of these elements into a myth that compels assent to its validity depends not on contemporary history but, to the contrary, on the will to turn away from it and from the ceaseless passing of time that impels it.

However it may be mythologized as a pathway to the future, reading is always an attempt to return to what is already known. Because such a return to the past is impossible, reading always, at one level, represents loss. In Baudelaire's writing, loss is met with rage and transformed into a spectacle of violence. But far from being unique, such a transformation is merely another instance of the pattern pointed out by Louis Marin (cited in the Introduction) as typical of hermeneutic mythology: the spatialization of a temporal problem.

Certainly Nerval, too, spatialized the problematic temporality of reading by making himself into a spectacle, both in life and through the narrators of his stories and the personae of his poems (most notably, among the poems, in "El Desdichado"). There is much truth in Pierre Gascar's suggestion that his friends foisted the role of writer-as-spectacle upon the biographical Nerval; nonetheless, Sarah Kofman is no doubt right in arguing that Nerval willingly embraced this role.

With Baudelaire, however, the question of manipulation by fellow writers scarcely arises. He was most interested in creating a bizarre persona for himself and was highly successful in manipulating contemporary writers into "buying" it; Sainte-Beuve is a conspicuous example.[13] Nearly all of Baudelaire's poetry, in both verse and prose, concerns the "I": its sensations, its perceptions, the changes it undergoes. Baudelaire's poetic work thus complies with the norms which, as Jonathan Culler has shown, shape Western lyric.[14]

But Baudelaire's poetry modifies in an important way the hermeneutic myth that had long brought the poetic persona onto the stage to revel in emotions that the reader was imagined to share. This imagined, potential sharing, traceable in vernacular lyric as far back as the troubadours, represents a hermeneutic crux. The relation between poet and reader is claimed to be intimate (for example, erotic or fraternal).

---

13. See Charles-Augustin Sainte-Beuve, "Des prochaines élections de l'Académie" (On the coming elections to the [French] Academy), in *Nouveau Monde*, 6th ed. (Paris: Calmann Lévy, 1885), vol. 1, where Baudelaire is made the representative of both eccentricity and opium "and a thousand detestable drugs." It should be clear that I am reading Baudelaire (as Sainte-Beuve did) in the context of romanticism and not as the first modern poetic voice. Baudelaire is, more obviously than most, a poet whom one can read either looking backward or looking forward, depending on whether one's bent at the moment of reading is more strongly exegetical or interpretive.

14. Jonathan Culler, "The Modern Lyric: Generic Continuity and Critical Practice," in Koelb and Noakes, *Comparative Perspective on Literature*, pp. 284–99 argues that Western lyric poetry is consistently read as concerning attitudes and that this reading convention determines admission into the lyric canon.

Their similarity is the very ground of the poem, its reason for being. Yet this similarity is, from a logical rather than a rhetorical viewpoint, a fiction, created by the reading of the poetic text according to those Western hermeneutic conventions that apply to the lyric. Fictional similarity between poet and poetry reader comes into being as a powerful weapon in the war that literature wages against time. The temporal gap that unfailingly and necessarily divides poet from reader appears to be erased by this fiction. The more a writer understands that such erasure of time, such merging of past (author) and future (reader), is impossible, the more fervent will be the effort to create the illusion that, on the contrary, it *is* possible. The work will thus reflect a deep ambivalence about time.

When Baudelaire precedes the famous words "my image, my brother" with the even more famous (because innovative and shocking) "*hypocrite* reader" (emphasis mine), he twists the convention of shared emotion into the somewhat different form of shared "evil."[15] This shift explicitly indicates a degree of moral doubt about the value of what is shared and who is sharing it, which in turn implicitly marks a degree of hermeneutic doubt about the character of the hermeneutic process itself. Baudelaire dramatizes this doubt most conspicuously in "Epigraph for a Condemned Book" (a title that alludes to the condemnation of *Les Fleurs du mal*). In this short poem, ambivalence about hermeneutic "sharing" and about the hermeneutic "sharer" is laid out in the form of two successive options. The octave describes the reader who will not understand the book, instructing him to throw it away; the sestet, at least through the middle of the last line, describes the reader who will share:

> Lecteur paisible et bucolique,
> Sobre et naif homme de bien,
> Jette ce livre saturnien,
> Orgiaque et mélancholique.

15. I have translated *mon semblable* as "my image" rather than as Joanna Richardson's "kinsman," in *Baudelaire: Selected Poems* (Harmondsworth: Penguin, 1975), p. 29, or Roy Campbell's "my twin," in *The Flowers of Evil: A Selection*, ed. Marthiel Mathews and Jackson Mathews (New York: New Directions, 1955), p. 5, since the French word emphasizes not family relationship but similarity in form. Translations below from *Paris Spleen* are from *Paris Spleen, 1869*, trans. Louise Varèse (New York: New Direction, 1970).

Si tu n'as fait ta rhétorique
Chez Satan, le rusé doyen,
Jette! Tu n'y comprendrais rien,
Ou tu me croirais hystérique.

Mais si, sans se laisser charmer,
Ton oeil sait plonger dans les gouffres,
Lis-moi, pour apprendre à m'aimer;

Âme curieuse qui souffres
Et vas cherchant ton paradis,
Plains-moi! . . . Sinon, je te maudis!

(Reader domestic, tolerant,
Sober, unsullied, honest man,
Cast down this book Saturnian,
Voluptuous and virulent.

If rhetoric you have not learnt
From Satan's artful lexicon,
Cast it away, then, simpleton!
You'd think me worse than vehement.

But if, remaining free from spells,
Your eyes can plumb the hellish deep,
Read me, and learn to love me well;

O soul who wants to know, and weeps,
And goes in quest of paradise.
Have pity! . . . Or receive my curse!)

[1:137; Richardson, p. 187]

The use of the first person pronoun here is complex. Its first appearance, in line 8, suggests that one important result of reading "this
book" (line 3) will be the reader's formation of an opinion about the
author. This notion differs radically from that of Dante, who emphasizes from the second line of the *Commedia* that the character based on
himself is important only insofar as he represents Everyman ("of our
life") and who feels obliged to offer justification on the one occasion
where his name appears in the poem (*Purgatorio* xxx).

By contrast, Baudelaire describes *Les Fleurs du mal* as a tool for the
reader who wishes to encounter the poet. Indeed, he goes further. In
"Epigraph," the authorial persona is actually equated with the text in
line 11 ("Read me"), and reading becomes an apprenticeship in reader-

author love ("and learn to love me"). The reader is described as having three options: not reading the book at all ("Cast down this book"); reading it and making a negative judgment about the author for lack of suitable rhetorical training; or reading it to fall in love with the author.

The second option implicitly alludes to what I have been describing as the exegetical model of reading (reconstructing the author, the author's viewpoint, and so on, through study), rejecting from participation in this model the unqualified reader. The third option proposes what I have described as interpretive reading, based on an implied sympathy between reader and author. In this instance, both possibilities imply voyeurism: either the viewing of the emotional contortions of a hysteric or the contemplation of a subject worthy of love and pity who nonetheless cannot be embraced because he is not really a subject but rather a text.

The figure of the poet as a spectacle being observed by a voyeuristic reader recurs frequently in Baudelaire's poetry over the entire span of his career. The long poem "Bénédiction," appearing as the first poem after "Au lecteur" in all three editions of *Les Fleurs du mal*, immediately follows the famous final line of "To the reader" and by implication introduces the "hypocrite reader" to the collection as a whole. In it, "the Poet" is satirized as a kind of Christ figure dedicated to the ideal, even while he is cursed and ridiculed by those closest to him: his mother (in an extended parody of the Magnificat) and his wife. When one whose vocation is to write is seen as ridiculous or is in some other way "misunderstood" even by such an intimate audience, the writer indeed becomes a spectacle.

The quasi-self-parody that opens *Les Fleurs du mal* thus implies a generalized inability to communicate on the part of the poet, an inability invoked repeatedly in Baudelaire's work. Nowhere is it rendered more succinctly than in the prose poem "Les Yeux des pauvres" ("The Eyes of the Poor"), first published just three years before Baudelaire's death. In this little fable, the narrator describes a day when he and his mistress "had duly promised each other that all our thoughts should be shared in common, and that our two souls henceforth be but one." In the evening, seated in an opulent cafe, they note a poor man with two ragged children staring through the window, a spectacle that moves the narrator and makes him feel a bit ashamed. Turning to look at his mistress's eyes "to read *my* thought in them" (emphasis Baudelaire's), the narrator is shocked to hear her say that she finds these people "insufferable" and wants him to ask the proprietor to chase them away. The narrator concludes: "[That's] how incommunicable thought is, even between two people in love!"(1:319, Varèse, 52–53).

So much, then, for the reader who will "learn to love" the poet and understand his words.[16]

Rhetoric Reversed:
The Reader Seduces the Author

It is no accident that the "other" in the fable of non-understanding just discussed is a woman. While the final, contemptuous line of the poem "Au lecteur" has become famous as an indicator of authorial ambivalence toward the reader, it is far from being Baudelaire's most characteristic presentation of the reader. On three occasions, Baudelaire treated the reader not as hypocritical brother but as woman.

As I noted in Chapter 4, male authors troubled by the temporality of reading have often created fictive readers who are female. The Judaeo-Christian tradition's inversion of the individual's biological history, to make of woman not the mother out of whom the son is born but rather the temporally second sex, provides the foundation for this specifically literary commonplace. Indeed, in Genesis, Eve is already a late-coming reader of a text written by God and by Adam the name-giver: a reader who chooses not to "read" the Tree of Knowledge as its Creator has decreed.[17] Thus, the difference between moment A, when there was a single truth to which all assented, and moment B, when more than a single choice presents itself, is converted into a difference between character A and character B; and B is dressed in a female body, while A remains in the normative body of a man. This translation of a temporal opposition into a sexual one is presented in an especially telling fashion in Baudelaire's work, for he suggests not only what an author stands to lose to the temporality of reading but also what it is an author has to

16. The prefaces which Baudelaire sketched for the second and third editions of *Les Fleurs du mal*, but never published, also complain of readers' lack of understanding of the poems while hinting at the poet's enjoyment of being made into a spectacle: "Every sin, every crime I have related has been imputed to me. Hatred and contempt as forms of amusement"; "If there is any glory in not being understood . . . I have . . . deserved that glory. . . . I have one of those happy characters that enjoy hatred and feel glorified by contempt" (Mathews and Mathews, *Flowers of Evil*, pp. xi, xiv-xv).

17. See Noakes, "On the Superficiality of Women," for more on this topic.

gain by spatializing, even sexualizing, his apprehension of that temporality. That is, he provides a perspective helpful in understanding the roots of the myth of the destructiveness of the latecoming reader. The development of this myth conforms to the pattern, identified by Marin and previously discussed here, of the spatialization of a temporal problem. It also exemplifies a pattern that Sarah Kofman points out in her book on Nerval and that I cited in discussing Boccaccio. What she calls "the Renaissance ritual" is the creation of a myth in the past (or the future) that responds to all the author's whims, like the most desirable mother/lover. The nightmarish obverse of this myth is the non-compliant, manipulative woman.

Baudelaire's relation to his fictive reader, whether female or male, is marked by a mutual abusiveness. He understands his violence toward the fictive reader to be justified by the violence the reader does him. Baudelaire sees the reader as the source of enormous pressure on him, the pressure to narrate, to link discrete moments of writing time into one continuous reading time. Still, the reader engenders a plethora of interpretations that leave behind them a sense not of bounty but of lack. The communal relation between two minds that reading seems to promise is, for Baudelaire, an illusion; reading is an activity in which two hostile parties face and stare past each other at their respective fantasies, not unlike the narrator and his mistress in "The Eyes of the Poor."

The background to Baudelaire's view of the author-reader relationship as abusive, often involving abuse of one sex by the other, is complex. His treatment of *Madame Bovary* is helpful to an understanding of it. One might think that Gustave Flaubert's novel, exactly contemporary with *Les Fleurs du mal* (both first appeared in book form in 1857), provides an example of a very different way of representing the reader, as a helpless victim of seduction for which literature has prepared the way. Baudelaire did not see the heroine in this light, however. Having watched Flaubert, like himself, brought to trial for his work—to be acquitted, while he was not—Baudelaire, two months after the condemnation of his own book, published an essay on *Madame Bovary* that reflects on the relationship among Flaubert, the reader, and Emma.

Baudelaire's reading of Emma contrasts with the more common contemporary view—successfully developed by Flaubert's attorney—that her example would not corrupt the young girls and married ladies who read of her, but rather warn them away from such a life as Emma's.[18] The attorney painted, for the court's benefit, a sentimentalized picture of Emma as a girl improperly educated in the wrong kind of school and led astray when the wrong kinds of novels were surreptitiously put into her hands.

In the first half of the nineteenth century, the notion that the clever novelist had the power to seduce female readers, a notion drawn primarily less from Dante's Francesca than from such key preromantic figures as Sade[19] and Rousseau,[20] had even become a commonplace of melodrama. The following interchange appeared in August Lefranc's *Le Système de mon oncle*, staged in Paris in 1838 (according to a friend of Baudelaire, Jeanne Duval—who later became Baudelaire's mistress—played the maid, Thérèse):

> THERESE *(tenant un gros paquet de livres)* Voici, Monsieur, tout ce qu'il y a de mieux en nouveautés.
> FAUCHEUX *(arrachant les livres des mains de Thérèse)* Des romans . . . des romans, voilà ce qui l'a perdue . . . voilà ce qui m'a aliéné sa tendresse.

> (THERESE *[holding a heavy package of books]* Here, sir, are all the best new books.
> FAUCHEUX *[tearing the books out of her hands]* Novels . . . novels, that's what ruined her . . . that's what took her away from me.)[21]

18. Dominick LaCapra, *"Madame Bovary" on Trial* (Ithaca: Cornell University Press, 1982), pp. 41-51.

19. Especially relevant are the Marquis de Sade's "Idée sur les romans," *Oeuvres complètes* (Paris: Cercle du Livre précieux, 1964), 10:3–22, and the intermittent addresses to the reader of *Juliette*, explaining the effect that alternation of narrated orgy and narrated landscape is to have on the reader.

20. Jean Jacques Rousseau, *Emile*, bk. v, pt. 1, presents a girl like the heroine Sophie in every respect, except that she has been corrupted by falling in love with the hero of François Fénelon's *Télémaque*. Cf. Nerval's *Sylvie* (1853), pt. VIII, where Sylvie trembles at the line in Rousseau's *La Nouvelle Héloise*: "Any girl who reads this book is lost" (Nerval, *Oeuvres*, 1966, 1:259). Sylvie's romantic quotation is incorrect in its implication that, according to Rousseau, it is the reading of the novel which will destroy morality. The preface to *La Nouvelle Héloise* states at the outset that any girl who has read even one page is already lost—not through the influence of the novel, at which she has not yet arrived, but rather because of the predisposing elements in herself that made her go beyond the book's warning title.

21. This unpublished work is cited by Claude Pichois, "A propos des 'Yeux de Berthe,' du nouveau sur Jeanne Duval?" in *Baudelaire: Etudes et témoignages* (Neuchâtel: La Baconnière, 1967), p. 67.

Banalization of Flaubert's novel by its interpretation through such a melodramatic stereotype held no appeal for Baudelaire, for he did not share the common view of Emma as a weak woman led astray by novels and, moreover, did not readily see the author as a superior figure with a responsibility to guide the reader. Several critics, he says, objected that *Madame Bovary* was immoral because it lacked a character who could "diriger l'intelligence du lecteur" (direct the reader's understanding; 2:81). Baudelaire argues instead that it is the reader's work to grasp the total logic of the novel and draw conclusions from that. Moreover, while some thought, in particular, that such a reader as the type represented by Emma stood in need of someone to direct her understanding of the novels she read,[22] Baudelaire unabashedly admires her, not just as a literary character but as an intellectual and moral personality. What is more, he suggests that her creation might not have been entirely subject to Flaubert's conscious control: "inconsciencieusement peut-être" (perhaps unconsciously; 2:82). Emma is, for Baudelaire, not a reader-character seduced by authors but a reader-character stronger than her author. To create Emma, he asserts, Flaubert had to strip himself of a fundamental aspect of his identity, his masculinity, and "se faire femme" (make himself woman; 2:81);[23] the author gave her his "male" blood, and "madame Bovary est *restée* un homme" (Madame Bovary has *remained* a man; 2:81, emphasis added). The choice of "has remained," rather than "has become," even suggests that Emma's (male) character somehow preexisted Flaubert's creation of the novel.

Thus, in Baudelaire's view, *Madame Bovary* is a great success as a novel precisely because the author has been seduced and dominated by his reader-character. Emma has taken over the author's role in that she creates her own life from other novels. Baudelaire thus chooses to see this reader-character as anything but powerless. Far from taking

22. Emma's reading habits and her tendency to model her life on the romanesque are especially prominent themes in chaps. 6 and 9 of *Madame Bovary*.

23. Flaubert himself encouraged the idea that he became Madame Bovary; see his letter to Taine in *Correspondance*, rev. ed., 5th series (Paris: Conard, 1929), p. 350. And in writing to thank Baudelaire for his review, Flaubert created a *dédoublement* similar to that which supposedly linked him to Emma: "You entered into the secret workings of the book, as if my brain were yours" (*Correspondance*, 4th series [1927], p. 229). On the problematics of gender in Madame Bovary, see also Naomi Schor, *Breaking the Chain: Women, Theory, and French Realist Fiction* (New York: Columbia University Press, 1985), pp. 3–28.

Emma Bovary to be passive and naive, he overflows with praise of her imagination, energy, decisiveness, and above all her taste for seduction and domination. According to Baudelaire, she not only takes over from Flaubert these admirable masculine attributes but also provides a paradigm for the activity of poets in general, even though she is a reader rather than a poet: "Madame Bovary se donne; emportée par les sophismes de son imagination, elle se donne magnifiquement, généreusement, d'une manière toute masculine, à des drôles qui ne sont pas ses égaux, exactement comme les poètes se livrent à des drôlesses" (Mme. Bovary gives herself; carried away by the sophisms of her imagination, she gives herself magnificently, generously, in a wholly masculine manner, to rogues who are not her equals, just as poets give themselves over to hussies; 2:82).

Such readers as Emma seem to be the only ones who interested Baudelaire. Emma-as-read-by-Baudelaire is indeed her author's hypocritical "brother," one who takes from him his birthright and leaves him her own. More than a mirror image, she is a kind of vampire, taking the author's blood and becoming the powerful figure he can no longer be. Baudelaire clearly relishes the notion of such metamorphosis when the author in question is Flaubert and not himself.

Powerless readers, without Emma's imagination and will to seduction, simply do not interest Baudelaire. In his essay "Les Drames et les romans honnêtes" (Respectable plays and novels; 1851), he had shrugged: "If the reader does not carry within a philosophical and religious guide who accompanies him in the reading of the book, too bad for him" [2:42]. The attitude here anticipates "Epigraph for a Condemned Book." The reader susceptible to being seduced is for Baudelaire just not very attractive game.

It is no accident that the readers waved aside in the essay on respectable plays and novels and in the "Epigraph for a Condemned Book" are male ("lect*eur*"). They exert no erotic pull for Baudelaire. Only the powerful reader, the woman who has the wit to move out of the secondary, latecoming position in which conventional literary structure places her and to take over the author's place, elicits his respect. At the same time, of course, her presence is the greatest reminder of his failure.

Baudelaire's ambivalence toward the reader's domination no doubt arises in part from his identification of himself as both a reader and a writer, and thus someone who can delight in taking control over another's words while at the same time realizing ruefully that still another reader will come to control *his* words. Whether at any given moment his viewpoint is that of reader or of writer, his obsession remains the failure of communication between these two, a failure that time builds into the reading process, one more fundamental than the barriers created by sex, education, or class. In the only near-novel he ever wrote, La Fanfarlo, he rendered this failure as an erotic one, treating the battle of author and reader against time as if it were an episode in the battle of the sexes.

This little-known story must be read by anyone seriously interested in Baudelaire's poetic development because it marks the starting point to which he returns, with a characteristic twist, in the prose poems that close his career. For a writer who began when the novel was king and when Balzac, the magician of "How One Pays One's Debts," was king of the novelists, this story represents a wistful flirtation with the genre that offered financial success (to Balzac, not Baudelaire), the best chance to please readers, and a simultaneous opportunity to deprecate its claims to power, in this case expressed through reversals in the relations of the story's characters. In the dedication of his prose poems, at the very end of his career, Baudelaire compares the novel with what he is offering (in this turn from verse back to prose), and once again he deprecates the novel even as he marks the pull it exerts on him: "Nous pouvons couper où nous voulons, moi ma rêverie . . . le lecteur sa lecture; car je ne suspends pas la volonté . . . au fil interminable d'une intrigue superflue" (We can cut where we want, I my reverie . . . the reader his reading; for I don't tie the will . . . to the endless thread of a superfluous plot; 1:275).

La Fanfarlo (1847) plays with the idea of plot and with the theme of the lady endangered by the novel by turning that theme upside down, making the virtuous, provincial female reader seduce a writer by means of the "plot" with which he had planned to seduce her. She, indeed, turns out to be a reader who rejects reading. The writer turns out to be a foolishly interpretive reader. Finally, the woman who gives the story its title emerges as a clever exegetical reader.

The provincial lady, Madame de Cosmelly, is first mentioned as someone who sometimes absentmindedly holds a book she is not reading (1:556). Thus initially classed as a reader, she seems, in her distraction, unlikely to be one whom an author might fear. At the end of Baudelaire's story, however, it becomes clear that her *refusal* to give herself over to this book is significant.

The writer, Samuel Cramer, watches her idly, for he too is a distracted reader who in the last analysis will show the mark of what he does *not* care to read: "books useful only to minds possessed of an immoderate taste for truth" (1:555). Cramer recalls "the whole youthful novel" of their one-time romance. He soon comes to think he can relive this "novel" by seducing her with the romanesque performance of a gallant service, at her request: she wishes him to save her marriage by separating her husband from the actress La Fanfarlo. Cramer attracts La Fanfarlo's attention by writing; he spends three months attacking her in the press, simultaneously seducing himself into a wild passion for her. But she reads his hostile reviews exegetically, critically, rather than literally; she understands that his dreadful attacks may be so many weekly bouquets from a seeker of favors (1:71). When Cramer separates Monsieur de Cosmelly from La Fanfarlo, he loses his rival's virtuous wife, who at once takes her husband back to the provinces. La Fanfarlo, too, gets the best of Cramer: he supports her by cranking out learned books while she thrives and grows fat (1:80). The story comically sets forth the terms of an ironic perspective that shapes Baudelaire's view of the relation of reader and author. Imagination appears as a faculty that makes clever, interpretive readers into fools.

As much as a figure of the writer, Cramer represents the reader who appropriates as his own what he has read; after reading a beautiful book, he is likely to think it beautiful enough to have been written by himself and to conclude, "c'est donc de moi" (therefore, it is by me) (1:554). This parody of the interpretive reader/author is quite explicit self-parody. The entire story is written with pens borrowed, in utter frankness, from Laurence Sterne, Balzac, Gautier, and others. A gloss directs Baudelaire's reader to identify him with Cramer: as first published, the story was signed "Charles Defayis," and an accompanying note confesses that the author has previously been known in the literary world under the name of Charles Baudelair Du Fays.[24] The story itself opens by identifying Samuel Cramer as one who formerly signed himself Manuela de Monte-verde (1:553).

Baudelaire thus draws an important parallel between his protagonist's "plotting" in the service of seduction and his own activity as a writer. He identifies Cramer's imaginative erasure of the distance between his "youthful novel" and Madame de Cosmelly and the present, on the one hand, with (for example) his own account of the distance

---

24. The note is reprinted in Baudelaire, *Oeuvres complètes*, ed. Yves-Gérard Le Dantec and Claude Pichois (Paris: Pléiade, 1961), p. 1641.

between Sterne's time and his own, on the other. Moreover, in Madame de Cosmelly, Baudelaire presents a reader fixed firmly in her own moment, unresponsive to the temporal erasures writers attempt and uninterested in giving herself over to a book. When Cramer reads to her from his work, she interrupts twice, with a sigh and then with an imprecation. Finally, she bursts into tears, and Cramer, thinking that his own language has brought forth her beautiful tears, regards them proudly "as his work and literary property" (1:562). But she is reacting not to Cramer's words but to something remembered from her own past. With Cramer's full attention, she begins her story, which goes on for twice as long as his prose, and ends thus: "You see what it is, a banal story . . . a provincial *novel!*" (1:68, emphasis added). Thus, the reader of novels is metamorphosed into a novelist, a reader stealing a writer's place from him—much like Madame Bovary, as Baudelaire will later read her.

Cramer's credulity as a reader of Madame de Cosmelly's "novel," together with his credulity as a writer, is summarized by Baudelaire as a belief in his public (1:69). Baudelaire's disillusionment with such belief must not be read exclusively as a change in the educational and class background of his readers any more than as a distrust of readers of a particular sex. The lack of belief in his public to which he alludes both early and late in his career is based on his constant concern with the temporal disjunction that both impels and limits reading. As an attempt to bridge the always temporal gap between author and reader, reading must necessarily disappoint faith.

Strange Siblings: The Reader as Virgin and Addict

Baudelaire created still one more female fictive reader. Though a reader in only a metaphorical sense, she largely conforms to the stereotype presented by Flaubert's lawyer: a helpless innocent corrupted by what she reads. Even this more traditional figure, however, permits Baudelaire to reflect once more on the powers of the reader and rehearse his ambivalence about the temporality of reading. Again, the tension between past and present that reading inevitably brings to life is transformed into spatial terms.

Baudelaire's innocent female reader appears in the essay entitled "De l'Essence du rire, et généralement du comique dans les arts plastiques" (On the essence of laughter, and generally on the comic in the plastic

arts; 2:525–43), first published in 1855 but thought to have been written over the course of the preceding decade.[25] In the second section of
this essay Baudelaire retells the myth of the Fall, describing the face of
prelapsarian man as "simple et uni" (simple and uniform; 2:528), not
deformed by either tears or laughter. The emphasis is on singleness, in
both expression and feeling. He goes on to demonstrate the effects of
the Fall by describing a contemporary, fictional example of a prelapsarian soul encountering civilization. He gives her the highly suitable
name "Virginie," taken from Saint-Pierre's well-known novel *Paul et
Virginie*. She arrives in Paris with only a very few visions stored in her
eyes: again, her innocence, like Adam's, is rendered as nonmultiplicity.
Her fall consists in her chance encounter with a caricature. Unlike
more sophisticated readers who confront caricature, she fails to laugh.
On the contrary, she is troubled by it; its complexity distresses and
even frightens her. Baudelaire explains that her "artless mind [is] used
to understanding intuitively things as simple as itself" (2:529). Virginie's fall thus consists in the movement from a mind that is simple
and uniform, to one that is complex and multiple. To read the caricature properly, she must have many images in her mind. Virginie will
respond as the caricaturist intended, by laughing, only when she has
been in Paris long enough to understand the possibility of two points
of view.

Virginie's failure to laugh thus serves to prove the principal thesis of
the essay, stated in the fourth section: that "the power of laughter lies
in the one who laughs, and in no way in the object of laughter" (2:53).
Nonetheless, the narrative of Virginie lingers on and tends to undercut
this later explicit statement about the "power" of the interpreter. Although Virginie, like the female readers in *La Fanfarlo*, exemplifies the
reader as someone who has the sole power to give or withhold a
reading, she draws no pleasure or advantage from that power. Moreover, when called upon to put her power to use, she responds like one
who has been attacked rather than one who triumphs. She is entirely
unlike Madame de Cosmelly, who also withholds the reading that
Cramer as author would like her to give to his poems; but Madame de

25. Richard Klein, "Baudelaire and Revolution: Some Notes," in *Literature and Revolution*, ed. Jacques Ehrmann (Boston: Beacon Press, 1970), a reprint of *Yale French
Studies* 39, relates Baudelaire's Edenic tale in this essay to his disillusion with the ideals
of the revolution of 1848 and his conviction, after Louis Napoleon's *coup d'état* in 1851,
that all hope of political change was utopian (see esp. p. 93).

Cosmelly does so deliberately, while Virginie simply fails to understand.

Because of Baudelaire's profound awareness of the ambivalence of reading, even his seemingly universal descriptions of it are called into question by their contexts. Virginie is presented as a kind of equivalent to Christine de Pizan's non-clerkly reader on the road to a qualitatively richer reading style. But, in part because Baudelaire creates her in a period of postrevolutionary disillusionment with learning and its promises, his portrait of her "progress" contrasts sharply with Christine's optimistic picture of the reader of increasing sophistication. "Virginie a vu; maintenant elle regarde" (Virginie has seen; now she looks; 2:529). The second verb implies what one might call a "studied" gaze, paralleling the notion presented in earlier chapters that one inevitably brings to reading more than just natural intelligence. Baudelaire remarks with a hint of irony: "Certainly, Virginie is a great intellect," but it is clear that intelligence alone does not suffice. Necessary as well are acquired skills appropriate specifically to reading as it is taught in a particular culture at a particular time. Baudelaire asserts that Virginie will indeed eventually learn to know the culture that is the caricature's context and thus learn to read the caricature properly: that is, learn to laugh at it as its author intended. "No doubt, if Virginie stays in Paris and acquires learning, she will learn to laugh. . . . When Virginie, fallen from grace, has sunk by one degree of purity, she will begin to form an idea of her own superiority, she will be more learned from the world's viewpoint, and she will laugh" (2:529–30). The imaginative superiority that will enable her to laugh, then, corresponds to a moral decline. Baudelaire conceives imagination and morality as inversely related to each other. Virginie will have stored inside her a multiplicity of images that will make her a better reader of caricature and, at the same time, a worse human being. As a virginal reader she was content with "few images and few memories"; once she has acquired a host of both during a period of obviously unwholesome city life, she will become an experienced reader and simultaneously a fallen woman.

To say that she will have a greater number of images in her mind to assist her in reading is to say, in semiotic terms, that she will have at her disposal a greater range of interpretants.[26] But all interpretants

---

26. In sign theory, an interpretant is the entity that mediates a subject's attempt to understand a sign. Its relation to temporality is discussed under "Exegesis, Interptetation, and Semiotics" in the Conclusion.

come from the past, and a past as idyllic as Virginie's *was*, pre-carica-
ture, is strictly the stuff of fairytales. Reading, then, implies an imaginative muliplicity that is not only morally but also and especially
temporally compromising. One cannot live *simply* in one moment
alone when reading.

This little fable of a reader's education, concomitant moral decline,
and temporal fragmentation stands in contrast to the earlier sketch of
the education of Prince Louis in which learning to read was conceived
of as helpful to salvation. It has another "moral" as well, for it dramatizes not only the development of the reader but also the power of the
text. Once again, the "scene of reading" depicted in Baudelaire's essay
on laughter differs significantly from that in *La Fanfarlo*. If, as Nathaniel Wing has pointed out, *La Fanfarlo* depicts the failure of the literary
text,[27] the Virginie fable ascribes to the text a triumph, albeit a partial
one. It is true that, like the poems Cramer gives to Madame de Cosmelly and his journalistic diatribes against La Fanfarlo, the caricature
Virginie sees fails to affect her as its author intended, for she does not
laugh at it. Still, unlike Cramer's work, the caricature is not dismissed
as ridiculous by an addressee on whom it has no impact. Indeed,
Virginie takes away a lasting and profound impression: "she will retain
from this impression an indefinable malaise, something like fear"
[2:529]. It may seem misguided to ascribe her malaise to the text, since
she would not feel it if she had been better prepared, more knowledgeable, when she first encountered it; in this sense, her interpretation of
the caricature—"the angel has sensed scandal in it"—may indeed be
said to originate more with her than with the text. It is certainly not
entirely of the author's making. Nonetheless, the reading "scandale"
cannot be simply a projection from her virginal mind. The caricature
does make a decisive impact on this simple reader quite apart from its
author's intention. Once created (as Dante knew), the text takes on an
independent life of its own.

The essay on laughter, which Baudelaire elaborated over the period
1845–55, thus depicts with great ambivalence one of the very few
readers to be found in his works whom he presents as "simple" (in the

27. Nathaniel Wing, "The Poetics of Irony in Baudelaire's *La Fanfarlo*," *Neophilologus*
59 (1975), 165–89. Specifically, Wing finds in the story "a far reaching examination of
the artist and the nature of artistic creation" (p. 169), the first episode of which portrays
"the negative function of literature" (p. 170; see also p. 175), while the second suggests
that literature is degraded if it is oriented toward a practical end (pp. 180, 185).

French sense of both "simple" and numerically "single," rather than "double," in mind). She is, when she encounters the caricature, very far from the hypocritical reader of "Au lecteur" or the prudent Madame de Cosmelly. Moreover, she is presented in a context of fable within an essay whose concluding assertion implicitly denies her reality: the assertion that there is "in the human being[28] the presence of an enduring duality, the power to be at the same time oneself and another" (2:543). A character wholly devoid of duality, Virginie is thus an entirely hypothetical figure, a reader so simple she could not possibly exist, because duality is, for Baudelaire, essential to humanity. What's more, Baudelaire does not much like her, as his sarcasm indicates: "Dieu, elle l'a connu dans l'église des Pamplemousses" (God she has met in the church of the Grapefruits; 2:529).

Scorning the reader of ideal (and fictive) simplicity, who carries with her almost no past, Baudelaire finds appeal in the notion of the reader of infinite complexity. Lengthy interpolations in his translation of De Quincey's *Confessions of an English Opium Eater* celebrate a reader who, especially with the aid of mind-altering substances, has promethean powers of association and historic re-creation. Father Time shrinks to nothing in the face of this reader's feats. He[29] is far more successful in the struggle against time's ravages than even such an indefatigable and often optimistic humanist as Boccaccio ever dared hope to be.

The palimpsest, a figure often used by the humanists, in fact provides the pretext for Baudelaire's reflections on the subject of the power of the reader to conquer time through the proliferation of what Baudelaire calls "images."[30] This figure is set forth in Baudelaire's expanded translation of a section of De Quincey's work titled "The Palimpsest."[31] The palimpsest symbolizes both the dream and the nightmare of every humanist: the dream, in that it holds out the possibility of recovering a text that time has almost but not quite obliter-

---

28. In an earlier version Baudelaire had written *l'homme* (man); one may infer that he deliberately extended his concept of the essential duality of man to apply it also to women.

29. I use the male pronoun alone because the epic quality of this reader's deeds accompany in Baudelaire's imagination features that Western tradition associates with "maleness."

30. These are essentially the same as interpretants, in semiotic terms; see n. 26 above.

31. Thomas De Quincey, *Works* (Boston: Houghton Mifflin, 1876), 1:225ff. Baudelaire's translation of this section begins at 1:505 in *Oeuvres complètes*. Its expansion with respect to the original text suggest still another meaning for "palimpsest" here.

ated; the nightmare, in that the text's marginal visibility teases the reader with the thought of the inexorable process of destruction time impels. The inherent ambivalence of the concept of palimpsest is completely evaded by Baudelaire in the *Opium Eater* translation, however, (one is tempted to ask whether under the influence of his subject matter).

In his gloss on De Quincey's assertion that not one of the "ideas, images, feelings" that have fallen on the reader's brain has ever been lost, Baudelaire claims that the human memory is not merely similar but indeed superior to any palimpsest. It triumphs over time even when time is aided by a furious author who burns his own unpublished works—a figure even more appalling than the Time who chewed up books in Boccaccio's proem to the *Genealogy* (see Chapter 4):

> Toutefois, entre le palimpseste qui porte, superposées l'une sur l'autre, une tragédie grecque, une légende monacale et une histoire de chevalerie, et le palimpseste divin créé par Dieu, qui est notre incommensurable mémoire, se présente cette différence, que dans le premier il y a comme un chaos fantastique, grotesque, une collision entre des éléments hétérogènes; tandis que dans le second la fatalité du tempérament met forcément une harmonie parmi les éléments les plus disparates. Quelque incohérente que soit une existence, l'unité humaine n'en est pas troublée. Tous les échos de la mémoire, si on pouvait les réveiller simultanément, formerait un concert, agréable ou douloureux, mais logique et sans dissonances.
>
> Souvent des êtres, surpris par un accident subit, suffoqués brusquement par l'eau, et en danger de mort, ont vu s'allumer dans leur cerveau tout le théâtre de leur vie passée. Le temps a été annihilé, et quelques secondes ont suffi à contenir une quantité de sentiments et d'images équivalente à des années. . . .
>
> Un homme de génie, mélancolique, misanthrope, et voulant se venger de l'injustice de son siècle, jette un jour au feu toutes ses oeuvres encore manuscrites. Et comme on lui reprochait cet effroyable holocauste fait à la haine, qui, d'ailleurs, était le sacrifice de toutes ses propres espérances, il répondit: "Qu'importe? ce qui était important, c'était que ces choses fussent *créées;* elles ont été créées, donc elles *sont.*"
>
> . . . Et si dans cette croyance il y a quelque chose d'infiniment consolant, dans le cas où notre esprit se tourne vers cette partie de nous-mêmes que nous pouvons considérer avec complaisance, n'y a-t-il pas aussi quelque chose d'infiniment terrible, dans le cas futur, inévitable, où notre esprit se tournera vers cette partie de nous-mêmes que nous ne pouvons affronter qu'avec horreur? Dans le spirituel non plus que dans le matériel, rien ne se perd.

(Between the palimpsest which bears, superimposed one on top of the other, a Greek tragedy, a monkish legend, and a chivalric tale, and the divine palimpsest created by God, which is our incomparable memory, however, there is this difference, that in the first there is a kind of grotesque and fantastic chaos, a collision among heterogeneous elements; while in the second, temperament necessarily pre-determines a harmony among the most disparate elements. No matter how incoherent an existence may be, such incoherence does not trouble its human oneness. All the echoes of memory, if one could awaken them simultaneously, would unite in a concert, either pleasant or painful, but logical and without dissonances.

It has often happened that beings, surprised by a sudden accident, violently suffocated by water, and in danger of death, have seen illuminated in their brains the entire spectacle of their past lives. Time has been annihilated, and a few seconds have been capable of containing a quantity of feelings and images deposited over years. . . . A man of genius, depressed, misanthropic, and wanting to take revenge for the injustice of his century, one day throws onto the fire all his still unpublished works. And as he is reproached for this dreadful holocaust committed out of hatred which, moreover, was the sacrifice of all his own hopes, he answers: "What does it matter? What was important was that these things had been *created*; they have been created, therefore they *are*." . . . And if there is in this belief something infinitely consoling, when our mind turns back toward the part of ourselves we can contemplate with pleasure, is there not also something infinitely terrible, in the inevitable future case in which our mind will turn toward the part of ourselves we can face only with horror? In the spiritual as in the material world, nothing is lost.) [1:505–7]

The association of human memory with a palimpsest draws upon related notions that held great appeal for Baudelaire throughout his career. The terms in which he ascribes this superiority to a harmony the human temperament creates in memory's echoes recall the images of especially the first two stanzas of what is perhaps his most famous poem, "Correspondances":

> La Nature est un temple où de vivants piliers
> Laissent parfois sortir de confuses paroles;
> L'homme y passe à travers des forêts de symboles
> Qui l'observent avec des regards familiers.
>
> Comme de longs échos qui de loin se confondent
> Dans une ténébreuse et profonde unité,
> Vaste comme la nuit et comme la clarté,
> Les parfums, les couleurs et les sons se répondent.

(Nature is a temple, in which living pillars sometimes utter a babel of words; man traverses it through forests of symbols, that watch him with knowing eyes.

Like prolonged echoes which merge far away in an opaque, deep oneness, as vast as darkness, as vast as light, perfumes, sounds, and colours answer each to each.)

[1:1]

In both "Correspondances" and the *Opium Eater* text, diverse echoes are described as resolving themselves into a kind of unity. But the untroubled unity in which these echoes are asserted to culminate elicits more praise from Baudelaire in the *Opium Eater* text than in the some what earlier poem.[32] Whereas in "Correspondances" one finds the verb *chanter*, "to sing," the later text employs a word connoting a higher degree of order, *concert*. Moreover, it reinforces this connotation of order with the modifiers *logique*, "logical," and *sans dissonances*, "without dissonances."

Around 1860, Baudelaire's interest in such echoes of meaning from the past and their recovery and resolution in a present unity was especially keen. The *Opium Eater* text represents only one of the points around which this interest revolved. Examination of others of Baudelaire's works from this period will show that his exuberant characterization of the epic powers of memory in the *Opium Eater* text represents an indulgence in wishful thinking, which the author was not long able to sustain. No sooner did he assert man's power to "annihilate time" than he fell back in despair at the recognition that neither individual nor cultural memory has such promethean capabilities. Indeed, if memory were so powerful as Baudelaire here depicts it, there would have been no need for the invention of writing. Writing's very existence recalls the limitations of memory, to which writing is often claimed to be an aid. But it is a lack of need for writing which Baudelaire goes on to suggest in his gloss on De Quincey.

Baudelaire's treatment of the surge of memory said to accompany drowning differs markedly and tellingly from De Quincey's, for it deals not with the memory alone but rather with the relation between memory and writing. The Englishman's treatment of the topic is anecdotal, somewhat polemical, never straying far from the concrete. He talks a good deal about the light that appears to the mind at the moment of drowning, comparing it to Saint Paul's vision on the road to

32. De Man, *Rhetoric of Romanticism*, p. 252, dates it prior to 1855.

Damascus, and he twice uses the word "resurrection" to describe the return of memories thought to have been lost. Baudelaire avoids such Christian associations and confines his reflections on memory while drowning to a relatively abstract philosophical and literary level. His assertion that "time has been annihilated" is far stronger than anything in De Quincey.[33]

The claim that human memory can "annihilate" time marks one of the two opposing extremes that seem, around 1860, to form the limits of Baudelaire's thoughts on the relation between the mind and time. It is simply the obverse of the notion that time annihilates man. They are sibling notions, two halves of the same ambivalence, like the opium addict reader and Virginie. These twin notions are of obsessive concern to Baudelaire because of his concern with the temporal dimension inherent in reading.

This is suggested by the bookish nature of the hypothetical anecdote, cited above, that Baudelaire introduces as a kind of substitute for De Quincey's tale about a little girl who almost drowned in a country pond. Baudelaire's substitute anecdote of the author who destroys his works implies that what is written exists not by virtue of its continuation in a written (much less published) state but rather by virtue of the prior existence of the creative act that preceded the writing. Thus, once a writer has written something, it makes no difference whether these writings continue to have any physical existence, and whether they are ever read is a question not even raised. The reader is left in a most peculiar situation by this state of affairs: on the one hand, Baudelaire gives the reader limitless powers to recall every image ever perceived in a lifetime; on the other, he makes the reader of no consequence whatever to the continuing life of the writings of a "man of genius."

The ambivalence that continues to distinguish Baudelaire's thoughts about the relation of time, writing, and "the human" emerges explicitly in his balanced rhetorical question about the attitude "we" (*nous*) should take toward the infinite powers of human memory. The self-congratulation of earlier paragraphs is slightly mitigated by the assertion that the horrifying will be remembered along with the pleasurable. No thought is given here to what Freud would come to designate by the term "repression." Moreover, the dread of remembering

---

33. Cf. *Works*, 1:111, for the earliest version of this anecdote in De Quincey, and see also his lengthy discursive note: there is nothing comparable to Baudelaire's assertion about the annihilation of time.

everything seems not very important, for Baudelaire immediately drops the notion rather than going on to develop it. His emphasis remains the denial that time brings any loss of human ideas or images. What is important is that the "holocaust" of time is entirely overcome, no matter what dreadful consequences this victory may bring.

Memory, Time, and the Poet

Yet just months after the translation from De Quincey was published, Baudelaire completed "Un Fantôme" ("A Phantom"), a cycle of four sonnets that resurrect this notion of the human senses, the memory, and especially the reader triumphing over time.[34] The sonnet cycle, however, rejects the notion as it draws toward its end with a new temporal holocaust. The first sonnet, entitled "Les Ténèbres" ("The Shadows"), revisits the shadowy scene of Plato's cave in that it is set in "caveaux" (more like "burial vaults" than caves or *cavernes*). These "caveaux" must be understood to be allegorical because it is an allegorical figure, "le Destin" (Fate), who has relegated the speaker to them. In these underground vaults the speaker does not simply watch shadows on the wall, as in the well-known Platonic scene: the "je" is instead like one condemned to paint upon the shadows.

Although no source of light that would cast the shadows is explicitly named, two sources are implied. The first is the fire that the "caveaux" must contain, because the speaker, when not painting, is occupied in boiling his heart so that he can eat it. The second is the phantom named in the title of the cycle, a specter whose gender is female—"C'est Elle!" (It is She!)—who gives off—"Par instants brille" (At times there glimmers)—an intermittent light. This specter is paradoxically "noire et pourtant lumineuse" (black and nonetheless luminous). The speaker can make out the identity of the spectral visitor who brings him something other than a self-destructive (heart-eating) light only after the passage of a certain length of time:

> Par instants brille, et s'allonge, et s'étale
> Un spectre fait de grâce et de splendeur.
> A sa rêveuse allure orientale,

---

34. The manuscript of "Un Fantôme" (A Phantom) is dated March 1860 (*Oeuvres complètes*, 1:1516). The translation from De Quincey had been published on January 15 of that year.

Quand il atteint sa totale grandeur,
Je reconnais ma belle visiteuse:
C'est Elle! noire et pourtant lumineuse.

(At moments there glimmers, and lengthens, and stretches out / A
specter made of grace and splendor. By its dreamy oriental allure, /
When it reaches its full size, / I recognize my beautiful visitor: / It is
She! black and nonetheless luminous.)

[1:38]

Whereas the quatrains are concerned with establishing the spatial setting of the poem, the tercets are given over to temporal development
as the reader follows the speaker, waiting for the identity of the specter
very gradually to unfold.

The cycle continues the image of the speaker as a painter on shadows
in the third and fourth sonnets, "Le Cadre" ("The Frame"), and "Le
Portrait." But the second sonnet, the often anthologized "Le Parfum"
("The Perfume"), seems to turn away from the development of this
visual metaphor. It opens with a gesture that seems also to turn away
from the allegorical setting of the first sonnet, taking a conversational
tone in its first line and addressing directly to the reader what could
well be a merely empirical question: "Lecteur, as-tu quelquefois re-
spiré" (Reader, have you sometimes breathed) (1:39).

At first reading, the connection between the first lines of this sonnet
and what immediately precedes it is far from obvious, since visual
imagery has been entirely abandoned for the olfactory. The connection, however, is indeed established at two levels. First, "Le Parfum"
evokes a gradual development over time of a sensual experience. Second, this temporal development is compared to an increase in magni-
tude from very small to very large. As the speaker in the first poem has
had to wait over a period of time for the specter to grow to a size that
permits recognition, so the reader is asked in the second poem whether
"he [*sic*]" has savored a perfume slowly, with "lente gourmandise"
(slow gluttony; Richardson, p.85). As in the first poem the specter
"s'allonge" (lengthens), so in the second a speck of incense comes to fill
an entire church. The past restored is described as an intoxicant, recalling the exhilaration with which Baudelaire evoked man's complete
ability to recover the past in his elaboration of *Confessions of an English
Opium-Eater.*

The crux of this second sonnet is the conjunction "ainsi" (thus),
which begins line 7, relegating the preceding six lines—comprising a

direct address to the reader and an exclamation—into a prologue for the description of erotic love presented in the sonnet's last eight lines:

> Ainsi l'amant sur un corps adoré
> Du souvenir cueille la fleur exquise.
>
> De ses cheveux élastiques et lourds,
> Vivant sachet, encensoir de l'alcôve,
> Une senteur montait, sauvage et fauve,
>
> Et des habits, mousseline ou velours,
> Tout imprégnés de sa jeunesse pure,
> Se dégageait un parfum de fourrure.

(Thus the lover on an adored body / Gathers the exquisite flower of memory. / From her elastic and heavy hair, / A living sachet, censer of the bed-alcove, / An odor rose up, savage and wild, / And from the clothes, muslin or velvet, / All permeated with her pure youth, / There escaped a perfume of fur.)

[1:39]

The reader, who is the addressee of this poem, is here explicitly compared ("ainsi") to a male lover who uses a woman's body as a kind of ground, a meadow more than a canvas, on ("sur") which to gather a memory. A part of the woman's body, her hair, becomes a thing—a sachet or censer, a tool that the male lover wields in his attempts to bring the past into the present. This very concrete, even reified woman corresponds to the allegorical (note the capitalization) "Elle" of the first poem in the cycle, who serves as a source of light for the casting of shadows on ("sur") which the speaker can paint. In these two poems, the female figure is neither subject nor object of the events the poems describe, but simply an essential aid to the painting-on-shadows, a tool to use in the intoxicating recovery of the past. She is a text.

The status of "Le Parfum" as an exploration of the kind of human effort toward temporal recovery which makes use of texts is, tangentially, confirmed by its many similarities to "Correspondances," which is commonly read as a kind of aesthetic manifesto. The lexicon is, once again, very reminiscent of "Correspondances." "Les Ténèbres" establishes for "Le Parfum" a setting similar to that of "Correspondances," not only in that the more famous poem alludes to "une ténébreuse . . . unité" but also in that both "Les Ténèbres" and "Correspondances" open with personifications ("Nature," "Destin"), making clear that both "Correspondances" and the cycle "Un Fantôme" are allegories.

Both poems evoke incense; instead of a temple, "Le Parfum" mentions "une église" (a church); the adjective "profond" is used in a similarly evocative and vague way in both poems; the phrase "les transports de l'esprit et des sens" (the transports of the spirit and the senses) suggests the same category of experience as the lover gathering the flower of memory on the adored body. Moreover, the lover in "Le Parfum" is engaged in the same kind of activity as "l'homme" (the man) passing through the forest of symbols, the gathering together of echoes. The forest in "Correspondances" is associated as well with what is "sauvage," "fauve" (savage, musky), the "fourrure" of "Le Parfum." In addition, the intermittent and not entirely easy liberation suggested by "laissent parfois sortir" (sometimes let out) is similar to the action described in "Le Parfum" with the verb "se dégageait." Above all, both sonnets are to a large extent permeated by the image of perfume (compare the last six lines of "Correspondances"). Both "Correspondances" and the cycle "Un Fantôme" are indeed allegories which concern representation. The happy vision of man's ability to recover the past in unified form which these allegories imply is a recurrent one for Baudelaire. But it is not enduring (as further investigation of his writing about this notion around 1860 will show).

The third poem in the cycle, "Le Cadre," once again seems to mark a major shift in kind within "Un Fantôme," for it presents itself on first reading as merely descriptive. When this poem about "the frame" is read within its own "frame"—that is, in relation to the poems that precede and especially the poem that follows it—it nonetheless becomes clear that "Le Cadre" is much more than a description of the way in which a young woman's surroundings once seemed to set off and complement her beauty. The first stanza appears to celebrate the advantageous effect on a painting of a beautiful frame, but its concluding line is ambiguous when read in the context of the cycle as a whole:

> Comme un beau cadre ajoute à la peinture,
> Bien qu'elle soit d'un pinceau très-vanté,
> Je ne sais quoi d'étrange et d'enchanté
> En l'isolant de l'immense nature . . .

(As a beautiful frame adds to the painting, / Even though it is the work of a much-acclaimed brush, / A certain something which is strange and enchanted / By isolating it from immense nature . . .

[1:39]

In one sense the last line implies that isolation from nature is advantageous to the painting because it gives it an exotic and magical quality. But in its larger context the line also suggests that the beautiful woman's isolation from nature can be only apparent. The tercets of the preceding sonnet have dwelt on a quality in the woman's body which is not only natural but even animalistic: "sauvage," "fauve," "fourrure." The last poem in the cycle will go on to show that, yet again, like every "Mignonne" of French poetic tradition,[35] this woman and her beauty will decay, along with the passion and the sensual transports that she and the lover have shared and—worst of all so far as the lover/painter/poet/reader is concerned—even along with his ability to remember her beauty in all its vivacity, his power to "gather the exquisite flower of memory" ("Le Parfum," line 8).

The second stanza, again on first reading, appears to complete the simile begun in the opening stanza by enumerating elements in the "frame" that surrounded the young woman and suggesting, twice over, that these inanimate things somehow had a will, which they put at the service of her beauty. This anthropomorphization, however, is once again revealed as an illusion not only implicitly by its own inherent impossibility but also, explicitly, by the hardly innocuous verb "semblait" (seemed) in the last line:

> Ainsi bijoux, meubles, métaux, dorure,
> S'adaptaient juste à sa rare beauté;
> Rien n'offusquait sa parfaite clarté,
> Et tout semblait lui servir de bordure.

(Thus jewel, furniture, metals, gilding, / Adapted themselves precisely to her rare beauty: / Nothing clouded her perfect clarity, / And everything seemed to serve her as trimming.)

[1:39]

The stanza's conclusion implies that the central position the woman assumed when seen in "her" frame was only a semblance of importance, just as the isolation from nature that the frame seemed to give her was only an apparent isolation. The irony of the stanza when read in relation to the following sonnet is that the elements making up the frame (jewels, furniture, and the like) appear to be subordinate to the

---

35. The allusion is to Pierre de Ronsard's famous ode, "Mignonne, allons voir si la rose . . ."

woman, but are instead superior in that they are less subject than she to the ravages of time.

The third stanza seems to intensify the apparent claim of the second that the young woman's material surroundings have a will that they subjected to her domination. In fact, however, its first line is made up of a series of rhetorical retreats:

> Même on eût dit parfois qu'elle croyait
> Que tout voulait l'aimer; elle noyait
> Sa nudité voluptueusement

(Sometimes one would even have said that she believed / That everything wanted to love her; she immersed / Her nakedness voluptuously)
[1:39]

The rhetorical double movement of this stanza is announced by "Même," implying not only that the relationship between the woman and her surroundings was imbued with an emotional charge but also that in thinking so both she and "one" were going too far, that not the relationship but the view of it was touched with excess. The phrase "on eût dit" questions everything that depends on it by casting it into the realm of hypothesis; it implies an "if." "Parfois" also hedges, raising a question: if such an ideal relationship between the woman and her surroundings actually existed at all, why would "one" have said so only sometimes? The verb "croyait" marks semantically not only belief but necessarily its opposite, doubt. It implies, "Yes, so she believed, but was she right?" The imperfect tense of the verb also calls the correctness of her belief into doubt, because it necessarily implies that at some point she stopped believing "that everything wanted to love her."

Especially telling is the placement of the verb "noyait" at the end of a line, a strategy that draws attention to it and at first leaves its meaning open to doubt, because this transitive verb is detached from the complement it requires by that very line-end position. So isolated, the verb is menacing; it suggests death by drowning. Only the appearance of the complement in the next line makes clear that it is to be read metaphorically rather than literally.

The threat of the verb's literal meaning must, indeed, be read retrospectively as an omen from the viewpoint created in the next (and last) poem in the cycle, where the reflexive form "se noya," meaning "drowned," appears. Again, like "noyait" in "Le Cadre," "se noya" functions metaphorically, but in "Le Portrait" it belongs to not one but two major metaphors. The first functions only in the poem's fourth line: "De cette bouche où mon coeur se noya" (Of that mouth where my heart drowned). The second metaphor, however, is the more comprehensive one of death, which dominates the poem as a whole, thus retrospectively reshaping the entire cycle and particularly such a detail as the use of "noyait" in "Le Cadre."

The last tercet of "Le Cadre" and especially its last word are unsettling:

> Dans les baisers du satin et du linge,
> Et, lente ou brusque, à chaque mouvement
> Montrait la grace enfantine du singe.

(In the kisses of the satin and linen, / and, whether slow or abrupt, in each movement / Showed the childlike grace of the monkey.)

[1:40]

For one thing, "singe" (monkey), when applied to a black mistress, must from today's viewpoint be seen as racist, again casting a peculiar reflection on the rest of the cycle. The white man's presumption of superiority over nature, a prominent motif in the essay on laughter, is called into question in this poem. The connotations that Baudelaire elsewhere associates with "singe" may be applied to the word here. In the essay on laughter (2:532) the monkey is classed with the parrot among both the most comical and the most serious of animals.

In "Le Cadre," "singe" has a related double connotation, reflected in the relation between "grâce" and "enfantine." The mistress's smell was characterized in "Le Parfum" as "sauvage," "fauve," "de fourrure," thus implying that she has animal-like traits; but these traits are seen from a viewpoint that regards animals as "graceful" rather than, for example, "beastly." It is nonetheless set at the end of a sentence which by implication characterizes the movements of the monkey as having the human quality of grace, especially the grace of a particular kind of human, a child. The comical quality of the monkey resides in this childlike quality; "enfantine" (childlike) implies that the speaker views the creature so described from above. The complex description moves from the human to the animal back again to the human, describing a person by comparison to an animal who is in turn described by relation to a person. It establishes a continuity where it is more conventional to erect a wall—between the animal world and the human world.

What is torn down by this description is precisely the "frame" that separates (or, to use the poem's stronger verb, "isolates") from the world of animals—"immense nature"—the human world of "jewels, furniture, metals, gilding." The last line of "Le Cadre" thus indicates that the isolation from nature the frame purportedly creates is merely an apparent isolation, for the nature which was, according to the first stanza, shut out of the portrait is by the poem's last word discovered to be the very subject of the portrait, in the center of the frame. Within the context of the sonnet cycle as a whole, this reversal is what is most unsettling about the word "singe." It suggests that the vision of the woman framed by the trappings of civilization is not fixed, like a painting in a museum, but transitory—part of nature and thus part of its cycle, its movement through time, toward decay.

The word "enfantine" also recalls the "jeunesse" (youth) of "Le Parfum," thus setting the stage for the last poem in the cycle. "Le Portrait" suggests that it is indeed the loss of the period of time associated with the woman's "jeunesse" that is the concern of the entire cycle of sonnets. The "frame" through which the poet in "Un Fantôme" looks is not made up of "bijoux, meubles," and so on, but rather of the imperfect tense; that is, the speaker is looking at what is past, looking backward, at shadows.

The title "Le Portrait" would seem to imply a culmination of the movement developed through the first three sonnets in the cycle, from the evocation of the speaker as painter, the description of the difficult "canvas" on which he must paint, and his wait for a source of light in "Les Ténèbres"; to an extended evocation of this light source, transferred to the olfactory realm, in "Le Parfum"; to a discussion of the frame and its relation to the object represented in "Le Cadre." But once past the title, the reader finds not so much an account of the portrait as of its destruction. The concluding poem evokes absence rather than the imitative presence its title implies.

"Le Portrait" returns to both the mode (allegory) and the imagery (painting) established in "Les Ténèbres." It concerns the triumph of time and the failure of the speaker / painter / poet to bring memory back to life:

> La Maladie et la Mort font des cendres
> De tout le feu qui pour nous flamboya.
> De ces grands yeux si fervents et si tendres,
> Ce cette bouche où mon coeur se noya,

De ces baisers puissants comme un dictame,
De ces transports plus vifs que des rayons,
Que reste-t-il? C'est affreux, ô mon âme!
Rien qu'un dessin fort pâle, aux trois crayons,

Qui, comme moi, meurt dans la solitude,
Et que le Temps, injurieux vieillard,
Chaque jour frotte avec son aile rude . . .

Noir assassin de la Vie et de l'Art,
Tu ne tueras jamais dans ma mémoire
Celle qui fut mon plaisir et ma gloire!

(Sickness and Death convert to ashes / All the fire that burned for us. / Of those great eyes, so passionate and so tender, / Of that mouth where my heart drowned, / Of those kisses powerful as a balm, / Of those transports more piercing than rays, / What remains? It is dreadful, o my soul: / Nothing but a very faint sketch, made with three pencils, / Which, like me, is dying in solitude, / And which Time, hurtful old man, / Each day rubs with his rough wing. . . / Sinister assassin of Life and of Art, / You will never kill in my memory / Her who was my pleasure and my glory!)

[1:40]

The last tercet is of particular interest. In the version above, first published in October 1860, it represents a sudden change from the movement of the first three stanzas, a change marked by the three suspension points. It is oratorical, a shaking of the fist against time's inevitable passage and effects. But the published tercet says just the opposite of the final tercet as it appears in the manuscript dated March 1860:

Comme un manant ivre, ou comme un soudard
Qui bat les murs, et salit et coudoie
Une beauté frêle, en robe de soie.

(Like a drunken yokel, or like a ruffian / Who bumps into walls, and soils and elbows / A frail beauty, in a silken gown.)

Several of Baudelaire's editors have felt obliged to comment on this striking change from manuscript to published version. Le Dantec remarks: "One may suppose that the poet must have long hesitated over the sacrifice of this fine tercet (a Guys!) and its replacement by the other, more logical but how banal! The trace of this struggle is marked by the points of suspension which end and prolong the preceding line, even while emphasizing an inevitable gap and a scruple over not wanting to perpetrate a sonnet with seventeen feet, called an *estrambote*."[36]

Jules Crépet also found the tercet as published "banal" and "plein de trémolos" (full of tremolos) and preferred the manuscript version (1:903). Claude Pichois, editor of the most recent critical edition published in the standard Pléiade series, explains Baudelaire's revision by his desire to establish a transition to the following poem ("Je te donne ces vers . . ."), which he reads as promising the aging mistress that she will not die entirely because she will live on in his verse (1:903). The juncture between "Je te donne ces vers . . ." and "Un Fantôme" is, however, not nearly so straightforward as Pichois's explanation alone would imply. Baudelaire's hesitation between the two variant tercets, entirely opposite in meaning, marks the great ambivalence of this juncture.

Because of its placement as the concluding poem in a cycle of four sonnets, "Le Portrait" must be read in relation not only to what comes after it but primarily to what has gone before. Specifically, it returns to the setting and situation established in the first poem in the cycle, treating the light source which in "Les Ténèbres" had cast the shadows on which the speaker was condemned to paint. In "Le Portrait" this light source, "the fire," has been turned to cinders, so that even the shadows are imperiled, if not destroyed entirely. The "grâce," "splendeur," and "allure" attributed to "Elle" in the first poem of the cycle become in the last poem a list of features ("yeux," "bouche," "baisers") that exist only in a very pale sketch; the emphasis is less on the beauty of these features than on the loss of that beauty. The speaker/painter/poet, in a kind of burial vault in the first poem, is in the last one also dying in isolation. The principal difference between the two poems is that in the first the coming into being of the specter of "Elle" is celebrated, while in the last the sketch of her is every day being gradually rubbed away.

The final tercet that Baudelaire chose to publish celebrates the triumph of memory over time. It breaks away from the image, established in the first tercet, of "Time" as a harmful old man rubbing the sketch away with his boorish "wing" to insist that the speaker will triumph over "Time." The variant tercet preserved in the manuscript,

---

36. Le Dantec and Pichois, eds., *Oeuvres complètes*, p. 1517, alludes to Constantin Guys, the artist who won Baudelaire's praise in his essay "Le Peintre de la vie moderne."

however, develops the harmful old man into a "drunken yokel" or "ruffian" and the boorish wing into an elbow or a drunken body that knocks against walls. The speaker of both final tercets detests "Time," who is depicted as either an assassin or a ruffian. But in the published version the speaker asserts a form of victory over "Time" which does not occur in the manuscript variant. The weakness of "Elle" and the delicacy of her garb are, in this variant, clearly no match for the "soil" applied by "Time."

The Pathos of Interpretation Loosed from Exegesis

With Virginie, the third instance of a female fictive reader whose own mind, interests, and history control (and, in this case, limit) her reading of a text to a greater extent than does the text's author, Baudelaire creates a link between what might otherwise seem a literary-sexual image of only marginal importance to his work and a theme that may properly be seen as of fundamental importance to the entire body of his verse and prose poems: the loss that accompanies the exhilaration of a fertile imagination. Virginie is happy with her few images, as the proverbial Wise Man is happy with few books, as indeed Adam was happy with the few guiding ideas God had given him and the single names he had given to the creatures around him. The introduction of more images, more books, more ideas about the meaning of the Tree of Knowledge, all acquired with the passing of time, may open up a new world of possibilities but also means exile from the peaceful simplicity of a single, uniform perspective.

The ambivalence marked by the contrast between Virginie and the reader evoked in the *Opium Eater* translation reappears in the discrepancy between the two versions of the final tercet of "Le Portrait." As I have indicated, the discrepancy is resolved at this point in the text of *Les Fleurs du mal* in favor of the notion already enthusiastically endorsed in Baudelaire's version of *Confessions of an English Opium Eater*—that memory will triumph over time. Nonetheless the contrary notion expressed in the manuscript version continues to play a prominent role elsewhere in the collection. It is especially important to a poem written, once again, early in 1860—one in a contrasting pair. "Obsession," two manuscripts of which were mailed to two publishers

in February 1860, was not published until May of that year(1:980).[37]
But it shares all the preoccupations concerning the struggle between
the poet and time that Baudelaire's works of the first months of 1860
display.

As Paul de Man has shown, "Obsession" may be understood as
Baudelaire's reading of his earlier and more famous "Correspondances."[38] Like much of Baudelaire's work, this pair of poems appears
to celebrate the poet's copious imaginative life only to invert that very
plenitude into a form of lack. "Correspondances" (the first two stanzas
of which appear above) presents Nature as speaking to the various
senses a multiple, babelic language that resolves itself into unity. If one
were to read the first stanza in isolation from what follows, one would
imagine an inhospitable "Nature": the words "parfois" (sometimes)
and "confuses" (faint) indicate an inconsistency and opacity that would
make interpretation difficult, while the ancient image of the "forêt"
(woods) immediately evokes the human struggle to understand (compare Dante's "dark wood"). However, no one reads the first stanza
alone, and with the second stanza Baudelaire has turned to celebrate
"unité."

But "Obsession" calls this celebration into question, by returning to
the mood hinted at in the first stanza of "Correspondances" and radically transforming its images almost word for word:

> Grands bois, vous m'effrayez comme des cathédrales;
> Vous hurlez comme l'orgue; et dans nos coeurs maudits,
> Chambres d'éternel deuil où vibrent de vieux râles,
> Répondent les échos de vos *De profundis*.
>
> Je te hais, Océan! tes bonds et tes tumultes,
> Mon esprit les retrouve en lui; ce rire amer
> De l'homme vaincu, plein de sanglots et d'insultes,
> Je l'entends dans le rire énorme de la mer.

---

37. Pichois notes (1:980) that "almost the whole poem seems to feed upon a reading
of De Quincey." His source is Michèle Stäuble-Lipman Wulf's critical edition of *Un
Mangeur*, published in *Etudes baudelairiennes* 6–7, which I have been unable to consult
(1:1368).

38. Paul de Man, "Anthropomorphism and Trope in the Lyric," in *Rhetoric of Romanticism*, pp. 239–62. Cynthia Chase, "Getting Versed: Reading Hegel with
Baudelaire," *Studies in Romanticism* 22 (1983), 241–66, translates the Baudelairean concept of the creative imagination into semiotic terms.

Comme tu me plairais, ô nuit! sans ces étoiles
Dont la lumière parle un langage connu!
Car je cherche le vide, et le noir, et le nu!

Mais les ténèbres sont elles-mêmes des toiles
Où vivent, jaillissant de mon oeil par milliers,
Des êtres disparus aux regards familiers.

(Great woods, you terrify me like cathedrals! You roar like an organ,
and in our condemned hearts, those chambers of eternal mourning in
which death rattles vibrate from the past, the echoes of your *De profun-
dis* repeat their responses.

Ocean, I hate you: my mind is full of your leaping and pan-
demonium. In the enormous laughter of the sea I hear the bitter laughter of man defeated, full of sobs and blasphemies.

How you would please me, O Night, without those stars whose
light speaks a language I understand! For my quest is for emptiness,
blackness, and bareness.

But the very shadows are canvases in which—leaping in thousands
from my eyes—live vanished beings with familiar gaze.)

[1:75–76]

The speaker in "Obsession" is tormented by a universe in which he
can find no silence or, rather, by what Jonathan Culler has termed "the
dictatorial imagination."[39] Like Virginie, whose eyes store the images
of her history, the speaker's eyes have stored up "vanished beings"
whom he projects by the "thousands" into "the very shadows." Many
other poems in the "Spleen et Idéal" section of *Les Fleurs du mal* voice
the poet's despair at the multiplicity of memories and images from
which he cannot escape. The "shadows" that "are canvases" in "Obsession" parallel closely the shadows on which the speaker must, regret-
fully, paint in "Les Ténèbres." In "Spleen (II)," the speaker who laments, "J'ai plus de souvenirs que si j'avais mille ans" (I have more
memories than if I had lived a thousand years) compares his brain to a
bureau swarming with the detritus of the past. "Alchimie de la dou-
leur" (Alchemy of sadness) provides a particularly dramatic image of
this problem. It presents Midas as symbol of the poet who loses what is
most valuable by his inescapable powers of alchemy. "Le Cygne"
("The Swan"), well known as a meditation on poetic history, also
ambivalently celebrates and laments the life of imagination which that

39. Culler, "Modern Lyric," p. 296, citing Hugo Friedrich. In semiotic terms, the
speaker is encumbered by so many interpretants that he can reach no stable interpretation.

history creates, for it evokes a city changing as much through the abilities of the speaker to read literary references as moral messages into it as through the action of the agents of urban renewal.

This theme of abundant imaginative transformation, which leaves behind it sadness and even torment, helps explain why the powerfully imaginative readers Baudelaire evokes in his narrative and essayistic prose are sometimes women. Women are for Baudelaire the focus of the same kind of love/hate relationship he has with his own imagination.[40] At the same time that these imaginative readers create, they also destroy. There is some uncertainty, always, about the identity or value of just what it is that has been lost through the productivity of the poetic-readerly imagination, but there is always connected with it at least a degree of ruefulness.

The recurrent motif of the female reader in Baudelaire, then, forms but a small element in a larger obsessive theme, which might be called (echoing "Alchemy of Sadness") the "Midas theme." In turn, both motif and theme represent aspects of a larger problem that Baudelaire was not alone in recognizing. He presents imaginative activity (whether its object be nature, a cityscape, or a book) as an intensely pleasurable orgy that veils the approach of death as it erases the march of time. Yet in the midst of this orgy the profligates know that something is lacking and wish to escape their imaginative powers in order to find something—they know not what—that has been lost. Their compulsion to imagine is as pathetic as it is pleasurable.

Baudelaire's female readers and Midas theme exemplify the problematic character of the extreme interpretive pole in reading. Interpretive reading knows no limits, and its infinite expansiveness is cause for rejoicing. At the same time, its limitlessness paradoxically sets a limit to the possibility of meaning. Such unbridled interpretation as Baudelaire celebrates cannot be carried on without an attendant sense of loss.

This aspect of Baudelaire's work may thus be read as emblematic of a viewpoint that I ascribed to Boccaccio. Boccaccio may be read as pushing the exegetical pole of reading to its fullest limit and also finding at that extreme a sense of loss. He, and humanists after him, recognized with pain that a text once fallen into the hands of a reader

---

40. An excellent development of this theme in the late Middle Ages appears in the work of SunHee Kim Gertz, "Woman as Word: Rhetorical Creativity in the Middle Ages" (diss., University of Chicago, 1983).

can never be put together again. The goal of exegetical reading is always out of reach, though the ideal which that goal establishes sets a clear limit, a limit that the extreme interpretive reading Baudelaire admired and regretted completely lacks.

Baudelaire, to be sure, was himself not a wholly interpretive reader, as Boccaccio was by no means always exegetical. Reading always, of necessity, occurs in the space between exegesis and interpretation. It is the shuttling back and forth from one to the other that gives reading its energy. While readers can only hope in vain to realize Boccaccio's dream, they are nonetheless safe from Baudelaire's nightmare.

One must ask, however, why Baudelaire evoked that nightmare again and again. Why did he so often celebrate or lament "the dictatorial imagination" rather than finding ways to rebel against it? Certainly, it seems to exert an erotic pull for him, as his repeated exploration of it through figures of female readers seems to suggest.

An answer that is less biographical and psychological may be sought, however, in speculations not about Baudelaire's literary personality, but about that of his readers. The pairing of "Correspondances" and "Obsession" opens a crucial avenue to this answer. Perhaps Paul de Man came as close as he ever did to advancing any concept of literary genesis, and thus of literary history, when he wrote of this pair of poems:

> ["Correspondances"], and it alone, contains, implies, produces, generates, permits (or whatever aberrant verbal metaphor one wishes to choose) the entire possibility of the lyric. Whenever we encounter a text such as "Obsession"—that is, whenever we read—there is always an infra-text, a hypogram like "Correspondances" underneath. Stating this relationship, as we just did, in phenomenal, spatial terms or in phenomenal, temporal terms—"Obsession," a text of recollection and elegiac mourning, *adds* remembrance to the flat surface of time in "Correspondances"—produces at once a hermeneutic, fallacious lyrical reading of the unintelligible. . . . If mourning is called a "chambre d'éternel deuil où vibrent de vieux râles" [chamber of eternal mourning in which death rattles vibrate from the past], then this pathos of terror states in fact the desired consciousness of eternity and of temporal harmony as voice and as song. True "mourning" is less deluded. The most *it* can do is allow for non-comprehension and enumerate non-anthropomorphic, non-elegiac, non-celebratory, non-lyrical, non-poetic, that is to say, prosaic, or, better, *historical* modes of language power.[41]

41. de Man, "Anthropomorphism and Trope, " pp. 261–62.

What I have identified as Baudelaire's concern in early 1860 with the conquering of time through the power of the imagination to multiply is here described by de Man as the production of "a hermeneutic, fallacious lyrical reading of the unintelligible." De Man's rhetoric suggests a motive for Baudelaire's obsessive (the term is most appropriate) return to celebrate and deplore the powers of the imagination, a motive that goes far beyond the situation of Baudelaire as an individual. When one encounters (as one daily does) the unintelligible, the impulse is to invent a "lyrical reading."

Jonathan Culler has taken not just the pairing of "Correspondances" and "Obsession" but Baudelaire's poetry in general as exemplary. Observing that this particular body of poems is frequently cited as marking the beginnings of modern poetry, he nonetheless insistently moves the focus from the poems to the reading of them, much as de Man does. Taking "lyric" as his topic, he works from an assumption that goes beyond the limits usually associated with this term: "Genres are . . . treated as models that function within a particular culture to generate readings."[42]

The argument I have tried to develop in this book shares something with these two related analyses of the production of the lyric, even though the latter is a generic category I have scarcely invoked. In the present chapter I have more often stressed the importance of the novel, even suggesting that the drama of perceptions and attitudes legible in *Les Fleurs du mal* constitutes a kind of novel *manqué*, designed to fascinate as character development in a novel fascinates. But my concern has been less with the goals and personality of the writer than with those of the reader. I have sought to establish that the literary personality of the reader *has* a historical character, in order to create a theoretical framework that might make it possible to identify features of this historical character within a cultural system.

According to de Man, *"whenever we read"* (emphasis mine), the relationship "Correspondances/Obsession" is reenacted; memory is brought forward to explain what is not memory but rather invention. But this very listening for what will never be heard "contains, implies, produces, generates, permits (or whatever aberrant verbal metaphor one wishes to choose) the entire possibility" of reading.

I have been asked why I have chosen to end this book with works from the romantic period (and, one might add, in a sense with a poem, "Correspondances," that is often read as marking the end of romanti-

42. Culler, "Modern Lyric," p. 292.

cism). This literary-historical question requires a complex answer in a book that calls literary history into question. Certainly I could have recounted a historical narrative that would end instead with Protestantism, identifying it with a shift from exegesis to interpretation (or vice versa). Alternatively, I might have closed with Paul Hazard's "crisis of the European consciousness" in the late seventeenth and early eighteenth centuries. An endpoint in the twentieth century would also have had much to recommend it. Yet the problem that my argument should, if it succeeds, make compelling is this: the book has inescapably to start in the twentieth century, and also to end there. Its narrative shape would, no matter what choices I made, *always* be fictive. Indeed, I originally placed the chapters on romanticism first, and in a sense they still belong there conceptually in that they set forth the theoretical nature of my argument without encouraging a misreading of that argument as historical in a positivistic sense. Nonetheless, I think the late Paul de Man was right in persuading me that ordering my argument nonchronologically would be a serious rhetorical mistake.

Romanticism represents, in the rhetorical structure I have tried to devise, not a chronological end but a conceptual frame that structures mid-twentieth century literary thought. I have argued that romanticism is rather a reading style than a period designation.[43] As others have observed, much influential American theoretical work in the last forty years is grounded in readings of romantic poetry (one thinks not only of Harold Bloom, Paul de Man, and Geoffrey Hartman but also back to Cleanth Brooks's *The Well Wrought Urn*). It is the romantic ambivalence about interpretation and the exegetical longing, seen in the philological labors of the scholarly contemporaries of romantic poets, which still impels the oscillating movement that gives to reading the form it appears to have at this moment.

43. For a full treatment, see my essay "Self-reading and Temporal Irony in *Aurélia*."

Conclusion: Between
Exegesis and Interpretation

> The terminology of traditional literary history, as a succession
> of periods or literary movements, remains useful only if the
> terms are seen for what they are: rather crude metaphors for
> figural patterns rather than historical events or acts.
>
> PAUL DE MAN, *The Rhetoric of Romanticism*

In the foregoing chapters I have tried to address a series of texts
both exegetically and interpretively. Now it is time to draw back and
look at the whole of what has been set forth, not in an effort to describe
the historical development of reading—since such a description necessarily remains beyond my reach—but rather in an attempt to describe
more clearly the conceptual model of the implication of reading in
history, and of history in reading, that my argument proposes.

It is also time to discuss other conceptual models that complement
the one presented here, models drawn especially from semiotics and
semiotically based Bettian hermeneutics but also from deconstruction,
phenomenology, historically based hermeneutics (Gadamerian and
Marxian), and feminism. My postponement of such discussion of alternative theoretical models to this concluding chapter invites a charge
of egregious historical distortion, since all these other models not only
precede mine chronologically but have been essential stimulants to my
own questions and formulations. Yet my ungraciousness in delaying
acknowledgment of them may, I think, be excused by my desire to
make the beginning and middle of this book, at least, as accessible as
possible to those who are seriously interested in the cultural position of
reading but are not specialists in literature, much less in contemporary

literary theory. If some parts of what follows must employ a vocabulary less accessible than that used in earlier chapters, a pathway into
them has nonetheless been opened, I hope, by means of an imaginative
evocation of what a specialist in theory might more readily approach
conceptually.

In Chapter 1, I pointed out a contrast between the images of the
reader whom Dante and Baudelaire address and asked whether the
difference between them might not be partially explained by changes
in the historical circumstances of readers and reading which occurred
between the fourteenth and nineteenth centuries. At this point, however, it may be more useful to bear in mind the contrast between
Boccaccio—rather than Dante—and Baudelaire. Boccaccio and Baudelaire may be taken to stand, respectively, at the two opposite poles
that form the limits of this study. Boccaccio represents the would-be
perfect exegete; Baudelaire, the would-be infinite interpreter. Boccaccio, at least in the *Genealogy* if not elsewhere, takes the text to be a
dismembered body that it is the able reader's task to heal; Baudelaire
suggests a view of the text as a body that the able reader will subject to
limitless metamorphosis. Each nonetheless finds built into the aspira-
tion toward the "best" form of reading, whether exegetical or interpretive, a source of distress and even despair. Boccaccio recognizes that he
will be able to put back together only a hump-backed monstrosity, not
the perfect, original body he seeks; Baudelaire understands that if the
text can become anything, it is also nothing.

None of the other three writers discussed here takes such an extreme
position as Boccaccio and Baudelaire do in certain of their texts. Nerval sees clearly the legitimacy and necessity of both exegetical and
interpretive aspirations but presents himself as shattered by their ten-
sions: "[This madness] is the fault of my readings." Both Dante and
Christine, by contrast, are paradigmatic figures each of whom develops a model of reading that comprises both exegesis and interpretation
without taking the two to be mutually competitive and destructive.
Christine might be said to see these two types of reading as symbiotically connected, while Dante's notion is fully dialectical.

My study of these five quite different figures has unearthed a broad
range of images for representing the temporality of reading. Dante
contrasts mortal and immortal reading, depicting the earthly reader's
lot as a continual hunt for scattered pages which will end only when
the original Author returns to bind them into a single volume. Boccaccio, too, employs the notion of binding scattered fragments but sees

them less as parts of a book ultimately to be perfected than as parts of a mutilated corpse. Dante, Boccaccio, and Christine each adapt the gloss to represent their varying notions of appropriate ways in which readings converge or diverge from the text. Nerval associates the temporal discrepancy between text and reader with sickness. Baudelaire returns repeatedly to the notion of mutual attempts at seduction on the part of author and reader.

All these models are in some way dichotomous in structure. The basis of each is a perceived gap between author and reader, which is in turn derived from a gap between past and present or present and future. In some of the models (Dante's, Christine's, and—to a more limited extent—Boccaccio's and Nerval's) the opposition is softened and the gap bridged by the notion that author and reader, past and present, have common interests, values, or dispositions. Nonetheless, most of them connote loss, pain, and even violence.

The goal of this study has been to show that dichotomous models of the temporality of reading are not only misleading but even deleterious when they fail to incorporate some means of resolving the dichotomy. Just as a model of reading as a temporal process need not remain dichotomized, moreover, an understanding of reading fully cognizant of its complex temporality need not be painful: the sense of loss, which has been evoked in many forms in these pages, arises only from an approach to the temporality of reading that personalizes or in some other way spatializes it inappropriately.[1] Reading then becomes, for example, a matter of competing for a rung on a ladder above or closer to someone else's position; or perhaps a struggle to hold onto, seize, or reclaim property.

Far preferable to such spatialization of the reading process would be its full *semiotization*. When applied to reading, the term is inherently

---

1. In his *Blindness and Insight*, Paul de Man sets forth a model that is ironic rather than dichotomous; that is, it posits that every text comprehends two conflicting voices but does not imply that these two voices cancel each other. This model depicts the voice of blindness and the voice of insight as together generating meaning and indeed goes so far as to locate the resolution of the blindness/insight dichotomy in the text's author (the crux of de Man's disagreement with Derrida in the chapter on Rousseau). The point is well made by Koelb, "The Authority of the Text," *Blindness and Insight* has nonetheless been taken, rather more than less frequently as time goes by, as describing every text as a kind of agon that brings about the destruction of both voices. This reading derives from precisely the kind of inappropriate spatialization, indeed personalization, of the pair "blindness/insight" which the present study has sought to criticize in the quite different realm of the timeliness (rather than the rhetoric) of reading.

redundant in that reading is already among the most sign-centered of activities; but it must be used here to stress the need to undo the ill effects of the stripping away from reading of its full semiotic character over a period of many centuries.[2] Reading has, in Western culture, been a principal victim of the failure to adopt and progressively refine an adequate notion of the sign. It is still common today for "clerks" (for example, teachers of literature) as well as lay people to accept as the whole truth the attractive but dangerous half-truth that *words* represent *things* (or events, ideas, attitudes) and that reading is thus a matter of correctly leading the mind from the perception of the former to the apprehension of the latter.

Exegesis, Interpretation, and Semiotics

Charles Sanders Peirce, a younger contemporary of Cardinal Newman, was the first since the late medieval speculative grammarians to offer an abstract model of sign structure which not only calls this misleading half-truth into question but also provides a useful concept that goes beyond such questioning.[3] He proposed to modify

2. In a chapter of his *Inventions* titled "The Originality of Texts in a Manuscript Culture," Gerald Bruns makes a similar point from a hermeneutic perspective.

3. Some of the following material appeared earlier in "Literary Semiotics and Hermeneutics: Towards a Taxonomy of the Interpretant," *American Journal of Semiotics*, 3 (1985), 55–65. Its tracing of a thread from Peirce to Emilio Betti, in the interests of chronological coherence, is not meant to exclude more recent contributions to a semiotically informed hermeneutics. For example, in 1974 Julia Kristeva, apparently drawing on Bakhtinian concepts, argued that linguistics should be deflected "toward a consideration of language as articulation of a heterogeneous process, with the speaking subject leaving its imprint on the dialectic between the articulation and its process. . . . what is implied is that language, and thus sociability, are defined by boundaries admitting of upheaval, dissolution, and transformation. . . . the dramatic notion of language as a risky practice, allowing the speaking animal to sense the rhythm of the body as well as the upheavals of history, seems tied to a notion of signifying process that contemporary theories do not confront." See "The Ethics of Linguistics," in Kristeva's *Desire in Language: A Semiotic Approach to Literature and Art*, ed. Leon S. Roudiez, trans. Thomas Gora, Alice Jardine, and Leon S. Roudiez (New York: Columbia University Press, 1980), pp. 23–35 (quotations from pp. 24–25, 34). Dean MacCannell and Juliet Flower MacCannell, in *The Time of the Sign: A Semiotic Interpretation of Modern Culture* (Bloomington: Indiana University Press, 1982), have powerfully demonstrated how concepts of sign structure and models of societal interaction are closely related. More recently Teresa de Lauretis has proposed a decentering of semiotics by means of feminism; its implications go far beyond her ostensible topic, film; see *Alice Doesn't: Feminism, Semiotics, Cinema* (Bloomington: Indiana University Press, 1984).

radically the traditional binary definition of the sign by introducing a third essential element, which he called the "interpretant." Now the "interpret*ant*" is by no means the same thing as the "interpret*er*," although the two are frequently and readily confused.[4] An interpreter, in literary semiotics, is a human subject; the interpretant is an abstract entity necessary to the production of a sign—necessary, in other words, to reading. In naming the interpretant, Peirce posited an entity that mediates the relations between other sign elements (namely, the element that signifies and the element that is signified) when a sign is produced: that is, when something stands for something else to somebody. Although one's first impulse may be to equate the interpretant with a psychological occurrence in an interpreter's mind, it is unnecessary and in fact quite limiting to give in to this impulse, for the concept is potentially much richer, especially when employed in the analysis of the timeliness of reading.

The interpretant is better thought of as a function of the sign rather than of the interpreter: a member of the same class as the word rather than a gesture by the reader. Indeed, it is one of the necessary components of the existence of the sign, an existence that does not depend on whether or not the interpreter attends to it. Umberto Eco has elaborated helpfully upon Peirce's definition of the interpretant.[5] According to Eco, if every sign is made up of (1) an object that is represented, (2) a representation of the object, and (3) an interpretant, then the interpretant is a representation of the object which is other than the representation first mentioned. That is, number 3, the interpretant, is the same kind of thing as number 2, the representation, in that both of them refer to the same object, number 1. Yet although numbers 3 and 2, the interpretant and the first-mentioned representation, are the same kind of thing—representations—they are necessarily different instances of representation. Their relationship is one of necessary non-identity, even though, from two points of view, they are congruent: each belongs to the same class of entities, representations; and each is a representation referring to the same object. Yet—and this is not a point that either Eco or Peirce stresses, though it is the very crux of what I am

---

4. In fact, Manley Thompson, *The Pragmatic Philosophy of C. S. Peirce* (Chicago: University of Chicago Press, 1953), pp. 295–96, argues that Peirce himself confounds the two, which would tend to confirm the present study's suggestion that readers resist seeing themselves as interpretants.

5. Umberto Eco, *A Theory of Semiotics* (Bloomington: Indiana University Press, 1976), pp. 14–16.

attempting to show—this description of the two representations as both congruent and non-identical cannot be understood by recourse to geometry alone, despite the geometric and mathematical implications of the two adjectives. There is always a temporal force in one representation or the other, which creates the dynamism of the relation between them. Before I explain what I mean by "temporal force" and "dynamism" in this relation, however, it is necessary to examine in more detail the Peircean concept of the interpretant.

One of Peirce's definitions of the sign, organized to start from the interpretant rather than to move toward it, may help to clarify the meaning of the term: "A sign is 'anything which determines something else (its *interpretant*) to refer to an object to which itself refers (its *object*) in the same way.'"[6] Thus, sign production, in the necessary generation of the interpretant, is intrinsically an act of repetition, of intended replication. The repetition is potentially infinite, for the interpretant takes on the property of what I have called the "first" representation in becoming itself a sign, which then requires an interpretant, and so on and on. The "temporal force" in sign production, therefore, might be described as the intention of replication. Even if one conceives of a momentary instance of sign production without any passage of time— that is, without any history—the *expectation* of repetition itself nonetheless depends on the *concept* of time. For this reason, I would argue, sign production, or semiosis, cannot be rightly understood without analysis of its inherent temporality.

Bettian Hermeneutics: A Taxonomy of the Interpretant

A major advance in developing Peirce's groundbreaking but still unstable and embryonic concept of the interpretant in such a way as to make it potentially fruitful in the study of the timeliness of reading appeared in the work of Emilio Betti.[7] Betti saw Peirce's triadic concept of the sign as a cornerstone of hermeneutics (which may be defined, as specified in the Introduction, as the study of the relation between exegesis and interpretation). Betti argued that hermeneutics must discriminate among three kinds of interpretant: in his terms, three different "criteria of cognition drawn forth from the mind." Each

6. Ibid., p. 69.
7. Emilio Betti, *Teoria generale della interpretazione*, 2 vols.(Milan: A. Giuffrè, 1955).

kind of interpretant is, in Betti's hermeneutic theory, the basis of a different kind of interpretation (a term Betti employed in a general sense, not the one used throughout the present study): that is, a different kind of reading.

The first interpretive type Betti called "normative interpretation": it aims to bring about a decision, a new behavior, or the adoption of some sort of position in practical life. Its basis would thus be an interpretant which, though necessarily derived from the past ("drawn forth from the mind") like all interpretants, would nonetheless also project itself toward the future. Such an interpretant should be thought of not simply as an object that takes on its characteristic function when it is apprehended as congruent with another object but rather as an entity that the human desire for replication of experience (which may be designated, for example, as "stability," "timelessness," "enduring value") endows with the ability to "live on," to "mean," both in a time posterior to its own conception and also in relation to decisions or behaviors occurring in a still later time. The normatively oriented interpretant operates in the United States, for example, in the evolution of constitutional law. Betti's "normative interpretation" represents a specification of what I have throughout this study been calling by the more general name of "interpretation."

The second form of interpretant forms the basis of what Betti called "merely re-cognitive interpretation," or interpretation as an end in itself. Its basis would be an interpretant moving only from past to present, though of course the seeking out of an interpretant that may be taken to replicate what is read, heard, or seen in the present may be a lengthy process. Throughout the present study, "merely re-cognitive interpretation" has been called "exegesis."

Betti's third form of interpretant, "reproductive or representative interpretation," has as its end to make that which is interpreted understood by someone else. Like normative interpretation it would be founded on a process of discovery of interpretants oriented toward the future rather than limited to the present. The interpretant characteristic of reproductive interpretation, however, would differ in its more limited scope from one that characterizes normative interpretation. It is oriented toward a future "reader" ("future" in the sense that a first interpreter endeavors to make something clear to another interpreter who appears after the first interpreter's initial act of interpretation), yet it does not seek to continue to shape the second interpreter's understanding after the moment in which first and second interpreters reach a common interpretation. Should the first interpreter thus seek to control not only the second interpreter's understanding of a given sign but also his or her later behavior, the first interpreter would move beyond the realm of reproductive interpretation into that of normative interpretation.

When the temporality of sign reading is taken to be of paramount importance, as in the present study, it is helpful to modify the order in which Betti presents his three forms of interpretation. One might then see re-cognitive interpretation as the most elementary; reproductive interpretation as occupying the next level of complexity and building upon re-cognitive interpretation; and normative interpretation as the most complex of all, building upon the other two. The latter two "build upon" what has gone before in the sense that the process of semiosis, or generation of interpretant-signs, is continuous from one to the next. The three basic kinds of interpretant in question thus act upon one another. The interaction is not unidirectional, however; its movement is characteristically oscillating, moving back and forth and back once again.

Two recent major contributions to the study of semiotics have proposed, if only in passing, notions useful to the analysis of the temporality of the interpretant. Michael Riffaterre has stressed the importance of what he calls "split-second, semiconscious retroactive reading" in the formulation of links among words in a single text:

> Retroactive reading . . . appears to be the method for decoding dual signs: first, because the sign refers to a paradigm, and a paradigm can be recognized only after it has been sufficiently developed in space so that certain constants can be perceived; second, because any stumbling-block sends the reader scurrying back for a clue, back being the only place to go; third, because the correction made backwards via the proximate homologue creates the ghost or parallel text wherein the dual sign's second (or syntactically unacceptable) semantic allegiance can be vindicated. . . . in the reading of poetry there is an initiatory period and a delay in realizing what a given text is actually about.[8]

That Riffaterre feels obliged to bring up, in a chapter on interpretants, the temporality of the reading process is by no means a casual matter, although it may seem so in the overall context of his presentation. Change is essential to the interpretant; it cannot be adequately de-

8. Michael Riffaterre, *Semiotics of Poetry* (Bloomington: Indiana University Press, 1978), pp. 91, 109.

scribed without recourse to a concept of time. To emphasize the fundamentally temporal character of the interpretant, and thus of reading, this book began (Chapter 1) by showing how the interpretant changes—that is, metamorphoses itself into another, and still another, interpretant—not only within the time of the reading of a single poem (as Riffaterre points out) but also over larger units of time—and thus requires description not only across the life span of an individual but across larger periods of time.

Eco's discussion of symptoms also focuses attention on the temporality of the interpretant. He points out that if we see smoke, we take it as a sign of fire because of a convention established within the community by past experiences of smoke, implying that the temporal quality of pastness is necessary to the interpretant. Eco in fact gives greater weight to the temporality of the interpretant than did Peirce. In Peirce's view, inference can occur without semiosis—that is, there exist for Peirce acts of interpretation that can take place entirely in a framework of the present—whereas for Eco, only a convention rooted in the past makes a sign a sign. When Eco stresses the centrality to his semiotics of the notion of meaning as a cultural unit, he is necessarily pointing to the temporal dimension of the interpretant. Although he does not discuss this dimension in detail, he alludes to it whenever he treats the "dissolving of cultural units," the "passing on [of a] torch," the "successive" nature of interpretants in infinite semiosis.

The interpretant must be conceived of as intrinsically and necessarily dynamic rather than static. When scholars debate, as they continue to do, whether there is a single valid interpretation of a text or a multiplicity of them, they are troubled by this dynamic quality of the interpretant, what I propose to call its "alternativity." "Alternativity" indicates the interpretant's tendency to posit more than one possible meaning, to produce more than one possible linked idea. It is a corollary of the interpretant's temporality because the interpretant characteristically looks forward to more than one meaning. The very fact that readers *expect* a text to mean something—that is, look to its (hypothetically existent) meaning as something to be discovered in the *future*, at a moment *after* the initial perception of its words—shows how deeply rooted in temporality the interpretant must be.

The Time of the Interpretant

The dichotomous images characteristically employed to describe reading by writers concerned with its temporality—mortal/immortal, gloss/text, dismemberment/wholeness, seducer/victim (as well as exegesis/interpretation)—are inadequate precisely insofar as they remain dichotomous. The pair "lady's reading/gentleman's reading" is by far the most enduring, and notorious, image to mask the timeliness of reading.[9] What is needed to begin to account for reading more adequately is a concept, like Peirce's interpretant, recognizing that there is something *between* such poles which constitutes reading and without which reading could not be.

The most misleading of such dichotomies is, certainly, the traditional one between author and reader, characteristically set into the dichotomous matrices of past and present (or, what is the same thing from an authorial rather than readerly point of view, present and future). It is in fact this past-author/present-reader (or present-author/future-reader) dichotomy that engenders all the others. From the conception of the author and reader as persons who form two basic elements in the reading process comes the notion of the person who dies versus the one who does not, of the person who marks a piece of paper with a pen versus the one who encounters the marks made, of the person who dismembers versus the one who is dismembered, and so on.

While no one would wish to deny that authors and readers are persons, one must also keep in mind that saying this is not saying enough, for in addition to being persons (who love, hate, and so on), authors and readers are also sign producers. It is in fact first of all in their capacity as sign producers that they participate in the reading process; their "personhood," so to speak, comes into play in reading only at one remove. The author-reader dichotomy, which in various manifestations has long plagued Western analyses of reading, ceases to be a dichotomy when the two are taken to be not different things but different instances of the same thing, sign production.

One must be careful, in considering this concept, not to reintroduce a false dichotomy by looking upon the author as an *earlier* sign producer and the reader as a *later* one. To think of the reader as temporally *second* is as correct (to refer once again to an insight that feminism contributes to hermeneutics) as thinking of Eve as formed out of

9. I have set out the numerous ways in which a gender dichotomy has been employed in Western tradition to mask a temporal problem in my essay "On the Superficiality of Women," which seeks to contribute to a semiotically informed feminist hermeneutics.

Adam's rib. The reader does not receive meaning from the author any more than a first woman learned the names of things from a first man. The myth of the reader as an empty vessel into which the author pours wisdom, long ago debunked by Socrates, is a myth few "clerks," particularly, would accept yet one that still tends to dictate the way Western culture deals with books (much as the story of Adam and Eve continues to affect sexual hierarchies). It is essential to bear in mind that readers necessarily and legitimately bring to the text interpretants that precede, in some form, their encounter with that text. If they did not, they could in no sense read it.

Reading is by nature a "timely" activity in the dual sense that (1) it is a process of sign production in which there occurs over time a series of substitutions of interpretants, backward and forward and back again, for the representation in the text (word, phrase, or symbol); and that (2) these substitutions take their orientation from the reader's expectation that the text means something, that he or she may be able to discover that meaning, that it meant something to its author. Even purely private reading, which is never to be discussed with another (an instance of Betti's "merely re-cognitive" interpretation) is thus temporal in character. This is all the more true of reading that is a prelude to discussion with others. A "timely reading" in the more conventional and limited sense of a reading that interprets the words of an earlier text to make them particularly applicable to a present situation—such as the reading I presented of Christine de Pizan's reading of Trojan legend—is thus not only entirely legitimate but necessary. All readings are, at some stage in their evolution, "timely," or interpretive, in this sense. But a reading whose impulse is primarily oriented toward the past is *also* "timely" in the sense that it bears in mind the temporal difference between the process of sign production in which the text was engendered and the process of sign production in which the exegetically oriented reading is itself engaged. Thus, I have sought in this study to enlarge the concept of "timely reading" beyond its conventional sense.

Reading is, nonetheless, commonly presented by Western culture not as a *timely* but as a *timeless* activity. Indeed, one school of thought sees the adjective "timeless" as the highest compliment one can pay a text. Similarly, reading is assumed to be a changeless activity. These two points of view converge to promote the notion that a reader can in any era pick up a "timeless" work and, once having remedied certain deficiencies in information, read it in the same way a reader would have done in the time it was written. Yet the *Aeneid* survived the Middle Ages, for example, not because it was timeless but because it was read as timely. Had it not been read as offering spiritual guidance to Christian readers, it would not have been recopied so often, and parts of it might have been lost. If Vergil's epic threatens in this century to become unknown to all but a few, it is perhaps because the work is more often now presented to readers as timeless rather than timely.

It might be useful to discard the image of book as body, as a synecdoche of its author's person, and replace it with the very different image of the book as clock. The numbers on a clock face are understood by all to be relative: twelve may indicate midnight or noon; it may further indicate midnight or noon on the eighteenth of April or the fourth of July; finally, it may indicate these hours on these dates in 1835 or 1972. It is easy to keep in mind that these numbers are elements in an ongoing process of sign production, and everyone who "reads" a clockface does so. Exactly the same is true of words in a book, and anyone who reads them must read them as but elements in the process of sign production. Yet rarely is this fact about books explicitly recognized. If it were, the broadly cultural consequences of such recognition would be considerable.

Before describing at least a few of these consequences, I must make clear that my emphasis on the need for more widespread understanding of the reading process as essentially semiotic in character should not be taken to imply that semiotic theory alone can provide the foundation for an adequate theoretical model of reading. Several other movements in twentieth-century reader-oriented theory bear centrally and directly on the problems that have been treated in this book.[10]

The first is deconstruction, fundamental to the approach I wish to suggest here because only deconstructive readings have rendered and can render visible the problem of temporality in the reading process; and because deconstruction's emphasis on the effort to touch what is repressed, when applied to the reading process, opens the way to a

---

10. For surveys and analyses of other reader-oriented theories, see Jonathan Culler, *Structuralist Poetics* (Ithaca: Cornell University Press, 1975); Paul de Man, "Literature and Language: A Commentary," *New Literary History* 4 (1972), 181–92; Harold Fromm, "Sparrows and Scholars: Literary Criticism and the Sanctification of Data," *Georgia Review* 33 (1979), 255–76; Gerald Graff, *Literature against Itself* (Chicago: University of Chicago Press, 1979); Steven Mailloux, "Reader-Response Criticism?" *Genre* 10 (1977), 413–31.

historicism that gives a more comprehensive account of the temporality of the reading process than do other forms of historicism. The second is phenomenological criticism, because by adapting to the purposes of literary criticism the analysis of perception proposed by phenomenology per se, it obliged the critical community to think of reading as a process, and one whose nature and structure was not to be assumed as given but rather to be investigated. The third is what in the United States has been called "The New Hermeneutic" and associated above all with the name of Hans-Georg Gadamer.[11] Although less useful to the analysis of "timely reading" than Betti's semiotically grounded hermeneutics, this movement nonetheless contributes an important analyis of the temporal discrepancy between text and reader, an analysis that is employed here after reconsideration in the light of Fredric Jameson's Marxian critique of Gadamer's related concept of the "fusion of horizons." The fourth is feminist theory, which continues to show the critical community that many of the literary functions to which it has often ascribed a natural or changeless character are instead learned and historically shaped. That current in feminist theory which today insists on the integration of the textual and the historical, while looking assiduously for the history which has been left outside History, does much to focus what is presently most useful in the other three critical movements just cited. In the four sections that follow, each devoted to one of these movements, I also point out the divergence of my own approach, from each one, while nonetheless endeavoring to make clearer just what it is I have taken from it.

Historicity in Deconstruction and the History of Deconstruction

In an interview published in 1967, Jacques Derrida defined the "deconstruction" of philosophy in the following terms:

> To "deconstruct" philosophy, thus, would be to think—in the most faithful, interior way—the structural genealogy of philosophy's concepts, but at the same time to determine—from a certain exterior that is unqualifiable or unnamable by philosophy—what this history has

11. Hirsch, *Validity in Interpretation*, p. 246, applies the term to Gadamer's approach. Richard E. Palmer, *Hermeneutics* (Evanston, Ill.: Northwestern University Press, 1969), p. 47, asserts that Gadamer accepts the identification of his work with that of New Hermeneutic theologians.

been able to dissimulate or forbid, making itself into a history by means of this somewhere motivated repression. By means of this simultaneously faithful and violent circulation between the inside and the outside of philosophy—that is of the West—there is produced a certain texual work that gives great pleasure. That is, a writing interested in itself which also enables us to read philosophemes—and consequently all the text of our culture—as kinds of symptoms (a word which I suspect, of course, as I explain elsewhere) of something that *could not be presented* in the history of philosophy, and which, moreover, is *nowhere present*, since all of this concerns putting into question the major determination of the meaning of Being as *presence*, the determination in which Heidegger recognized the destiny of philosophy.[12]

Although this passage would bear extended and detailed analysis, I present it simply as a reminder of the character of the Continental philosophical movement that gradually became known as "deconstructive" as it began to come to the attention of American students of literature. Derrida's definition of the deconstruction of philosophy then made it clear that deconstruction was centrally concerned with history, that it was a way of grappling with certain of the problems that history poses for thought.

The passage connects history to the deconstruction of philosophy as a future, indeed hypothetical, task ("this would be") in four ways. First, and most obviously, it defines deconstruction as a two-phase activity whose first part is the thinking through of a genealogy: that is, of a history, a history that traces births and deaths and the relations of ancestral generations one to another. Moreover, several of the words and phrases Derrida chooses in this definition of deconstruction suggest that great care is to be expended in the accomplishment of what others might have called an act of historical imagination, a degree of care that even some positivistic historians might applaud if the passage went no further: "structured" (structurée), which implies that deconstruction will reflect long enough and hard enough on the genealogy it thinks through for a structure to become visible; "the most faithful" (la plus fidèle); "the innermost" (la plus intérieure).

---

12. Jacques Derrida, *Positions* (Paris: Minuit, 1972), p. 15; according to a note (p. 9), this interview first appeared in *Lettres françaises*, no. 1211 (6–12 December 1967). The English translation is that of Alan Bass in *Positions* (Chicago: University of Chicago Press, 1981), pp. 6–7. Cf. Gayatri Chakravorty Spivak's remark that one of the things that interests her about deconstruction is "its emphasis upon 'history'": "Foreword: 'Draupadi,' by Mahasveta Devi," *Critical Inquiry* 8 (1981), 383.

Second, the passage describes the second phase of deconstruction as well by recourse to a notion of history: it is to be an investigation of what the first phase of deconstruction itself represses in its thinking-through of the genealogy of philosophy. This implies the centrality to Derrida's deconstructive project of a highly sophisticated notion of history. The notion is a dialectical one, for the two phases are to occur simultaneously (*en même temps*). A concept of the origin of history—that is, of an act (of repression) that is a starting point for a history of history—is posited by the phrase "making itself history by means of this repression," but because Derrida stresses so emphatically that the activity he envisages is to be dialectical ("this simultaneously faithful and violent circulation"), it is clear that this notion of origin is not to be associated with a simple, linear kind of historical thinking.

Third, the passage suggests the possibility of the recovery of something that has not been able to become a part of history. Although Derrida is hesitant about this urge toward recovery, as his parenthetical remark about "symptoms" makes evident, it is such an important impulse in the deconstructive writing he has already done by the time of writing this passage that he cannot exclude it from the elaboration of his definition of deconstruction, despite his uneasiness. The urge to recover what has escaped history has long been familiar to historians, as has the uneasiness that accompanies it. A number of them have, especially since the time of Wilhelm Dilthey, made their discomfort with it known. Reflections on the impulse Derrida mentions here, to "read" certain things as symptoms of what is lost, have been an important part of the territory of the historiographer since long before they were associated with the term "deconstruction."

Fourth, the passage alludes to and seems to concur with the view that Derrida's discipline, philosophy, has a destiny—a view that is based on a highly traditional, not to say classical, concept of history. To embrace a view of one's discipline which sees it as having a destiny and to define one's own project as part of the movement toward the fulfillment of that destiny is to be very concerned with history indeed, and in a way that must pervade one's work.

Clearly, deconstruction was, at about the time it began to play an important role in American literary theory, defined in terms heavily oriented toward the problems of history. Its translation in this country has, however, carried it further and further from explicit connection both with the problems of the thinking-through of the history of philosophy or of other disciplines and with the attempt to recover what is repressed by the very nature of historical thought. This distortion in translation has not been the fault of the translators: that is, of the half-dozen or so key theorists who first published deconstructive studies in the United States. Rather, it has arisen from patterns of thought inculcated in their literary-theoretical audience, patterns that have made it difficult for this audience to understand, or even remark, much of what deconstruction has to offer. Because of these patterns of thought, the aspect of deconstruction emphasized most forcefully in this country, both by those identified with this "movement" and by its critics, has been the insistence on "the priority of language to meaning."[13] Moreover, in dealing with this phrase and its implications, both friends and foes of deconstruction have given almost exclusive attention to forms of "language" and the analysis and classification of the circuitous paths by which people connect them to "meaning" (by reference, for example, to the tropes of rhetoric or to the defenses of psychoanalysis). They have apparently not paid much attention to the analysis of the temporal elements suggested by "priority."

The form of priority conceived not simply from a logical viewpoint but also from a temporal one has been of central concern to the foregoing chapters. It has not, however, been central to other responses to deconstruction. It is not difficult to understand why deconstruction should, in America, have most readily been legible as an effort to grapple with language and meaning, rather than with time. The New Criticism turned literary study away from literary history; therefore, when deconstruction began to attract interest here, it necessarily engaged students of literature on the grounds they then occupied, rather than on grounds they had abandoned some time before.

Deconstruction appeared to some to be not primarily a critique of American literary history but rather a critique of American New Criticism in its latter-day forms. It is not surprising, then, that Gerald Graff should decry deconstruction as a mere extension of the New Criticism.[14] People read all books, whether novels or studies of literary theory, by reference to categories and notions retained from reading

13. The phrase is quoted from Geoffrey Hartman's preface to Harold Bloom, Paul de Man, Jacques Derrida, Geoffrey Hartman, and J. Hillis Miller, *Deconstruction and Criticism* (New York: Seabury Press, 1979), p. vii. Hartman also suggests (p. ix) the reasons for which I put "movement" in quotation marks. Indeed, if there is any element common to theories associated with "deconstruction," it is the denial of the possibility of such commonality of meaning as "movement" implies.

14. Graff, *Literature against Itself,* pp. 144–46.

others; they would find incomprehensible any book that had no contact with the familiar. Studies associated with the word "deconstruction" have been written and read in terms often reminiscent of New Critical studies, though the terms have been used in different ways. Although both kinds of critical work focus, for example, on semantic details, New Critical studies see each text as embodying only one complete, coherent (albeit often ironic) structure, whereas deconstructive studies see each text as embodying two, each of which contradicts the other.[15] Because New Criticism has used tools similar to those that deconstruction took up, even while following an entirely different blueprint, the New Criticism effectively prepared the American critical public to respond to, if not agree with, the deconstructive approach to language. But at the same time the antihistorical polemics of the New Criticism created an environment that seriously impaired the ability of much of that public to see the challenges that deconstruction presents to literary history. Even those who have understood that the exploration of the temporality of written language is essential to deconstruction have necessarily had to write in dialogue with New Critical thought patterns. The meaning of what they have written has thus emerged only through a New Critical, antihistorical filter.

But the effort to understand how one can responsibly and rigorously think about and in time, as well as about and in language, is nonetheless a major current in the work of those leading theorists who contributed essays to the volume *Deconstruction and Criticism* (see note 13). Harold Bloom's efforts to understand the responses of the poet to earlier poems led to the first major change in a very long time in the way literary history is practiced in this country. And it is Bloom who contributes the first essay in this (alphabetically arranged) collection, extending still further his study of the importance to the poet of the "return to origins" (p. 2) and applying his notion of defense to the attitude of "deconstructionist criticism" itself toward its intellectual antecedents (pp. 12–13). The collection is, indeed, framed by reflections on the history of deconstruction: in the final essay J. Hillis Miller also concerns himself with that history and suggests that deconstruction's understanding of its historical role as a move toward liberation is

---

15. The deconstructive view of the text is analogous to the psychoanalytic view of passages in a patient's narrative as ambivalent: such a narrative embodies two contradictory structures, neither of which need be regarded as more true, right, or privileged than the other.

inaccurate (p. 229). Thus, the volume that is sure to be taken as the "manifesto" of deconstruction begins and ends with gestures toward the thinking-through of deconstruction's own history—gestures which, if they are not the most radical that those associated with this "movement" have ever made in this direction, are certainly perfectly explicit and, no doubt, symptomatic of a self-reflexive historical awareness.

By far the longest piece in the collection, standing at its center, Jacques Derrida's "Living On" takes its title from its concern with, among other things, the dual temporality of the text: "A text lives only if it lives *on* [*sur-vit*], and it lives *on* only if it is *at once* translatable *and* untranslatable" (p. 102n). Geoffrey Hartman, after pointing out (p. 186) that theorists of reading from I. A. Richards to Wolfgang Iser have failed to concern themselves sufficiently, and in a sufficiently complex way, with the relation of history to reading, proceeds to criticize certain kinds of attempts "to disclose the structure of 'timely utterance'" (p. 207), among them Derrida's. As Hartman stresses in his preface, with telling accuracy even at the level of grammar, the contributors to this volume "differ considerably in their approach [*sic*]" (p. ix).

If neither the title ("Shelley Disfigured") nor anything else about Paul de Man's contribution tells a concern with time so explicitly and straightforwardly as the Derrida and Hartman contributions, his essay nevertheless shows that concern in its very structure. De Man stresses that language has as its end, its goal or purpose, the creation of history (pp. 62–63). One corollary of this would seem to be the notion that it is the desire for history which calls language into existence and, particularly, that without the desire for history there is no written language. In short, de Man's analysis would seem to imply an explanation of the origin of language, a history of language, which de Man himself would be obliged to criticize, perhaps following lines similar to those suggested by Derrida's definition of the deconstruction of philosophy. Rhetorically, de Man goes on to write the following question: "How can a positional act, which relates to nothing that comes before or after, become inscribed in a sequential narrative?" (p. 64). He then emphasizes that when we ask why we desire so to inscribe—why we desire to create narratives, histories, stories, reasons—we do the very thing we are asking "why" about and therefore close off the question. While de Man's essay, then, does not announce itself as a struggle with history and even takes a rather condescending view of "archaeological labor," it encounters very forthrightly just those problems of history that are uniquely concerned with language, especially language semiotically conceived, and that cannot be understood by analogy with such extralinguistic endeavors as archaeology.

De Man addresses the relation of history to literature more directly in the chapter of his *Allegories of Reading* that deals with Nietzsche's *The Birth of Tragedy*.[16] In this chapter, titled "Genesis and Genealogy," he argues quite rightly that the genetic model is yet another example of rhetorical legerdemain. But although it is certainly pertinent to my own discourse, as I have repeatedly pointed out, it is not that conclusion that I wish to discuss here but rather some observations from the opening paragraph of the chapter. These observations may serve to suggest why and how the argument of this book diverges from deconstruction as generally understood in the United States, even though deconstruction opens the way to this argument:

> In literary studies, structures of meaning are frequently described in historical rather than in semiological or rhetorical terms. That is, in itself, a somewhat surprising occurrence, since the historical nature of literary discourse is by no means an *a priori* established fact, whereas all literature necessarily consists of linguistic and semantic elements. Yet students of literature seem to shy away from the analysis of semantic structures and feel more at home with problems of psychology or of historiography. The reasons for this detour or flight from language are complex and go far in revealing the very semiological properties that are being circumvented. They explain the methodological necessity of approaching questions of literary meaning by way of the nonlinguistic referential models used in literary history. This is one of the means, among others, to gain access to the enigmas that lie hidden behind the more traditional problems of literary classification and periodization.

This passage, removed from its context and without any discussion of the meaning or structure of the important phrase "detour or flight from language," may be read as an indictment of historical descriptions of meaning within "literary studies"—that is, of what is termed in this book "exegesis." The word "flight," as it stands here, implies that the formulation of such descriptions is cowardly. The ground for this accusation is the negatively but emphatically made assertion that "the historical nature of literary discourse is by no means an *a priori* established fact."

16. Paul de Man, *Allegories of Reading* (New Haven: Yale University Press, 1979), pp. 79–102.

What I have contended is that all "literary discourse" *that is read* has, a priori, a "historical nature." When I finish writing this sentence and go back to read it over before going on to write the next one, I demonstrate ipso facto that read discourse has a historical nature. My sentence is old, already past (this is true, even leaving aside the sense in which the words were old before I ever put them into a sentence). I have claimed, relying on a semiotic concept of language, not merely that read discourse has a historical "aspect" or historical "character" but that its very "nature" is historical. Drawing upon de Man's notion that the desire for history calls language into being, I have argued that temporality is an inextricable part of the writing and the reading of language, and that to study written and read language without giving an account of its temporality is in itself a very dangerous, though tempting, form of flight.[17] I hope I have shown that reflection on the timeliness of reading—on, so to speak, the modes of priority of language to meaning—is a necessary aspect of the study of literary language. Without deconstruction's opening-up of the whole question of the "timeliness of utterance," to paraphrase the Hartman essay just cited, it would have been impossible to do so.

As a corollary I have urged that critical writing must seek ways to make the temporal structure of reading visible, if only for brief moments. To that end I have proposed a historicism that is not anti-deconstructive but rather assumes deconstruction. The most obvious and easily reproducible means of rendering the temporality of language visible, suggested in Chapter 1, is certainly a perilous undertaking, doomed to the pattern established by Pygmalion. Yet Pygmalion, according to Ovid, got something valuable from his creation: a son. The kind of activity undertaken in the first chapter of this study is likewise meant to bear fruit, in the encouragement of the awareness of reading as a semiotic and temporal process. This awareness is, I have argued, repressed always by the very nature of reading, which is—even ety-

---

17. John Brenkman, "Deconstruction and the Social Text," *Social Text*, no. 1 (Winter 1979), 186–88, voices similar concerns in stressing the need to "reopen deconstructive reading to the problematic initiated by Freud and Marx." Cf. also, in the same journal ("Reification and Utopia in Mass Culture," pp. 130–48), Fredric Jameson's juxtaposition of what he calls the "means/end" restructuring of the reading process, typical of "instrumentalized culture," and the kind of reading process that sees a poem as "at every point . . . vertical to itself, self-contained" (p. 132), exemplified in Auerbach's treatment of the *Odyssey* in *Mimesis*.

mologically—a matter of gathering words together rather than keeping them distinct.[18]

Temporality in Phenomenological Criticism

Still another conceptual model of reading which both complements and differs from the one presented here is provided by phenomenological criticism. Phenomenology's principal gift[19] to reader criticism is the concept—or perhaps the reminder—that reading is a process: an activity shaped to a specific end, subject to malfunction at any of various points, deserving of attention and study. When Edmund Husserl and then Maurice Merleau-Ponty raised questions about the process of perception, emphasizing the need to describe it and understand its workings as a necessary prelude to any other philosophical activity, they set a standard that many literary critics have been striving to meet ever since. Although these two were concerned not with the understanding of texts but with the perception of the world, which is quite different, their focus on the complexity of the perceptual process served to remind students of literature that the process of "perceiving" a text is not so simple either and may indeed be more complex than the perceptual process phenomenologists have studied.

18. Charlton T. Lewis and Charles Short, *A Latin Dictionary* (Oxford: Oxford University Press, 1879), s.v. *lego*: "to bring together, to gather, to collect"; in a figurative sense, "overhear," "catch with the eye," "to read." A similar point is made by Umberto Eco, *The Role of the Reader* (Bloomington: Indiana University Press, 1979), p. 31, but Eco makes temporal consciousness in reading "neurotic": "The fabula is always experienced step by step. Since every step usually involves a change of state and a lapse of time, the reader is led to make an intermediate *extensional* operation. . . In fact, such disjunctions occur at every sentence of a narrative step, even within the boundaries of a single sentence. . . . But the condition of a neurotic reader compelled to ask Whom? What? at every occurrence of a transitive verb. . . is usually neutralized by the normal reading speed." What I have proposed in this study is an effort against such "neutralization." The kind of reading Eco valorizes negatively as "neurotic" I have instead proposed as a distant, indeed unattainable, goal.

19. Among the many contributions to the understanding of literary temporality of a movement so extensive and diverse as phenomenology, I have chosen to focus on Maurice Merleau-Ponty and Georges Poulet because they are more widely read in this country than others. Other phenomenological explorations of temporality meriting particular study include the following.

Maurice Blanchot, *L'espace littéraire* (Paris: Gallimard, 1955), chap. 6, "L'oeuvre et la communication": in the section headed "Lire" the central image for reading is the

It is this aspect of phenomenological criticism, the suggestion that reading is a process, which I see as a contribution, and perhaps the most fundamental contribution of all, to the approach this book has taken.

---

resurrection of Lazarus; Blanchot describes reading as a "miracle," a "liberating decision," an act that is "innocent." In the preface to his *Lautréamont et Sade* (Paris: Minuit, 1963), p. 11, steadfastly advocating the notion (rejected here as antitemporal) that the critic's goal is his own disappearance in the act of reading, Blanchot nonetheless makes some interesting remarks on the relation of criticism to "the disciplines which are called 'historical.'"

For Mikel Dufrenne, *Phénoménologie de l'expérience esthétique,* 2 vols. (Paris: Presses Universitaires de France, 1953), the historian's approach to an object has nothing to do with entering into an aesthetic relation; he sees art as something that escapes history (cf. Benedetto Croce). He claims (1:305) that any aesthetic object implies both time and space, but does not call that pairing into question. He discusses music as his preferred example of temporal art, but gives no account of the temporality of language. Most relevant to the concerns of the present study is his brief discussion (1:306–7) of time as constitutive of interiority and of the self, on which it nonetheless depends.

Roman Ingarden provides the most extensive account I know of the temporality of reading from a phenomenological perspective. In a book first published in Polish in 1937, enlarged and translated into German in 1968, and finally made available in English in 1973, Ingarden takes the analysis of language as his point of departure. *The Cognition of the Literary Work of Art,* trans. Ruth Ann Crowley and Kenneth R. Olson (Evanston, Ill.: Northwestern University Press, 1973), chap. 2, "Temporal Perspective in the Concretization of the Literary Work of Art," emphasizes the sequential nature of the reader's encounter with the parts of a work and the role of memory in dealing with this sequential process. Ingarden is also concerned (pp. 118–19) with the changes that seem to take place in past events when they are recalled several times and (pp. 105–7, esp. 107) with what the reader experiences as the integration of the present moment into the whole of time. In his analysis of memory, Ingarden formulates a distinction between two kinds of temporal perspective (p. 115) which anticipates my distinction between "exegesis" and "interpretation"; he applies it to narrative time and asserts that "for each type of perspective there is a corresponding mode of reading, which is, to a certain extent, forced on the reader" (p. 127).

An early theoretical work by Jean-Paul Sartre, *L'imaginaire: Psychologie phénoménologique de l'imagination* (Paris: Gallimard, 1940), contains a section titled "Nature of the Analogon in the Mental Image," in which Sartre identifies two kinds of mental activity in the reader's encounter with a book: that without mental image, occurring "when the reader is very involved"; and that which gives rise to images, occurring "at stopping-points and glitches in the reading" (p. 127). This second kind of activity in reading, he says, expresses a desire for transcendence (p. 132). The pattern is one of movement from an experience of temporal discontinuity in reading (*arrêts*) to the postulation of the possibility of an escape from time, a pattern that anticipates in a general way one of the arguments of this book. The methodology, on the other hand, based on reports of experiments in the psychology of reading, anticipates that of Norman Holland and David Bleich.

The ground of my *departure* from phenomenology may be set forth most clearly in the context of some discussion of what is perhaps the best-known work of phenomenological literary criticism in this country, Georges Poulet's *Etudes sur le temps humain (Studies in human time)*. This elegant study is based upon a consistent turning away from just that issue which is of most urgent concern here: textual temporality and its relation to the reader's temporality.[20] Indeed, it is perhaps this very exclusion of temporal consciousness that gives Poulet's essays their conviction, charm, and persuasive power.

The theoretical ground of Poulet's exclusion of temporal considerations from criticism may be found in the work of Merleau-Ponty,[21] who offers to an investigation of the timeliness of reading the notion of the perceiving subject's "situation." But he presents it so ambivalently that it is taken away while being given; indeed, the ambivalence of Merleau-Ponty's presentation of the notion of "situation" is even more telling than the notion itself. It is more influential as well, for it is this ambivalence that gives Poulet and other phenomenological critics license, so to speak, to turn away from the temporality of their own activity as readers.

The ambivalence is evident in the preface to *Phénoménologie de la perception*, which Merleau-Ponty opens by making himself a historian of the past accomplishments of phenomenology. Writing in a tradi-

20. The comparatively large number of translations of Poulet which appeared in this country in the 1960s indicates the interest of the American public in his work, even though it centered on French texts that were unfamiliar to many American critics. I think this interest is partly explained by the proximity of Poulet's techniques to those of "close reading," and by his use of those familiar techniques to move on to matters that the New Criticism excluded from consideration. That Poulet's turn away from the temporality of the subject is deliberate is shown by the following passage from the introduction to *Etudes sur le temps humain* (Paris: Librairie Plon, 1950), p. xlv, translated by Elliott Coleman, *Studies in Human Time* (Baltimore, Md.: Johns Hopkins University Press, 1956) p. 36: "To apprehend the present as the generative act of time in its concrete reality is then, without doubt, the tendency of our epoch. But as Jean Wahl has shown, nothing is more difficult, 'since our attention can be directed only to the past, and since whatever is new eludes the grasp of consciousness, and when seized by it becomes transformed into a thing of the past.' By the same token it is unavailing to go back . . . into the newness of a moment of historical genesis which precedes time, since it is—Bergson understood it so well—a sheer illusion the mind entertains in placing itself in the 'antecedent future.' If then the mind wishes to apprehend itself as creator, it must recognize in its act of creation an act of annihilation. . . . The creative act of time appears first then as a death of time itself."

21. I do not mean to imply a direct filiation between Merleau-Ponty and Poulet; I treat them in tandem for heuristic purposes only.

tional historical vocabulary and letting the French word *commencement* enunciate a traditional concept of genesis, he implies that phenomenology has, until his own time, remained "at an initial stage" (*à l'état de commencement*); only later in the Preface does he make it clear that this is not to be taken as a sign of the movement's weakness or failure, and that *commencement* is not to be taken in a genetic sense.[22] He sounds like a historian when he mentions as significant the difference between the early and later writing of Husserl, alludes to the works of Husserl's student, Eugen Fink, and traces Husserl's proximity to and departures from Kant. Toward the end of his preface he sounds like a prophet of the future of historiography as he envisions the possibility that "phenomenology can become a phenomenology of origins" and that it will enable the historian to take up again and assume "the *dimensions* of history."[23]

The preface's rhetoric of historical genesis and end—indeed, any notion of history within the *Phénoménologie*—must be founded on the concept of the "situation" of the intending subject, and this concept is not absent from the preface. Merleau-Ponty stresses its importance, describing it as crucial to the transformation of subjectivity into intersubjectivity: "The *Cogito* must reveal me in a situation, and it is on this condition alone that transcendental subjectivity can, as Husserl puts it, *be* an intersubjectivity" (*Phénoménologie*, p. vii; *Phenomenology*, p. xiii). Indeed, he presents the awareness of "situation" as that which differentiates the phenomenological concept of intentionality from the Kantian concept of relation to a possible object: "What distinguishes intentionality from the Kantian relation to a possible object is that the unity of the world, before being posited by knowledge in a specific act of

22. Maurice Merleau-Ponty, *Phénoménologie de la perception* (1945; rpt., Paris: Gallimard, 1967), p. ii. Page numbers provided first in the text refer to this French edition; English translations are taken from *Phenomenology of Perception*, trans. Colin Smith, (London: Routledge & Kegan Paul, 1962); the passage discussed above appears at p. viii. Merleau-Ponty's preface makes clear that *commencement* is meant in another sense and that this quality of remaining at a beginning state is by no means a sign of failure: "The unfinished nature of phenomenology [is not] to be taken as a sign of failure" (*Phénoménologie*, p. ix; *Phenomenology*, p. xxi); it is inevitable, for phenomenology's role is revelatory, and revelation is always new. But by writing of "beginning" in its traditional sense at the opening of a preface that spends much time orienting itself to the history of the movement to which the book's title claims connection, Merleau-Ponty opens to question his presentation of the concept of a beginning which is perceptually new.

23. *Phénoménologie*, p. xiii; *Phenomenology*, p. xviii. The emphasis is the author's. On this topic, note Merleau-Ponty's scorn for the historian and philologist (pp. i-ii).

identification, is 'lived' as ready made or already there" (*Phénoménologie*, p. xii; *Phenomenology*, p. xvii).

It is this sense of being in a world whose unity is, always, "*already
made*" or "*already* there" which constitutes the subject's "situation."
Merleau-Ponty is emphatic about its importance: "The world is there
before any possible analysis."[24] It is the sense that the unity of the
world is *already* established which, he says, gives knowledge its goal
(p. xiii). Yet despite his evident concern with history, he omits from
his elaboration of the concept of "situation" any notion of change or of
consciousness of this "already-made" character of the unity of the
world: that is, though he stresses that the unity of the world is already
made, what he proceeds to work with is the notion of unity itself, not
the notion that it is found "already there." When he rejects history's
traditionally objective modes of knowing in favor of "lived experience," he appears to forget that the sense of the world's unity as "already made" is an important part of the way experience is lived. When
he claims that philosophy cannot clarify, by analysis, the subject's
relationship to the world but can only bring this relationship to the
subject's attention, he denies as an aspect of this relationship any possibility that humans can notice change. From a phenomenological
standpoint, then, the oscillation between exegesis and interpretation
which, I have argued, constitutes the fundamental character of reading
as a "timely" activity could be neither attended to nor studied; the
absence from the concept of "situation" of any notion of change over
time forbids it. It is this very absence, I would suggest, that underlies
the appealing unidimensionality of Poulet's work.

My argument about Merleau-Ponty takes the same direction as the
one I made about deconstruction. Deconstruction has been presented
as an inquiry into "the priority of language to meaning" but has been
read, in the New-Criticism-shaped environment of the United States,
as focusing explicit attention primarily on language and meaning, ne-
glecting the issues suggested by the word "priority." Similarly, Merleau-Ponty makes the notion of "situation" the distinguishing feature
of phenomenological thought and defines "situation" as an indication
of the "lived experience" of the world's unity as "already made." Yet,

24. *Phénoménologie*, p. iv; *Phenomenology*, p. x. On the same page, Merleau-Ponty
terms naive a concept of subjectivity, "as yet untouched by being and time," yet Poulet
stresses in *Etudes* that the concept of the annihilation of time is basic to the critical
activity he proposes.

he does not probe that experience of the unity as "already made" or impel those who take their inspiration from him to probe it.

Timely Reading and the New Hermeneutic's "Historicity of Understanding"

The third movement whose bearing on reflection about the timeliness of reading I want to examine is the one least familiar to the American critical community. I think it is fair to say that it was introduced into literary circles in this country by E. D. Hirsch's essay "Gadamer's Theory of Interpretation," when it appeared in 1967 as an appendix to Hirsch's *Validity in Interpretation*.[25] It was only in 1975 that an English translation of Gadamer's major work, first published in German in 1960, became available in English, as *Truth and Method*.[26] This study has roots that go back through Heideggerian philosophy to German biblical philology, of which it provides a historical critique. Its title comments ironically upon, among other things, the positivistic notion that methods, particularly those of philology, are linked in a clear and direct way to the approach to truth.[27] Gadamer's work is important to both the social sciences and the humanities because it argues that the methods of the natural sciences are not the exclusive avenues to truth.

In some ways Gadamer's book and the tradition behind it are *this* book's most direct and essential ancestors;[28] for example, the effort undertaken in the present study might well be classed as what Gadamer would call *Wirkungsgeschichte*, the history of how reading "works itself

25. Hirsch, *Validity in Interpretation*, pp. 245–64; Hirsch notes that the essay was first published in *Review of Metaphysics* in 1965. Useful introductions to hermeneutic theory are provided by Palmer, *Hermeneutics,* and Peter Szondi, "L'herméneutique de Schleiermacher," *Poétique* 1 (1970), 141–55.

26. Hans-Georg Gadamer, *Wahrheit und Methode* (Tübingen: J. C. B. Mohr, 1960). Citations refer to this first rather than to the second (1965) edition; translations are from Gadamer's English *Truth and Method*, (New York: Continuum, 1975); and page numbers are given for both.

27. On "methods," see ibid., p. 279.

28. That tradition goes back beyond Friedrich Schleiermacher to the initiator of modern German biblical studies, Martin Luther. Hirsch (*Validity in Interpretation*, pp. 247–48) comments on the connection between Gadamer's and Luther's views of the relation between word and thing. H. G. Haile, "Luther and Literacy," *PMLA*, 91 (1976), 816–28, finds in Luther "an acute awareness of the polarity constituted by reader and text" (p. 826). He stresses that Luther was, on historical grounds, highly critical of biblical texts—"so much so that before the sixteenth century was out he would cer-

out."[29] Like Gadamer, I have attempted to move away from a positivistic historicism and toward a historical hermeneutic consciousness. In other ways, however, the tradition is more remote from the argument made here than that of deconstruction or phenomenology, because the terms this German tradition uses have almost nothing in common with those used in the mainstream of American criticism in the last fifty years. The relationship is like that between a foreign-born, foreign-language-speaking grandparent and an American-born, American-English-speaking grandchild: from the genetic viewpoint they share much, but their attempts to converse must remain clumsy and cut off from any feeling that the language being used can possibly make contact with the concerns of greatest importance. Moreover, despite the cross-disciplinary breadth of Gadamer's influence, attempts to integrate his ideas into literary criticism have been few. These differences between the relationship of the present argument to deconstruction and phenomenology and its relationship to the New Hermeneutic mean that the discussion in this section must follow a different pattern. Whereas in each of the other movements it was possible to find a basic principle (the *priority* of language to meaning, and the sense of the *priority* of the unity of the world) that lent itself directly to a description of the problem this study seeks to address, none of the basic principles of the New Hermeneutic lend themselves to such adaptation here. Even so close a similarity as that implied by juxtaposition of the phrase "the historicity of reading" to Gadamer's "the historicity of understanding" is a false one. While the lines my argument follows do intersect with Gadamer's, they always move in a different direction from his and never parallel it. They cross, recross, and cross again at several points: the image of the "horizon" of understanding; the temporal discrepancy between text and reader; and the attitude toward readers and texts which are seen as contemporary.

---

tainly have been excommunicated from the Lutheran Church, too, had he lived" (p. 823)—but was also committed to the application of biblical texts to practical, daily experience and to the encouragement of individual judgment in the understanding of scripture: two positions—apparently not, in Luther's mind, contradictory—suggesting the distinction made in this book between "exegesis" and "interpretation."

29. On the difficulty of translating the concept of *Wirkungsgeschichte* and Gadamer's own admission that a phrase based on it is excessively ambiguous, see Joel C. Weinsheimer, *Gadamer's Hermeneutics* (New Haven, Conn.: Yale University Press, 1985), p. xx. Weinsheimer departs from Gadamer's own translation, "effective history," by leaving the term always in German (e.g., p. 181).

Gadamer's explanation of the image of the "horizon" of understanding grows out of his analysis of the hermeneutical "situation,"[30] consciousness of which is necessary to the kind of historical understanding Gadamer proposes:

> Effective-historical consciousness is primarily consciousness of the hermeneutical situation. To acquire an awareness of a situation is, however, always a task of particular difficulty. . . . The illumination of this situation—effective-historical reflection—can never be completely achieved, but this is not due to a lack in the reflection, but lies in the essence of the historical being which is ours. . . . Every finite present has its limitations. We define the concept of "situation" by saying that it represents a standpoint that limits the possibility of vision. Hence, an essential part of the concept of situation is the concept of "horizon." [*Wahrheit*, pp. 285–86; *Truth*, pp. 268–69]

His explanation of this image is then developed with many thoughtful attempts to erase from it those associations that are not appropriate to an image used to represent an aspect of the consciousness of time. In particular, he emphasizes self-questioning as the force that builds a bridge, a form of tradition, linking (earlier) text and (later) reader. Nonetheless, the horizon image retains the limitations inherent in any spatial term used to evoke a temporal problem. To say this is not so much to criticize Gadamer as to point to his implication in a recurrent problem, emphasized at the very beginning of this study. As a spatial image, the "horizon" of understanding makes it possible to apply a geometric model to the problem of the relation between the temporality of the reader's[31] understanding and the temporality of the understanding by which the text was written: when understanding occurs, two "horizons" melt into one another, becoming congruent. Their congruence inevitably creates, to use the terms of Joel Weinsheimer's paraphrase, "a single shared horizon that embraces times."

---

30. Gadamer specifies (p. 285n) that he takes his notion of "situation" above all from Karl Jaspers and Erich Rothacker; it should not be confused with Merleau-Ponty's notion designated by the same term, although the two are certainly collaterally related.

31. I translate Gadamer's *wir* ("we") by "reader," though he does not apply the model presented here to language until the third part of his book. Hirsch's criticism (*Validity in Interpretation*, p. 260 n.7) of Gadamer's uses of this pronoun seems justified.

With such a concept, Gadamer resurrects a Hegelian notion of universal history.[32]

In making my argument, by contrast, I have tried to keep as a fundamental principle the impossibility of any blending of "horizons." The notion of a shared horizon transcending time is quite alien to my purpose. A discouraging principle to write and even to think from, the unpleasantness of this impossibility does not make it any less essential. Nor does this principle, although it would seem to do so, preclude either writing or thinking; rather, it gives them their peculiar energy. Indeed, my study may even be read as an exploration of this paradox.[33] Nor does it necessarily imply a retreat into solipsism or (to use a term rather casually flung about in literary-critical circles of late) nihilism. Why this is so may become clearer in an examination of Gadamer's account of the temporal relation between text and reader.

Gadamer's response to the recognition of temporal discrepancy between text and reader differs from mine in that though I would agree with him that this temporal discrepancy cannot be done away with, I cannot subscribe to his description of that discrepancy as a wholly fruitful thing: "Hence temporal distance is not something that must be overcome. This was, rather, the naive assumption of historicism. . . . In fact the important thing is to recognize the distance in time as a positive and productive possibility of understanding. It is not a yawning abyss, but is filled with the continuity of custom and tradition, in the light of which all that is handed down presents itself to us. Here it is not too much to speak of a genuine productivity of process" [*Wahrheit*, p. 281; *Truth*, pp. 264–65).

Temporal discrepancy is viewed in my study as entailing loss as well as productivity, break as well as continuity. Rather than the naive response of traditional historicism or the optimistic response of Gadamer, I propose that the subject seeking to be conscious of its own temporality and of that of the texts it encounters must be always

32. Weinsheimer, *Gadamer's Hermeneutics*, p. 183. This aspect of Gadamer's perhaps unwilling reliance on Hegel is pointed out by Weinsheimer (p. 183 n.43, and p. 160 n.18), following Wolfhart Pannenberg.

33. It is sometimes necessary for the theory of literature to explore such paradoxes rather than turn away from them in embarrassment; the most distinguished example is Kant's reflection on the fact that although there is certainly no disputing about taste, people continue to dispute about it.

making its continuity in the present, and consciously doing so, while deliberately encountering an ever-widening range of information from the past, information that announces its discontinuity with the present. Fredric Jameson has shown "that a Marxian conception of our relationship to the past requires a sense of our radical difference from earlier cultures which is not adequately allowed for in Gadamer's influential notion of . . . fusion of horizons."[34] My strategy shares with Jameson's a preference for the "semantic enrichment" that an enlargement of the scope of exegetical activity brings with it. It is thus very far from nihilism.[35] This strategy promises more authentically temporal moments, in thinking, reading, and writing, because it avoids Gadamer's one-sided emphasis on what is "inside" the "horizon" and convenient neglect of what inevitably remains "outside." The range of information that must be encountered must indeed remain "ever-widening" in that as one element of information becomes incorporated into the continuity being made in the present, it loses its character as temporally discrepant from the present; and different ones must be encountered to serve anew the old function, entirely essential to "timely reading," of recalling to the reader his or her temporal discrepancy from the text.

It is as categories of information that may serve this function, and not as objects of research directed toward empirical ends, that I have

34. Fredric Jameson, *The Political Unconscious* (Ithaca: Cornell University Press, 1984), p. 75 n.56.
35. One might be tempted to regard the reading strategy Jameson proposes in *The Political Unconscious* as an extreme form of exegesis. Indeed, certain of the directions he pursues are deliberately, to use his own term, "antiquarian": e.g., his methodological analysis of the history of readings of a text and their ideological character as a necessary element in the reading of the text. He makes quite plain, however, that such exegetical activity forms only one part of a dialectical relationship, finding its complement in "the tendency of much contemporary theory to rewrite selected texts from the past in terms of its own aesthetic" (p. 17). The latter tendency corresponds to what I am calling "interpretation." (Another example is David Bleich's *Subjective Criticism* [Baltimore, Md.: Johns Hopkins University Press, 1978]). Jameson urges that the current impasse between proponents of exegesis and of interpretation provides an "unacceptable option, or ideological double bind," from which criticism can emerge only by making use of "a genuine philosophy of history" (p. 18). The present study, to be sure, is not intended to propose such a philosophy but rather to describe in a more complex, accurate, and fruitful manner the character of reading and the dialectic between exegesis and interpretation which constitutes its temporal foundation. Yet I share with Jameson not only the view that criticism is currently polarized by an unwillingness to confront the peculiar and complex "timeliness" of the literary text but also an interest in the ideological character of reading: that is, in the social and economic factors that shape the character of reading in a specific time and place.

introduced such topics as the history of education and the history of literacy; for I do not propose, any more than Gadamer would, that investigation of the history of reading be adopted as a method leading to literary truth. Gadamer, indeed, treats both educational and literary history as well, and his purpose in doing so is certainly not empirical. In the third part of *Wahrheit und Methode* he writes a narrative of the emergence of the concept of language which sees the history of education in a central role.[36] He points out the importance of medieval linguistic thought, which presents a view of language entirely different from that of Plato.[37] He stresses the impact of the development of lay, vernacular literacy on notions about the relation of language to thought.[38] But Gadamer does not make explicit what the hermeneutic function of the investigation of such topics is to be—except, perhaps, by placing the historical narrative that he constructs around them at the end of his volume, where they stand as the consequence and fulfillment of the earlier parts rather than as an account of the pre-history or genesis—as they would if they opened *Wahrheit und Methode*.

The third area of concern that this study shares with Gadamer's has to do with the relation between readers and texts that are seen as "contemporary" and with the possibility that their very "commonality" is an issue. Gadamer's treatment of the judgment of contemporary works of art, as a special case, is limited to a discussion of

36. "The struggle between philosophy and rhetoric for the training of Greek youth, which was decided with the victory of Attic philosophy, has also this side to it, namely that the thinking about language becomes the object of a grammar and rhetoric that have already recognised the ideal of scientific concept formation. Thus the sphere of linguistic meanings begins to become detached from the sphere of things encountered in linguistic form" (*Wahrheit*, p. 409; *Truth*, p. 392).

37. "Thus we showed that the theological relevance of the problem of language in mediaeval thought constantly points back to the unity of thinking and speaking and also brings out an aspect of which classical Greek philosophy was not aware" (*Wahrheit*, p. 410; *Truth*, p. 393)

38. "The fact that, despite the scriptural importance of the confusion of tongues, the Latin Middle Ages did not really pursue this aspect of the problem of language can be explained chiefly by the unquestioned domination of Latin among scholars, and the continued influence of the Greek doctrine of the logos. It was only in the renaissance, when the laity became important and the national languages part of cultivated learning, that people began to think productively about the relation of these to the inner, i.e. the 'natural' word" (*Wahrheit*, p. 413; *Truth*, p. 395). It is not to the Renaissance, though, that this insight should be attributed; Dante, author of the *De vulgari eloquentia*, insisted in *Convivio* I.xii that only the words of the mother tongue could speak in a way "unified" by love.

the greater clarity with which the meaning of a work emerges when, because of the passage of time, it can be understood in a disinterested fashion.[39] But he does not present contemporaneity per se as creating a problem for artistic understanding; whatever problem there may be he attributes to "interest." Yet Hirsch is correct, I think, in seeing Gadamer's analysis of the historicity of understanding as pointing inevitably to a problem in the relation between contemporary reader and text which is truly temporal in nature.[40] This problem, which Hirsch treats as a *reductio ad absurdum*, seems to me an entirely serious one. I treat it as a particularly telling limit case termed "self-reading."

These are, then, the three most important ways in which the viewpoint adopted here differs from Gadamer's: it rejects as a goal the possibility of the total melting together of horizons of understanding; it accepts as inevitable and indeed emphasizes that temporal discrepancy inevitably entails loss as well as gain; and it takes instances of what is termed "contemporaneity" of reader and text to be central rather than peripheral to the task of temporal analysis. Despite these differences, the present study is intended as a contribution to that field with which Gadamer's name is, more than any other, currently associated. Hermeneutics, unfortunately, has so far failed to find any very visible lodging in the United States, perhaps because the so-called Betti-Gadamer debate has made it too easy for proponents of either to rigidify rather than refine their positions, perhaps because the field is so thoroughly occupied by disciples of Gadamer that any attempts to address hermeneutic issues which take their point of departure outside Gadamer's work do not seem pertinent. In either case, because I am convinced that a greater awareness of the temporal problems hermeneutics addresses is now more necessary than ever before to those who teach students how to read literature, I have tried to present those

39. In the same regard he also brings up his optimistic view of the productivity of temporal discrepancy.

40. Hirsch, *Validity in Interpretation*, p. 256: "Heidegger, on Gadamer's interpretation, denies that past meanings can be reproduced in the present because the past is ontologically alien to the present. The being of a past meaning cannot become the being of a present meaning, for being is temporal and differences in time are consequently differences in being. If this is the argument on which Gadamer wishes to found his doctrine of historicity, he should acknowledge that it is ultimately an argument against written communication in general and not just against communication between historical eras. For it is merely arbitrary, on this argument, to hold that a meaning fifty years old is ontologically alien while one three years or three minutes old is not. It is true that Heidegger introduces the concept of *Mitsein* which corresponds to the idea of cultural eras, but this does not solve the problem." Hirsch responds to this problem in the body of his text with a distinction between "meaning" and "significance" (pp. 6–9).

problems in an accessible way. Hermeneutics is too important to society for it to remain apart from the mainstream of debate about writing and reading.

From Hermeneutics through Feminism to Iristics

The fourth and last critical direction whose relation to the concept of timely reading I wish to discuss is feminist theory. In an earlier
section of this chapter, "The Time of the Interpretant," I mentioned
one of the ways feminist theory may contribute to what might be
understood as a hermeneutics newer than the (now old) new hermeneutic: feminist theory calls into question the notion that the author
is primary and the reader secondary, that Adam is created first and
names all the animals while Eve is created out of his rib and accepts the
language Adam has created. The mythic terms employed here may be
reformulated in order to emphasize how feminist theory underlies my
attempt to analyze the practice and theorization of reading: Eve must
be seen no longer only as the one who gives the originary, and wrong,
answer (to the serpent), but rather as one who originates questions (not
simply repeating someone else's, the serpent's, for example). This
book has been shaped by a female subject who thinks of her own
reading practice from a consciously female perspective. How clearly
this shaping will emerge for various readers I cannot know. It should
in any case be evident that a number of the book's most central concerns parallel or build upon those of recent feminist theory.

My use of non-canonical literature, especially in its most extreme
form, unedited texts and marginalia, is motivated by the belief that
what is received at any moment as canonical is so received because it
conforms to prevailing ideology and that it is therefore necessary to go
outside the canon to articulate whatever calls such ideology into question. Feminist criticism has been especially successful in showing how,
for example, the canon has been formed by an ideology that celebrates
conquest and has also begun to examine more subtle kinds of ideologically based canon formation.[41] In this book I have suggested ways in
which not only text selection but also other forms of reading practice

---

41. On the ideology of conquest and canon formation, see especially Jane P.
Tompkins, "Sentimental Power: *Uncle Tom's Cabin* and the Politics of Literary History," *Glyph* 2 (1978), reprinted in *The New Feminist Criticism*, ed. Elaine Showalter (New
York: Pantheon Books, 1985), pp. 81–104. Critiques of other kinds of ideologically
based canon formation are discussed below.

are shaped by dominant ideologies in particular times and places. While recognizing and documenting such forces for the homogenization of reading practices, however, I have stressed their inevitable variety. If my project has succeeded, it should create further occasions for the theoretical description of the reading experiences of many different women.[42]

The domain of feminist criticism to which this study is most closely affiliated is the critique of phallogocentrism which deconstructive feminism has developed. As Naomi Schor has indicated, this critique arose from and continues to re-enact a resistance to the binary modes of thought characteristic of structuralism. Schor has argued "that it is in textual details either overlooked or misprized by male critics that something crucial about woman's stake in representation is to be found."[43] Schor intends here details referring to the body, and my study of certain textual and corporeal images used by Boccaccio (and inverted in my treatment of Christine) supports her argument. I have here attempted to show, however, that it is not only or exclusively sexual fetishism that veils the foundation of a critical practice that assigns women to the position of misreaders in a dichotomized view of hermeneutic possibilities. Schor's insistence that not only broad structures but also textual details must be interrogated if accepted notions about representation are to be questioned finds more general confirmation in this book's work with such details as punning, page layout, and tense.

The form of binarism which has been questioned here is temporal in the widest possible sense: my study has dealt not with kinship, just one figure of temporal relation, but instead with multiple figures of time and their traces. Barbara Johnson has shown how, in order to repress differences *within* entities, a whole network of differences *among* entities must be created. These latter differences are presented as promising their ultimate resolution in a final act of understanding.[44] This book has concerned itself, from the epigraph to the Introduction onward, with the repression of temporal change within the reader and a series of resultant dichotomies in descriptions of reading: for example, male author/female reader; whole/dismembered text; past truth/present ignorance. I have also tried to establish the value of yet another pair

42. Compare de Lauretis, *Alice Doesn't*, p. 166.

43. Schor, *Breaking the Chain*, p. x.

44. Barbara Johnson, *The Critical Difference: Essays in the Contemporary Rhetoric of Reading* (Baltimore, Md.: Johns Hopkins University Press, 1980).

of concepts, exegesis and interpretation, as heuristic tools, while emphasizing that I do not seek to bring the two to some (fictive) moment
of resolution. Instead, I have pointed to the shuttling back and forth
between these two poles as an approximation of the most generalized
form of reading practice.

My entire project might well be seen as an outgrowth of Annette
Kolodny's precept that "[when we speak of reading] we are calling
attention to interpretive strategies that are learned, historically determined, and thereby necessarily gender-inflected."[45] Whereas there has
been a certain tendency, however, especially in American feminist
theory, to focus immediately and directly on the ways in which gender
has shaped "interpretive strategies," I am convinced that an understanding of the role of gender in reading cannot unfold without more
fundamental study of the historicity of reading. This gives me a somewhat different set of priorities from those of many American feminist
theorists. Gayatri Spivak has proposed that feminist theory investigate
the question "what is man that the itinerary of his desire creates such a
[phallogocentric] text?"[46] I have sought to begin to raise a related
question: what is man's reading that it creates such images of itself?
Both questions oblige feminist critics who would explore them to
return once again to the familiar, yet still puzzling, domain of canonical male writers and their texts, for, as Spivak also argues, feminist
criticism must strive "to rewrite the *social* text so that the historical and
sexual differentials are operated together" (p. 185, emphasis Spivak's).
The history of reading needs to be understood as a crucial component
of the "social text."

It must then be clear why I cannot concur with that tendency in
American feminist theory which argues that feminist criticism should
move primarily toward the study of female culture. The attractions of
such a strategy are enormous.[47] If, as I have emphasized, Christine de
Pizan presides both literally and figuratively over the center of this
book, it is in large part because I too feel pulled toward the exploration

45. Annette Kolodny, "A Map for Rereading: Gender and the Interpretation of
Literary Texts," *New Literary History* 11 (1980), reprinted in Showalter, *The New
Feminist Criticism*, 46–62; the passage quoted appears at p. 47.
46. Spivak, "Displacement and the Discourse of Woman," in *Displacement: Derrida
and After*, ed. Mark Krupnick (Bloomington: Indiana University Press, 1983), pp. 169–
95; the passage cited appears at p. 186.
47. See especially Elaine Showalter, "Feminist Criticism in the Wilderness," *Critical
Inquiry* 8 [1981], 179–205, reprinted in Showalter, *The New Feminist Criticism*, pp. 243–
70. Showalter thoughtfully reacts to what I believe is a misconception. Putative mas-

of those female texts that have always lain outside the curriculum wherever I have studied or taught. But I have not allowed this placement to become a hysterocentrism that would merely reverse the phallocentrism of many other treatments of hermeneutic theory. Spivak has asserted that deconstruction feminizes philosophical practice (p. 173). Hermeneutics, too, is in need of such "feminization," that is, of an opening to the most radical kind of questioning of the very "details" of its practice.

Such a new "new hermeneutics," the result of efforts to challenge the androcentric foundations of traditional hermeneutics, might well be called "iristics."[48] Just as *hermeneutics* is derived from the name of Hermes, the god who brought messages to men from Olympus, and especially from Zeus, so *iristics* would be formed from the name of Iris. Iris, it will be recalled, appears in the *Iliad* as the messenger of the gods, and especially of Hera. (In the *Odyssey*, however, she is completely displaced by Hermes and no longer mentioned.) Iris is thought originally to have been a personification of the rainbow, regarded as the fastest of all the messengers of the gods. In certain later poets she is no longer a virgin goddess but instead the mother of Eros. Her association with the infinite variety of colors suggests her suitability as an emblem of the relation between exegesis and interpretation which would mark variety as an analytical starting point rather than an afterthought.[49]

The Culture of Reading

Whether reading at present plays a less important role in Western culture than it has in certain past ages, I would not venture to say.

---

culine opponents who say that feminist criticism has no single theoretical foundation are simply waving a red herring; neither deconstruction nor semiotics nor hermeneutics has such a single foundation either. Feminism has both a conceptual unity as critique—as what is always fundamentally other—and rhetorical power as that which speaks with the fiction of the voice of a majority.

48. I owe this term to the suggestion of my colleague Gary Shapiro.

49. On Iris, see *Harper's Dictionary of Classical Literature and Antiquities*, ed. H. T. Peck (New York: American Book Co., 1896; rpt. 1923), p. 886. I thank Julie Vernon, a University of Kansas women's studies major, for bringing to my attention the following suggestive formulation from *The Woman's Encyclopedia of Myths and Secrets*, ed. Barbara G. Walker (San Francisco: Harper & Row, 1983), p. 450: "personifying. . .the many-colored veils of the world's appearances . . . [Iris was] a form of . . . both the organ of sight and the visible world that it saw."

Certainly it seems likely that more Westerners know *how* to read now than ever before. Still, the not infrequently voiced laments about the decline of literacy suggest that some sort of change is taking place, even though the lamenters may not have their fingers on what, precisely, that change is. One might well think back to Saint Louis, whose degree of literacy was considered quite remarkable by his contemporaries, and ask whether the decline in literacy is to be located among the "rulers." It is difficult to imagine any current elected official contributing, for example, to the vigorous exercise in both exegetical and interpretive reading that became *The Federalist Papers*—not because no one in Washington is currently as bright as Alexander Hamilton and his colleagues ("for mennys wyttes be as goode now as they were then") but rather because reading and writing are not regarded as sufficiently important, by either voters or vote getters, to justify a large expenditure of time on the reading of "classic" works or the development out of them of "timely" ideas. Another cause of current lament is the purported turn away from the liberal arts on the part of college students, who want, it is said, to study only what will enhance their chances for secure and relatively lucrative employment; because they do not expect prospective employers to value ability in critical reading and historically informed writing, the argument goes, they do not value it themselves.

Reading and books at present occupy a marginal position indeed in Western culture. This marginality may, however, derive less from the purported avarice of students or Babbittry of government leaders than from the extremism of "clerks." Professional readers, those who have the responsibility for teaching others how to read and especially for developing a high *quality* of literacy, have too often presented *either* exegesis *or* interpretation as the preferred form of reading. The polarization evident in theoretical approaches to literary history over the last two generations has contributed significantly to this unfortunate situation. In many schools and colleges exegesis was taught in the classroom; interpretation was left to the privacy of the dormitory room, where in many instances it no doubt withered away for lack of cultivation. The opposite tendency, to cultivate interpretive abilities while planting not even the seeds of ("irrelevant") exegetical ones, has flourished in some places rather more recently. Interpretive reading unaccompanied by exegesis, however, quickly becomes insipid, just as exegetical reading not vivified by interpretation is ultimately a dreary affair.

No "clerk," to be sure, ever engages in one without the other, yet often we speak, write, or teach as if we do. The failure of those whose profession is letters to convey accurately the temporal structure of their reading has serious consequences for those who are "scarcely clerks": clearly, they cannot learn both kinds of reading if taught only one. They, and their fellow citizens, are ultimately the poorer for it.

When such professional readers as high school teachers and college professors present reading as if it were an exclusively interpretive or exclusively exegetical activity, they fail to contribute to the development of qualitatively more advanced literacy, although they may in various ways be extending literacy *quantitatively*. In considering this problem, I think of a student who took the very first course I ever taught. He was a sophomore at an Ivy League university, a young man of great good will and ability with a voracious appetite for learning. While chatting with him one day about some problem or project he had in mind, I suggested that he might find it illuminated by a reading of James Joyce's *Portrait of the Artist as a Young Man*. His previously open face, for the first time, drew closed its shutters. He told me that he had read some Joyce, *Ulysses* (or perhaps *Finnegans Wake*, I can't remember which), for his high school Advanced Placement English course and found it "boring." I could well understand his judgment; he did not yet have the background to *make* a reading of *Ulysses* (or *Finnegans Wake*) interesting. But I'm quite sure he would have loved, and profited from, *Portrait*, had premature exposure to Joyce's more demanding works not created in him a prejudice against it.

The primarily interpretive reading skills this student then possessed would have been enough to permit him to read *Portrait*; he had yet to acquire the exegetical reading skills essential to the other two, and those who had obliged him to read one of them (to whom the words of Boccaccio—"delusio, ignominia," and so forth—apply) had not helped him to do so. Once at college, he had soon been introduced to exegesis—and learned to detest it. He described in terms (again) reminiscent of Boccaccio's his freshman literature teacher's explication of a passage from Dante, setting forth all its "intertexts": his teacher had, he said, "destroyed" it, "pulled it apart." It had been beautiful before it was subjected to exegesis; after exegesis, it was somehow "spoiled."

I surmise that this student's teachers, both in high school and in college, were trying in some way to make him more literate; they were exposing him to *more* books he hadn't read, more pertinent excerpts to help him with the books he was reading. I was doing the same thing myself when I suggested he read a different book by Joyce. Yet we all had, in one important way, contributed to blocking the qualitative development of his literacy skills by urging always that he encounter more texts without helping him acquire the understanding of hermeneutical principles necessary to deal with them.

In a passage cited in the previous chapter, Baudelaire remarks that a few books are enough for the wise man. Perhaps this means that one measure of wisdom is the ability to derive as much stimulation from a few books as the less enlightened derive from many; in other words, because the wise person knows how to do more with a single book, she or he does not require the continuing novelty of access to many books. It would follow that advanced training in literacy—for those, say, "en l'aage de quinze ans" and slightly above—would be doomed to fail if it merely brought the students to read more books, more classics, even perhaps a few books in a foreign language.

What is needed to give value to such quantitatively greater exposure to books is explicit education in the principles of hermeneutics. In particular, students need to be led, step by step, to see the necessity of both exegesis and interpretation and then to learn some of the methods of each. In the chapters on Saint Louis and Christine de Pizan I have already hinted at several of the problems that need (and have long needed) to be kept in mind with students moving toward advanced literacy. Above all, attention must be focused continuously and explicitly on the *process* of reading itself. This does not mean excluding study of such traditional topics as author, genre, or period but rather stressing that each of these is in fact encountered only as the result of the reading process. Students need to learn that there is not just one way to read, that reading (whether one recognizes it or not) is always a process of investigating and making choices. Such explicit study of the process of reading should help to make reading (once again) a less exclusively solitary and a more shared activity, in that readers who are more aware of the choices they make in reading should be better able to discuss the reasons behind and implications of those choices.

The development of such ability to discuss not just what one reads but the *prior* question of how one reads it is of capital importance to a culture that wishes to see itself as founded on the effort to reach consensus. Emilio Betti suggested that the effort to understand, and apply to the present, laws written in times past makes especially visible the nature of that hermeneutic activity carried out in a great range of other circumstances. It follows that if the hermeneutic awareness of the members of a society is carefully cultivated, as they are taught alternative means of making choices in the reading of all sorts of verbal structures from sonnets to speeches, they will be better able to contribute to the evolution toward an enriched consensus. And, perhaps, the poets will no longer find themselves banished to the margins of the republic.

Index

Library of Congress Cataloging-in-Publication Data

NOAKES, SUSAN.

   Timely reading.

   Includes index.

   1. Books and reading—History. 2. Books and reading
in literature. I. Title.

Z1003.N8 1988   028'.9   87-47862

ISBN 0-8014-2144-6